# BIRMINGHAM CITY
## MODERN DAY
# HEROES

# BIRMINGHAM CITY
# MODERN DAY HEROES

**Keith Dixon**

First published in Great Britain in 2011 by The Derby Books Publishing Company Limited, Derby, DE21 4SZ.

This paperback edition published in Great Britain in 2013 by DB Publishing, an imprint of JMD Media Ltd

© **Keith Dixon**, 2011

All Rights Reserved. No part of this publication may be reproduced, stored in a retrieval system, or transmitted in any form, or by any means, electronic, mechanical, photocopying, recording or otherwise without the prior permission in writing of the copyright holders, nor be otherwise circulated in any form or binding or cover other than in which it is published and without a similar condition being imposed on the subsequent publisher.

ISBN 978-1-78091-320-9

Printed and bound in the UK by Copytech (UK) Ltd Peterborough

# Contents

| | |
|---|---|
| Acknowledgements | 6 |
| Introduction | 7 |
| Preface By Mark Newton-Jones | 9 |
| Foreword By Mike Wiseman | 12 |
| Heroes And Villains | 14 |
| The Team Sheet | 15 |
| The Heroes (In Alphabetical Order) | 16 |
| The Final Word | 189 |
| Carling Cup League Final | 190 |

# Acknowledgements

This is my third book on Birmingham City to be published by Derby Books Publishing Company (previously Breedon Books), and I must thank the people there for their support and encouragement in taking me from a novice author into a published novice author. Alex Morton, Publishing Manager, Steve Caron, Managing Director and Matt Limbert, Senior Designer, have been instrumental in bringing *Birmingham City – Modern Day Heroes* to the retail bookshelves and the online warehouses. Many thanks.

As a part-time novice author, books get written when time permits, and therefore on occasions this can be either at unsociable hours or when the family might want me to do something else. Therefore to my wife, Julie, daughter Holly and son Harry please accept my grateful thanks and apologies for any disruption.

To my two older sons, Matt and Ben, thanks to them for being there together with their partners, Dell and Caz, and my two grandchildren, Caleb and Amy.

My thanks also go to Mike Wiseman and Mark Newton-Jones, two fellow businessmen who have The Blues at heart. As this book is about the players, I felt it appropriate for two high-profile supporters to be given the opportunity to write the Foreword and Preface respectively so they can reflect on what the players who have worn the royal blue in recent times mean to them.

While writing this book my father, Eric, died on Sunday 3 May 2010. He took me to my first Blues game, passing me over the turnstile while he paid and 'made arrangements' with the turnstile operator. He was a barber by trade and lived his life in the Blues' territories of Small Heath and Sheldon. Several Blues players of the 1950s received a 'short back 'n sides' for the princely sum of 1s 6d – including Len Boyd who played in the 1956 Wembley FA Cup Final sporting a 'Dicky' haircut. Thanks for everything Dad.

To all the players who answered my questions, daft as they may have sounded. Thank you.

The programmes used to illustrate my book are courtesy of Danny Drewry (midlandsmemorabilia.com) and my archivist Mike O'Brien.

Note: All extracts from *Big Fry*, by Barry Fry, are reprinted by permission of Harper Collins Publishers Ltd © 2001.

# Introduction

The selection of my Modern Day Heroes of Birmingham City was totally subjective and wholly personal. Included in my book are players with whom I have felt a connection when I watched them playing for the Blues. While there is little rhyme or reason to my choices, I wanted the book to include new content for the reader as no one wants to read the same material re-produced under a different guise therefore I decided that a number of obvious choices for the label 'Modern Day Hero' would be excluded because of the following reasons:

The players who were featured as a Birmingham City Legend in the Tony Matthews's book *The Legends Of Birmingham City* which was published in 2006. This decision resulted in the removal of the following players from my potential list of 'Modern Day Heroes':

Kevan Broadhurst
Steve Bruce
Steve Claridge
Julian Dicks
Mark Dennis
David Dunn
John Frain
Paul Furlong
Archie Gemmill
Michael Johnson
Vince Overson
Paul Peschisolido
Ray Ranson
Brian 'Harry' Roberts
Colin Todd
Jeff Wealands
Frank Worthington

The players that were profiled in my 2009 book *Birmingham City – 50 Greatest Matches* as for each featured game I wrote a Player Factfile. This decision resulted in the removal of the following players from my potential list of 'Modern Day Heroes':

Ian Bennett
D.J. Campbell
Alan Curbishley
Paul Devlin
Christophe Dugarry
John Gayle
Nigel Gleghorn
Andy Kennedy
Seb Larsson
Gary McSheffrey
Clinton Morrison
Martin O'Connor
Darren Purse
Paul Tait
Matthew Upson
Billy Wright

So before I started to compile the 'team sheet' I had removed over 30 obvious candidates including a Frenchman, a Canadian, a Swede, a Jamaican and a Scotsman – four English Internationals and some of the biggest characters ever to wear a royal blue shirt. So where did I start? What was my definition of a hero? The dictionary confirmed that a hero was 'a person who is admired for their courage or outstanding achievements' so not much help there, but perhaps the reference to courage was a clue! Therefore I decided that my definition of a 'hero' in the context of this book, is a player who is recognised by all Bluenoses as having a special quality which enabled him to make his own unique contribution to the History of Birmingham City Football Club regardless of the number of times he wore the shirt or his skills as a footballer. On this basis I gave immediate inclusion to most of the players who featured in the four biggest games in our recent history: Leyland Daf Final, Auto Windscreens Final, 2001 Worthington League Cup Final and 2002 Division One Play-off Final.

The three exceptions to these rules were Martin Thomas and Simon Sturridge who featured as a 'Legend' and Ian Clarkson who was profiled in '50 Greatest Matches'. Why? Because they gave me great interviews, which I felt must be available to my readers.

A much simpler task was to define 'Modern Day'. I wanted the book to be relevant to the fans who currently populate the terraces (sorry seats) of St Andrew's and therefore felt that any player who played prior to the 1980s would be outside of the living memory of the vast majority of the current Bluenoses, therefore I have ensured that every player included played for the Blues in the 1980s and after.

# Preface by Mark Newton-Jones

In the office of Mark Newton-Jones, Chief Executive Officer of Shop Direct Group hangs a framed Birmingham City shirt that is numbered 20 million and has his surname above it. It was presented to him by the Charities Trust in recognition of his contribution in helping to raise £20 million for children's charities. Regrettably for him this is the nearest he has ever come to having a squad number for his beloved Blues.

Mark tells his story:

I went to my first match when I was eight years of age on 27 December 1976 when we drew 0–0 with West Ham United in front of a crowd of over 39,000. The team was: Dave Latchford, Malcolm Page, Archie Styles, Howard Kendall, Joe Gallagher, Tony Want, Gary Jones, Trevor Francis, Kenny Burns, Terry Hibbitt and John Connolly.

Since then I have kept a programme for posterity from every game I've attended since that Christmas. In those days for Christmas we always had a 'big present' and, as an easily influenced eight-year old, I asked my Dad (Keith) for a Liverpool scarf and hat; after all they were the team of the 70's! On Boxing Day my Uncle Steve (Tunnicliffe) nearly choked on his cold turkey in disbelief of my supporting a non-Midlands side and promptly organised my first trip to St Andrew's the very next day!

Steve 'lifted' me over the turnstile bedecked in a hastily purchased blue and white scarf, we then walked up those seemingly giant steps to the entrance of the Kop and onto the terraces; I was totally overwhelmed by the vivid green pitch which appeared over the horizon before me. Wow! The ground filled up, the noise level rose and 'Keep right on' rang out. Wow, this is St Andrews. I'd got the bug!

My second 'Wow' memory was my first game under floodlights which was a (5–1) victory over Chelsea on Tuesday, 11 March 1980 at St Andrew's when Kevan Broadhurst, Kevin Dillon and Alan Ainscow (2) scored supported by an own-goal from Borota. Over 27,000 fans watched the following team: Jeff Wealands, Kevan Broadhurst, Mark Dennis, Alan Curbishley, Joe Gallagher, Colin Todd, Alan Ainscow, Frank Worthington, Keith Bertschin, Archie Gemmill and Kevin Dillon.

My final childhood football 'Wow' was my first visit to Wembley which was to watch an England v Wales Schoolboy international on 24 March 1979. We only went because a lad at our school (Light Hall in Shirley, Solihull) Kevin Ash, was playing for England. At the time I did not realise the Blues' connection within the Welsh side. In their team were Dean Holtham, Mark Bowen and Tony Rees.

Sadly, against the 'Wow Factor' was the terrible trouble with hooligans that was prevalent in the late '70s mainly outside the ground in the streets of Small Heath. I recall that there was even fencing running up and down the terraces of the Kop and Tilton Road preventing Blues' fans from getting to one another!

I had my regular 'spot' along with lots of other kids on the white wall half way up the Kop and level with the half way line just in front of the crash barrier; behind me getting crushed stood my Uncle, Dad and Grandad Roy and Grandad Aubrey. I remember craning my neck at half-time to see the black and white scoreboard as the scores appeared from the other games around the country – this generated great excitement within the crowd which was never the same once technology took over... I stood on the Kop for the last time on 16 April 1994; an emotional day of childhood adolescent memories... When the seats came the following season, my season ticket was for a seat as near as possible to my 'spot'!

My all-time hero has to be 'TF' and my first full 'penguin strip' Birmingham kit had a Number 8 on both the shirt and shorts. I'm sure I played better with it on!

Following on from 'TF' from those early days I remember Dave Langan, Ian Handysides and Garry Pendrey. Then for glamour and skill, we recruited the likes of Frank Worthington, Keith Bertschin and, of course, Alberto Tarantini (the first UK based Argentinian international).

Then there were the dark, but fun, days in the old Third Division, under the guidance of the legendary Barry Fry. I was a regional manager with Next in those days and although I didn't have to work Saturdays I often did and visited the store nearest to our opponents in the morning before the match – it worked out that I never missed an away game!

Those were the days when the patience of all Bluenoses was truly tested – if you were one of the 3,963 fans that stood in the chill of our vast Kop for the Anglo-Italian game in December against Ascoli Calcio along with my mates, Paul and Alan, then your loyalty can never be doubted. I'll tell you no amount of Bovril and pepper kept the cold out that night! It was December 8 1992 and we drew 1–1 thanks to a goal from Simon Sturridge. The Team was: Les Sealey, Ian Clarkson, Graham Potter, Paul Fenwick, John Frain, Trevor Matthewson, Ian Rodgerson, Paul Tait, David Speedie, Mark Sale (Sub: Louie Donowa) and Simon Sturridge.

In amongst the years of pain we had two amazing days out at Wembley – unfortunately, I missed the first but the memory of Paul Tait's golden goal and subsequent celebration in the Auto Windscreens Shield will stay with me for ever.

We finally started to climb the tables with the introduction of 'TF' as the boss and new players including Steve Bruce, Martin O'Connor, Andy Legg (he could give Rory De Lapp a few tips on long throw-ins), Paul Devlin, Paul Furlong, Chris Holland, Gary Ablett, Bryan Hughes and Barry Horne (now Professor of Science at one of my local schools, The King's School, Chester). The headmaster, Simon, is also a Bluenose!

A very proud moment for me happened early in 2003 when a letter landed at home from Birmingham City's Academy – my eldest boy (Mackenzie), then eight, had been spotted playing for his club, Binbrook FC, and was invited to the Academy. Some weeks later another letter arrived from the other side of the City with the same request. I couldn't believe it he actually wanted to play at both! I had a plan, I was sure his homework would get in the way of doing both so after a few games I gave him the choice – he picked claret and blue, but not for football reasons; the beans on toast after training at Villa beat the crisps and juice at Wast Hills!

Moving through the years it was the turn of Geoff Horsfield, Darren Purse, Kenny Cunningham, Andy Johnson (gutting to see him miss that penalty at Cardiff), Robbie Savage, Martin Grainger and Damian Johnson. In the main, as you can see, my heroes were the guys that gave 100 per cent for the shirt and while not always the most skilful you knew they were giving their all and they all became fans' favourites as a result. While talking of skill, the two players who possessed for me awe-inspiring talent were Christophe Dugarry and Mikael Forssell but for varying reasons they did not stay long enough to have a real impact on Blues' fortunes.

Fast forward to the team of today and I believe we possess the best central defensive partnership in the Premier League in Scott Dann and Roger Johnson – I sincerely hope we keep them both together on a long-term basis – and in Barry Ferguson we have one of the most intelligent playmakers I've seen in a Blue shirt.

Finally, history repeated itself two years ago when the younger of my two sons (Harry) decided he wanted to become a Liverpool fan (I put it down to pressure from his school mates and the nearest club to our new home being Liverpool). I had to act quickly; Birmingham v Liverpool at St Andrews, we were 2–0 up at half-time and adorned in his new scarf he announced Birmingham was his team. The two goals that were scored in the second half to earn Liverpool a draw didn't dampen his enthusiasm … thank heavens!

Lastly, two wishes for the future: firstly, some silverware for the trophy cabinet (anything will do!) and, secondly, which I guess will never happen, is for Blues to be shown as first match on 'Match of The Day' – then we really have arrived!

**Mark Newton-Jones** is the Group Chief Executive of Shop Direct Group, the UK's leading online and home shopping retailer.

Shop Direct Group was formed as the result of the merger of Littlewoods Home Shopping and Shop Direct, the home shopping business of Great Universal Stores plc, in 2005.

Mark's career in retail began at Next where he spent 18 years working in various senior management roles, the last five years of which were as the Director responsible for the Next Directory. During Mark's time at the helm, the Next Directory doubled in turnover and trebled its profits.

Mark moved to join Littlewoods Stores in 2003. He spent two years modernising and repositioning the Littlewoods high street business prior to divesting it from the Group. In 2005, he was appointed Group Chief Executive of the newly-formed Littlewoods Shop Direct Group, where he was instrumental in delivering the largest integration in Europe of two retail businesses, Littlewoods and Great Universal Stores.

# PREFACE

Renaming the business Shop Direct Group, Mark successfully completed the acquisition of Empire Stores in 2008. This was swiftly followed in 2009 by the purchase of the Woolworths brand, the launch of the Very brand, previously known as Littlewoods Direct and the entry of Littlewoods Europe into France, Spain, Germany and Portugal.

With a huge heritage, covering both the high street and home shopping, Shop Direct Group now sees its future firmly rooted online, with its 2009–10 Christmas trading statement announcing more than 65 per cent of sales transacted through the web (six-week period to 1 January 2010). It expects to exceed 70 per cent of sales online by end of FY 2010–11.

Today, Shop Direct Group has $c.9,000$ employees, annual sales of over £1.7 billion, more than 5 million customers and provides £1.45 billion of credit to its customers through its financial services business.

**Author's note:** I received a text message from Mark at 09.27 on 2 December 2010 the morning after we had beaten Aston Villa 2–1 in the quarter-final of the Carling Cup, it read 'Hi Keith…Great result…Wembley here we come!!! Shame about the morons after the game… Cheers Mark'

# Foreword
## By Mike Wiseman

Writing the Foreword has brought back so many memories of my involvement with the Blues and also given me a chance to reflect on my heroes.

The Wiseman family, through my grandfather David, my father Jack and myself, have been associated with Birmingham City Football Club since 1928, and while we have never seen our team raise the FA Cup at Wembley or win a League Championship our time has been filled with excitement, disappointments and a good many laughs.

My first trip to St Andrew's was on 12 February 1966 at the age of 10. It would have been at an earlier age, but Jack preferred me to play sport for my prep school on a Saturday rather than watch football. The game was a fourth-round FA Cup tie against Leicester City and we lost by two goals to one. The hero that day was unfortunately Derek Dougan who murdered us in front of a crowd of 46,680. I can recall the team as: Jim Herriot in goal, Cammie Fraser and Ray Martin at full-back, Ron Wylie, Winston Foster and Malcolm Beard as the halves and in attack we had Trevor Hockey, Alec Jackson, Bobby Thomson, Geoff Vowden and Denis Thwaites, who scored. There were a few heroes in that team!

Like so many fans, my all-time Blues hero was Trevor Francis. We got on well together, being the same age, and our friendship was forged when we both survived a drive to Preston North End in the back of my father's Jaguar XJ saloon.

'Jolly Jack's' driving was anything but heroic; he was extremely impatient and easily distracted which is evidenced by a tale witnessed by the old Blues secretary, Alan Instone. 'While on the way to Queen's Park Rangers, Jack offered a lift to a mouthy skinhead Bluenose who was thumbing his way to Loftus Road from the Coventry Road near St Andrew's. I advised him not to stop, but Jack would not pass a Blues supporter who needed a lift. Our passenger was very much "Jack-the-lad" at the start of our journey but having travelled the length of the M1 at 120mph with Jack talking to him and looking at him, he arrived in London a trembling nervous wreck!'

My overall football hero is Bobby Charlton who staked his claim to this status with his two magnificent goals against Portugal in the 1966 World Cup Qualifying stages. I am proud to say that Sir Bobby retains his hero status to this day as I have the pleasure of looking after him whenever Manchester United visit Small Heath. Few people have the privilege of calling one of their heroes a friend.

It is something of a cliché, but my father Jack Wiseman was my lifetime hero. He was a great man to have in a crisis and would never give up where the Blues were concerned. He virtually kept the club alive on his own when the Kumar's business empire collapsed with the BCCI banking failure. His optimism reigned supreme, as recently as our promotion to the Premier League in 2008–09 when after our failure to secure promotion against Preston North End at the last home game of the season, he wrote a note to the Board saying 'We will do it at Reading' (Note: Jack suffered a severe stroke and was unable to speak although he maintained his 'Swinging Thumbs Up' sign – a true hero.)

My father must have inherited his heroic qualities from his father, David 'Curly' Wiseman who was virtually tee-total until the age of 70. He needed major surgery to overcome a life-threatening condition, and the success of the operation resulted in a change of outlook by my grandfather. He took his first glass of real champagne at the age of 71, which resulted in him consuming a half bottle everyday at 11 o'clock in the morning. He lived to the ripe old age of 93!

The most heroic of Blues performances for me was the Promotion match at Orient on 2 May 1972 when we won promotion back to Division One thanks to a Bob Latchford goal. We had to survive a pitch invasion from Millwall fans during the 90 minutes and a bomb scare which threatened the after match celebrations. Heroism can sometimes be created by a simple stubbornness to conform, as was the case (no pun intended) when after the final whistle, David arranged for a case of champagne to be delivered to the Away dressing room. The Police came into the Board Room instructing everyone to evacuate the Brisbane Road ground due to a bomb warning. In the chaos that resulted we could not find my grandfather until we were eventually allowed back into the stadium to find him in the dressing room well on the way to finishing his first bottle. Despite repeated pleas by the Police, he had refused to move, telling the officer in charge that he was 86 years of age and if indeed the bomb did go off, what finer way to die than while celebrating his team's promotion with a glass of champagne in his hand!

Heroic or stubborn, let's give him the benefit of the doubt!

Enjoy the book.

**Profile of Mike Wiseman:**
Mike has been a director of Birmingham City Football Club since 1997 and was appointed as Vice-President in October 2009 by the new owners of the club. The Wiseman family has been connected with St Andrew's since 1928. Born in 1955, Mike graduated from Sheffield University with a degree in Economics, qualifying as a Chartered Accountant in 1982. He is Managing Director of a property company, Haunch Lane Developments Limited as well as being a Governor of University College Birmingham where he chairs the Audit Committee. His hobbies include golf, skiing and watching he Blues.

# Heroes & Villains

In the Introduction to this book I posed the question – how does one define a hero?

I decided that a Blues Hero is a player who is recognised by all Bluenoses as having a special quality which enabled him to make his own unique contribution to the History of Birmingham City Football Club regardless of the number of times he wore the shirt or his skills as a footballer.

You will appreciate as you get started on the book that the 'special quality' demonstrated by the players featured is 100 per cent positive but in going through the selection process I came across a number of players whose 'special quality' was less than positive and on some occasions downright devious.

With a club like Birmingham City a 'hero' can equally be defined as a 'villain' (with all the negatives a Bluenose would associate with such a name) -players who are signed and received by the fans with the eternal optimism required of being a Blues' fan only for them to let us down with either their negative attitude or failure to produce the goods on the field of play.

No place in this book for the ex-Manchester United players Steve Bruce signed – how betrayed 'Brucie' must have felt when his Old Trafford pals Nicky Butt, Dwight Yorke or Andy (sorry Andrew) Cole let the club down. They had no positive impact on the fortunes of the Blues other than reducing our bank balance as they used St Andrew's to extend their financial status rather than their playing careers.

No place in this book for Chris Sutton, Walter Pandiani, Muzzy Izzet, Mario Melchiot, Ferdinand Coly, Olivier Kapo, Mike Newell and Jesper Gronkjaer.

I know the selection of Robbie Savage will surprise some readers, but if the ex-Chairman can forgive him 'I loved Robbie Savage. I thought he was a fantastic character, and he was great for Birmingham City' then so can I.

Following his departure, the Blues midfield lost a unique ingredient – the ability to change a game! How often did Robbie turn a dire contest into a exciting battle with an outrageous tackle, a bit of afters with a defender or a pinpoint free-kick? 'Sav' was both hero and villain!

On the subject of Villains, I make no apology for including some players who have also donned the claret and blue of our suburban rivals, such as Noel Blake, Robert Hopkins, Liam Ridgewell and Peter Withe. Those included gave great service to the Blues and deserve their place in this book.

I have referred earlier to Tony Matthews' book *The Legends of Birmingham City* and by comparing this book with that publication you can demonstrate the changes which have taken place in football over the past 30 years:

Players no longer stay at football clubs for long periods therefore the average appearances for the Blues is dramatically reduced. The number of locally born players has diminished and been replaced by surnames like Dominguez, Forssell, Tebily and Nafti. The distractions of the late 20th century are evidenced in this book; a player electronically tagged by the authorities, and a convicted drug dealer makes the case.

Players look to have a career in football rather than a specific club and throughout the book it can be seen how St Andrew's has been used a stepping stone to a great career or a resting place for a player in the twilight of their careers.

Each player's entry includes:
His Heroic Claim To Fame
Player Vital Statistics
Playing Career in Table Format
His Career in Words

In the majority of cases there are insights into the player's personality via interviews and questionnaires entitled 'About The Man'.

# The Team Sheet

1. Dele Adebola
2. Ian Atkins
3. Dennis Bailey
4. Dave Barnett
5. Jon Bass
6. Keith Bertschin
7. Noel Blake
8. Stephen Carr
9. Simon Charlton
10. Aliou Cisse
11. Jamie Clapham
12. Ian Clarkson
13. Stephen Clemence
14. Gary Cooper
15. Tony Coton
16. Kenny Cunningham
17. Liam Daish
18. Kevin Dillon
19. Jose Dominguez
20. Louie Donowa
21. Nicky Eaden
22. Mikael Forssell
23. Kevin Francis
24. Howard Gayle
25. David Geddis
26. Jerry Gill
27. Martin Grainger
28. Julian Gray
29. James Hagan
30. Ian Handysides
31. Mick Harford
32. Martin Hicks
33. Scott Hiley
34. Chris Holland
35. Robert Hopkins
36. Geoff Horsfield
37. Bryan Hughes
38. Jonathon Hunt
39. Graham Hyde
40. Stern John

41. Andrew Johnson
42. Damien Johnson
43. Stephen Kelly
44. Jeff Kenna
45. Martin Kuhl
46. Dave Langan
47. Stan Lazaridis
48. Chris Marsden
49. Trevor Matthewson
50. Jon McCarthy
51. James McFadden
52. Tommy Mooney
53. Mehdi Nafti
54. Peter Ndlovu
55. Ricky Otto
56. Dean Peer
57. Jermaine Pennant
58. Kevin Phillips
59. Kevin Poole
60. Gary Poole
61. Franck Queudrue
62. Liam Ridgewell
63. Steve Robinson
64. Ian Rodgerson
65. Mat Sadler
66. Robbie Savage
67. David Seaman
68. Peter Shearer
69. Danny Sonner
70. Byron Stevenson
71. Simon Sturridge
72. Maik Taylor
73. Martin Taylor
74. Olivier Tebily
75. Martin Thomas
76. Nico Vaesen
77. Pat Van Den Hauwe
78. Mark Ward
79. Chris Whyte
80. Peter Withe

# Bamberdele 'Dele' Adebola

**Heroic claim to fame**
Scored four goals for Blues in four games in the period 28 February to 10 March 1998.

**Vital statistics**
*Date of birth:* 23 June 1975
*Place of birth:* Lagos, Nigeria
*Blues career:* 102 + 50 substitutes – 41 goals
*Blues debut:* First appearance on 7 February 1998 as a substitute (h) drew 1–1 v Middlesbrough. Crowd: 20,634
*First start:* 17 February 1998 (h) won 2–0 v Crewe Alexandra and he scored. Crowd: 5,559
*Team:* Bennett, Bass, Charlton, Bruce, Johnson (M), Marsden, McCarthy, O'Connor, Adebola, Hughes, Ndlovu
*Club honours:* Crewe Alexandra – Promotion to First Division 1996–97; Blues – Worthington Cup runner-up in 2001
*Representative honours:* Selected for Northern Ireland and Nigeria but withdrew on both occasions

**Playing Career**

| Club | From | To | Fee | Total Appearances incl (subs) | Goals |
| --- | --- | --- | --- | --- | --- |
| Nottingham Forest | 2009 | | Free | 40 | 4 |
| Bristol City | 2008 | 2009 | | 62 | 16 |
| Bradford City | 2004 | 2004 | Loan | 16 | 4 |
| Burnley | 2004 | 2004 | Loan | 3 | 1 |
| Coventry | 2003 | 2008 | Free | 182 | 36 |
| Crystal Palace | 2002 | 2003 | Free | 48 | 7 |
| Oldham | 2002 | 2002 | Loan | 5 | |
| Birmingham City | 1998 | 2002 | £1,000,000 | 152 | 41 |
| Northwich Victoria | 1994 | | Loan | 0 | |
| Bangor City | 1993 | | Loan | 4 | 2 |
| Crewe Alexandra | 1993 | 1998 | Trainee | 152 | 46 |

**Career in words**
Dele was raised in Liverpool, and as a schoolboy he played in the same representative side as Robbie Fowler. He was offered a YTS place at Liverpool but felt that Fowler presented too much competition and he accepted a similar offer from Crewe Alexandra.

He made his first-team debut in the old Third Division. At the age of 17 during the seasons of 1992–93 and 1993–94 he gained valuable experience on loan with Bangor City in the Welsh Premier League and Northwich Victoria in the Conference. In 1996–97 his 16 goals helped Crewe gain promotion to the First Division.

In February 1998 Blues signed him for a fee of £1 million. In his first full season (1999–2000) he scored 13 goals, but as he became less prolific he was put up for transfer and a proposed move to Las Palmas in the Spanish La Liga fell through due to medical grounds.

Although on the transfer list, his goals helped Blues to the Worthington Cup Final in 2001, he made six appearances plus two as a substitute, scoring five goals.

A serious knee injury resulted in him making no first-team appearances in 2001–02 season, and although he went on loan to Oldham Athletic towards the end of that season the writing was on the wall, and it was no surprise when Steve Bruce chose not to renew his contract.

He played one season for Palace under Trevor Francis, making 48 appearances in all competitions. Once more he was released at the end of that season and he moved back to the Midlands with Coventry City. Initially he failed to find any form and finished the season going on loan to Burnley, where he scored

one goal in three appearances. Slowly he was regaining his goalscoring knack, and after a loan spell at Bradford City, where he scored three goals, he won a recall to the Sky Blues first team, making regular starts in 2004–05.

On 30 January 2008 Dele signed an 18-month contract with Bristol City, despite Coventry wanting him to stay. He made his debut on 2 February in a 3–0 defeat away to Queen's Park Rangers. In 2008–09 10 goals from 42 appearances earned him the club's Player of the Year award.

He refused their offer of a year's extension to his contract and signed a two-year deal with Nottingham Forest on 30 June on a free transfer.

In March 1998 the then Northern Ireland manager Lawrie McMenemy discovered that Dele held British Citizenship and promptly selected him to play in McMenemy's first game in charge against Slovakia, but Dele had to withdraw due to injury. He was also selected in Nigeria's provisional squad for the 1998 World Cup but failed to make the final 22.

In Alan Sugar's autobiography *What you see is what you get*, published by Macmillan in 2010, he recalls the match as follows:

'After one particularly dismal performance under Graham's management – a Cup tie against Birmingham (again a lower-League team), when we got slaughtered 3–1 at home – the fans were frustrated and started chanting for my head. Ann was sitting next to me while the crowd were screaming, "Sugar out! Sugar out!". This wasn't the first time they'd chanted this, but on this occasion the whole stadium seemed to erupt; it was really frightening. Karren Brady, Birmingham's managing director, spoke to me after the match, saying how disgusted she was at the way the fans were treating me. She went to the trouble of writing an article in *The Sun* the next day, saying how unreasonable the fans were and how they'd forgotten all I'd done for the club. It was nice of her – she was genuinely upset at what she saw and felt very sorry for Ann too – but her words in *The Sun* fell upon deaf ears, as one would expect.'

(**Author's note:** Graham was George Graham and Ann is Alan Sugar's wife.)

### About the man
Mike Wiseman recalls: 'Dele started the call from Spurs fans to sack Alan Sugar [now Lord Sugar of *The Apprentice* fame] when he scored two goals at White Hart Lane in Blues' 3–1 shock win in round three of the League Cup on 31 October 2000 in front of 27,096 very disgruntled spectators. The chant "Sugar Out" echoed around the ground after Dele's second.'

# Ian Leslie Atkins

### Heroic claim to fame
Cost Blues a £10,000 fine when he played against Peterborough United before being registered.

### Vital statistics
*Date of birth:* 16 January 1957
*Place of birth:* Sheldon, Birmingham
*Blues career:* 114 + 3 Substitute – 9 goals
*Blues debut:* 27 August 1988 (a) lost 0–1 v Watford. Crowd: 12,656

# BIRMINGHAM CITY
## MODERN DAY HEROES

*Team:* Godden, Ranson, Roberts, Atkins, Bird, Trewick, Bremner, Langley, Whitton, Robinson (S), Wigley
*First Blues goal:* 17 September 1988 (h) won 3–2 v Sunderland
*Club honours:* Shrewsbury Town – Division Three champions 1978–79; Everton – Division One champions and European Cup-Winners' Cup winners 1984–85; Blues – Division Three runners-up 1991–92

### Playing Career

| Club | From | To | Fee | Total Appearances incl (subs) | Goals |
|---|---|---|---|---|---|
| Doncaster Rovers | 1993 | 1994 | | 7 | |
| Sunderland | 1993 | | | | |
| Cambridge United | 1992 | 1993 | | 2 | |
| Birmingham City | 1992 | 1992 | For both spells | 117 | 9 |
| Colchester United | 1990 | 1991 | | 41 | |
| Birmingham City | 1988 | 1990 | | See 1992 | |
| Ipswich Town | 1985 | 1988 | | 77 | 4 |
| Everton | 1984 | 1985 | | 7 | 1 |
| Sunderland | 1982 | 1984 | | 77 | 6 |
| Shrewsbury Town | 1975 | 1982 | | 279 | 58 |

### Career in words

Ian began his career as an apprentice with Shrewsbury Town after leaving Sheldon Heath Comprehensive School in 1973. He turned professional in January 1975, staying at Gay Meadow for seven years in which he made 279 appearances and scored 58 times. After helping them avoid relegation in the next three seasons he joined Sunderland for £80,000 at the beginning of the 1982–83 season. He was in the North East for two years before moving to Everton in October 1984 for £70,000 lasting just one year playing a squad role only in the 'Toffees' League title and European Cup-Winners' Cup victories. In September 1985 he went to Ipswich Town for £100,000. In three years he played 77 matches and scored four goals but was unable to prevent relegation to the Second Division. He joined Blues in March 1988 for £50,000. In the summer of 1990 Ian was appointed player-manager at Colchester United who had just been relegated to the GM Vauxhall Conference. After 12 months at Layer Road, in July 1991 he returned to St Andrew's as player-assistant manager under Terry Cooper. In December 1992 he was the manager of Cambridge United but they were relegated and he was dismissed in May 1993. He then had a second spell as a player at Sunderland before he ended his playing days at Doncaster Rovers in Division Three. In October 1994 he became manager at Northampton Town guiding them to promotion by winning the Division Three Play-off Final in 1996–97 in the following season they reached the Division Two Play-offs losing out to Grimsby Town. After relegation back to Division Three he resigned early in the 1999–2000 season. In January 2000 he became manager of Chester City but quit six months later after they were relegated to the Conference. Later he had a year-long spell in charge of Carlisle United between June 2000 and July 2001. In July 2001 he became Alan Cork's assistant manager at Cardiff City but was sacked in December 2001 and soon after joined Oxford United as Director of Football before being formally appointed as manager in April 2002. He was suspended in March 2004 and then dismissed the following month for talking to Bristol Rovers about becoming their manager which he subsequently did. He was there for just over a year before he was sacked after a poor start to the 2005–06

season. In April 2006 he became manager of Torquay United, having joined as an advisor to John Cornforth the previous month. On 27 November 2006 he was replaced as manager by former Czechoslovakian World Cup star Lubos Kubik and refused the role of Director of Football. He now works for Sunderland as a scout and was doing radio summaries for BBC Radio Suffolk in 2009–10 season.

### About the man
Mike Wiseman recalls: 'We were away at AC Cesna in Italy on 2 December 1992. When we arrived the fog was a real pea souper and we assumed the game would be off. Faced with this circumstance, Ian and I proceeded to enjoy some local wine and sambuca. Imagine the look on our faces when, with 45 minutes to go to kick-off, the fog cleared and it was game on! Luckily, Ian was assistant manager at the time and did not need to play and we won 2–1 in front of a dismal crowd of 2,090.'

# Dennis Bailey

### Heroic claim to fame
He scored the first-ever Division One hat-trick at Old Trafford – but not for Blues.

### Vital statistics
*Date of birth:* 13 December 1965
*Place of birth:* Lambeth, London
*Blues career:* 93 – 25 goals
*Blues debut:* 19 August 1989 (h) won 3–0 v Crewe Alexandra and he scored. Crowd: 10,447
*Team:* Thomas, Clarkson, Frain, Atkins, Sproson, Matthewson, Peer, Bailey, Yates, Langley, Sturridge
*Club honours:* Blues – Leyland Daf winners 1991

### Playing Career

| Club | From | To | Fee | Total Appearances incl (subs) | Goals |
| --- | --- | --- | --- | --- | --- |
| Stafford Rangers | 2002 | 2006 | | 1 | |
| Tamworth | 2001 | 2002 | | 2 | |
| Aberystwyth | 2001 | 2001 | Free | 0 | |
| Forest Green | 1999 | 2001 | £15,000 | 64 | 9 |
| Cheltenham Town | 1999 | 1999 | Nominal Fee | | |
| Farnborough | 1998 | 1999 | Free | | |
| Lincoln City | 1998 | 1998 | | 5 | |
| Gillingham | 1995 | 1998 | Free | 102 | 13 |
| Brentford | 1995 | 1995 | Loan | 6 | 3 |
| Watford | 1994 | 1994 | Loan | 8 | 4 |
| Charlton Athletic | 1993 | 1994 | Loan | 6 | |
| Queen's Park Rangers | 1991 | 1995 | £175,000 | 48 | 13 |
| Bristol Rovers | 1991 | 1991 | Loan | 6 | 1 |
| Birmingham City | 1989 | 1991 | £80,000 | 93 | 25 |
| Bristol Rovers | 1989 | 1989 | Loan | 19 | 10 |

### Career in words
Dennis will always be remembered for the fact that on 1 January 1992 he scored a hat-trick for Queen's Park Rangers at Old Trafford in a 4–1 win in the old Division One. He told BBC sport that 'without a doubt that was the highlight of my career. Manchester United had not lost at home in their race to win the First Division title and everyone considered us 'no hopers' but the Queen's Park Rangers side had one of those days and we could have scored at least two more goals possibly three.' Since 1992 the only other players at the time of writing this book to score a hat-trick at Old Trafford are Ronaldo who got

his treble in the Champions League against Real Madrid in 2003 and David Bentley on 1 February 2006 when he scored three for Blackburn Rovers to become the first player in the Premiership to score a hat-trick at Old Trafford. So Dennis' record stands as follows:

Division One – Hat-trick at Old Trafford – Dennis Bailey
Champions League – Hat-trick at Old Trafford – Ronaldo
Premiership – Hat-trick at Old Trafford – David Bentley

(**Author's note:** Southampton forward Egil Ostenstad was convinced he had scored three times at Old Trafford when the Saints beat the Red Devils 6–3 in October 1996, but the Football Association's goal panel declared that one of his three was an own-goal by Dennis Irwin.)

### About the man
#### How did you become involved in coaching disadvantaged young people?
When my football career was over I became a self-employed football coach and my church, Renewal in Solihull, was looking for a way of connecting with young people in local schools, so I volunteered. Many of the children come from tough backgrounds. After one match, a kid robbed the local shop.

#### What's the best thing about coaching disadvantaged kids?
Helping then develop social skills through the sport. Football is a great medium for encouraging kids to take responsibility and work as a team. It also builds confidence and leadership, on and off the pitch.

#### What's the worst thing about coaching disadvantaged kids?
Many of the kids at first can be difficult to control. They tend to swear a lot and spit, and often disagreements over the ball end in fights. I don't automatically get their respect, but it really helps being a footballer rather than their teacher or parent. They relate to you on a different level. And football teaches them to play by the rules.

#### What difference have you made?
I've banned swearing. As a result, their language is moderated, they have stopped fighting, and teachers tell me their concentration and schoolwork have improved.

#### What do you remember about your hat-trick at Old Trafford?
My teammate Andy Sinton scored an early goal, then I got another before they pulled one back. After half-time, they piled on the pressure, but against the run of play I scored our third. Their confidence collapsed after that and I snatched my third in the last minute. Following that defeat, United struggled to regain their winning form and Leeds United beat them to the League title.

THE HEROES

# David Kwame Barnett

**Heroic claim to fame**
Sent off in first full game for Blues v West Bromwich Albion on 28 December 1993.

**Vital statistics**
*Date of birth:* 16 April 1967
*Place of birth:* Birmingham
*Blues career:* 59
*Blues first appearance as substitute:* 1 January 1994 (a) lost 1–3 v Southend United. Crowd:10,731
*Blues debut:* 3 January 1994 (h) drew 1–1 v Oxford United. Crowd: 15,142
*Team:* Bennett, Hiley, Cooper (G), Barnett, Dryden, Whyte, McMinn, Lowe, Peschisolido, Saville, Smith (D)
*Club honours:* Blues – Auto Windscreens Shield winner 1995, Division Two champions 1995

## Playing Career

| Club | From | To | Fee | Total Appearances incl (subs) | Goals |
| --- | --- | --- | --- | --- | --- |
| Moor Green | 2002 | | | 5 | |
| Halesowen | 2001 | | | | |
| Forest Green | 2000 | 2000 | Loan | 3 | |
| Lincoln City | 1999 | 2000 | Free | 27 | 4 |
| Port Vale | 1998 | 1999 | Free | 28 | |
| Port Vale | 1998 | 1998 | Loan | 9 | 1 |
| Dunfermline | 1997 | 1998 | | 26 | 1 |
| Birmingham City | 1994 | 1997 | £150,000 | 59 including loan in 1993–94 | |
| Barnet | 1992 | 1994 | £10,000 | 72 | 3 |
| Kidderminster Harriers | 1990 | 1992 | Free | | |
| Walsall | 1990 | 1990 | Free | 7 | |
| West Bromwich Albion | 1989 | 1990 | Free | | |
| Edmonton Oilers | 1989 | 1989 | Free | | |
| Colchester United | 1988 | 1989 | | 30 | |
| Windsor & Eton | 1986 | 1988 | | | |
| Alvechurch | 1985 | 1986 | | | |
| Wolverhampton Wanderers | 1983 | 1985 | Youth | | |

## Career in words

He played for Wolverhampton Wanderers as a youth from 1983 to 1985 but when he was released he moved into non-League with Alvechurch for the season 1985–86 followed by a move to Windsor & Eton for the next two years. He moved back into League football with Colchester United in 1988 where he made 30 appearances at Layer Road. In 1989 he played for Edmonton Oilers in the Canadian Soccer League before returning to England to sign for West Bromwich Albion for the 1989–90 season. Before he could make a first-team appearance for the Baggies he moved to Walsall where he made five appearances. He slipped back into non-League football in 1990–92 with Kidderminster Harriers before moving onto Barnet where he made 59 appearances, scoring three goals. In the 1993–94 season he went to Blues on loan and made three appearances before signing permanently in 1994. He moved to Scotland to play for Dunfermline making 26 appearances and scoring one goal. He was a much-travelled professional and

continued to ply his services with Port Vale from 1998–99, recording 37 outings and scoring one goal and then onto Lincoln City where he finished his League career.

He joined Halesowen as first-team coach in March 2001 before leaving to join the coaching staff at Blues' Academy.

### About the man
Edwin Stein was an integral part of the Barry Fry regime that won the Division Two Championship in 1994–95 season. He had this to say about Dave Barnett's contribution to the triumph:

'Barnie started sluggishly. He had injury problems and took a while to get going. Once he did, there was no stopping him until he had awful bad luck against Brentford when he snapped his Achilles heel. What a lot of people didn't realise was that he worked on his game, on his touch and improving his awareness. It paid off and his partnership with Liam Daish was superb. Barnie's pace allied to Daishy's presence made them impregnable at times. It's pleasing that a Blues lad like Barnie has been rewarded with a medal. He got a lot of stick when he first came here, but eventually he won everybody over.'

# Jonathan David Bass

### Heroic claim to fame
Blues 1996 League Cup semi-final v Leeds United.

### Vital statistics
*Date of birth:* 1 July 1976
*Place of birth:* Weston-Super-Mare
*Blues career:* 72 + 8 Substitute
*Blues debut:* 4 October 1994 (h) drew 1–1 v Blackburn Rovers in League Cup round two, second leg. Crowd: 16,275
*Team:* Bennett, Bass, Frian, Ward, Barnett, Daish, De Souza, Shearer, McGavin, Dominguez, Donowa
*Club honours:* Blues – Division Two champions 1994–95

### Playing Career

| Club | From | To | Fee | Total Appearances incl (subs) | Goals |
|---|---|---|---|---|---|
| Salisbury | 2006 | 2009 | Free | 77 | |
| Bristol Rovers | 2005 | 2006 | Free | 12 | |
| Pahang FA Malaysia | | | | | |
| Hartlepool United | 2001 | 2006 | Free | 27 | 1 |
| Gillingham | 2000 | 2000 | Loan | 7 | |
| Carlisle United | 1996 | 1996 | Loan | 3 | |
| Birmingham City | 1994 | 2001 | Trainee | 80 | |

### Career in words
He began his career as a trainee with Blues, going on to make 80 appearances between 1994 and 2001, playing for Blues in League Cup semi-final v Leeds in 1996. He also played for Carlisle on loan, Gillingham on loan, Hartlepool United, Pahang FA in Malaysia and Bristol Rovers. He was released at the end of 2005–06, and he left the pro game to become a trainee quantity surveyor in the family business before joining Salisbury City in July 2006 on a part-time basis.

Jon's career spanned 17 years before his retirement while with Salisbury City who he had joined from Bristol Rovers at the age of 33 in 2006. The Whites were a full-time squad with Jon the only part-timer. He could not commit to a full-time contract as 'I was ready to go into other things. It had been quite a tough season physically and mentally. We've got a family building business, and that really requires my full-time effort now as opposed to travelling around the country.'

# THE HEROES

**About the man**
**What is your current job?**
I am currently working as a Junior Surveyor in the family building business. We have recently opened up a new arm to the business supplying and installing renewable energy technologies which is proving to be both exciting and challenging.

**Who was your favourite player as a boy? And why?**
Kenny Dalglish was my favourite player growing up – there was always the possibility of 'magic' on the pitch when he played, seemingly being able to create and score goals in equal measure.

**Which game in your career stands out in your memory?**
My debut at Blues stands out most in my memory. I was 18, not long turned Pro and had been called up to play against Blackburn at home in the second round of what's now the Carling Cup. It was the Blackburn team that went on to win the Premier League that season and Kenny Dalglish, my boyhood hero, was their manager. I can remember walking in at half-time 1–0 to the good and feeling like crying!! A dream realised. We ended up drawing 1–1 and I ended up injured for the next eight weeks due to the late 'give the young 'un a knock'-type tackle I sustained in the first 10 minutes from Jason Wilcox. The beginning of the ups and downs!!

**What's your best football experience?**
My best football experience was undoubtedly scoring my one and only competitive goal. It was the equaliser in a dour Tuesday night encounter against Rochdale while playing for Hartlepool, the celebration being far more spectacular than the goal! I got a lot of ribbing at Hartlepool for being very stiff and straight-backed, so my goal celebration consisted of me getting down on all-fours in front of the home fans with the lads taking it in turns to 'iron' my 'ironing board' back!

**Who was the best player you played with and why?**
The best player I ever played with was Steve Bruce. His reading of the game was second-to-none and considering his age and lack of pace at the time (he was in the twilight of his career while at Blues) he was rarely caught out of position. A natural leader and organiser on the pitch, it was a great pleasure to have played in the same back-four as Steve. Special mention must also go to Steve Robinson and Jon McCarthy who when playing in midfield in front of me, often did most of my running!

**If you could go back to your days at Blues what one thing would you do differently?**
As much as I loved my time at the Blues, I guess I should have left the club earlier. I spent a couple of seasons trying to regain my place in the side after the signing of the formidable Gary Rowett, however from that moment on my days were numbered, and I ended up playing a lot of reserve team football – looking back, probably too much. I don't think I ever re-captured the form I had then shown in my early twenties.

**What was your best moment while at St Andrew's?**
There were many brilliant moments for me while playing for the Blues, and I always look back very fondly on my time there. My debut aside, I guess highlights include playing in the televised semi-final of what's now the Carling Cup at home to Leeds, playing against Ryan Giggs and David Ginola in home friendlies against Man United and Spurs respectively, and winning 7–0 away at Stoke. All equally memorable!

**If you hadn't chosen football as a career what would you be?**
If I hadn't chosen football as a career, and although I never thought of doing anything else while growing up, I believe I would have followed in my father's and brother's footsteps and become professionally trained in Quantity Surveying before joining the family building business.

**What is your opinion of football today?**
I do believe that football today, running throughout the Leagues, has never been of a better quality or standard. This includes stadia and fan's facilities. That said, at the highest levels of the game anyway, I do believe that football has lost some of its credibility with the public. Due to the ridiculous sums of money being earned in wages, power is now fully weighted in the players' favour, and there is an unhealthy lack of respect shown by some of the players in their position of responsibility, as well as to authority, and thus the game suffers as a result. In my opinion, the players must never become bigger than the game itself.

**If you could be one of today's Premier League stars who would you want to be and why?**
If I could be a Premier League star today, I would be Steven Gerrard. On the pitch, he truly leads by example and has consistently performed at a very high level over a sustained period of time in a, relatively speaking, under-performing side.

# Keith Edwin Bertschin

**Heroic claim to fame**
Scored with his first kick in League football for Ipswich v Arsenal at Highbury in April 1976.

**Vital statistics**
*Date of birth:* 25 August 1956
*Place of birth:* Enfield
*Blues career:* 134 + 7 Substitute – 41 goals
*Blues debut:* 20 August 1977 (h) lost 1–4 v Manchester United. Crowd: 28,005
*Team:* Montgomery, Calderwood, Pendrey, Towers, Howard, Page, Jones (G) Francis, Bertschin, Hibbitt, Connolly
*First Blues goal:* 17 September 1977 (h) won 3–0 v Newcastle United
*Club honours:* Blues – Division Two Promotion 1979–80
*Representative honours:* England Under-21 – 3 appearances 1977–78

**Playing Career**

| Club | From | To | Fee | Total Appearances incl (subs) | Goals |
|---|---|---|---|---|---|
| Stafford Rangers | 1996 | 1998 | | | |
| Tamworth | 1996 | | | | |
| Hednesford Town | 1995 | | | | |
| Worcester City | 1994 | 1995 | | | |
| Barry Town | 1994 | | | | |
| Evesham United | 1993 | 1994 | | | |
| Solihull Borough | 1992 | 1993 | | | |
| Aldershot | 1991 | 1992 | | | |
| Chester City | 1990 | 1991 | | 19 | |
| Walsall | 1988 | 1990 | | 55 | |
| Sunderland | 1987 | 1988 | | 36 | 7 |
| Stoke City | 1984 | 1987 | | 88 | 29 |
| Jacksonville Tea Men | | | Loan | 14 | 3 |

# THE HEROES

| | | | | |
|---|---|---|---|---|
| Norwich City | 1981 | 1984 | 114 | 29 |
| Birmingham City | 1977 | 1981 | 141 | 41 |
| Ipswich Town | 1973 | 1977 | 32 | 8 |
| Barnet | 1972 | | | |

## Career in words
He began his professional career with Ipswich Town in 1973 after a year with Barnet previously. In 1978–79 broke the same leg twice After retiring as a player he worked as an agent before his appointment to the coaching staff at Blues. In November 2007 he followed Steve Bruce out of St Andrew's to Wigan. In June 2009 he followed Bruce to Sunderland.

## About the man
### What inspired you to take up coaching?
After finishing football, I could have probably stayed in the game with Walsall, but I had a massive operation and I left The Saddlers on the basis that my contract had changed and one or two things that were promised were not forthcoming. I had a quick spell at Chester and Aldershot and all of a sudden you find yourself at that sort of retirement age. I went into two or three different businesses – I ran an indoor five-a-side stadium, did a bit of finance with Cornhill and a sales job. Then I realised I was missing football. I got back involved doing a little bit of coaching at Walsall through Paul Taylor, the general manager at the time. I was working with him with the Under-15s and the Under-16s. At the same time I'd been given the opportunity to go into the football agency world with a couple of partners. It was around the time Steve(Bruce) arrived at Birmingham. Our families knew each other from old and we had played at Norwich City together. We got talking and he said 'Are you busy and would you ever consider a career change? I know you keep yourself fit and I know you're still involved with football with the agency, would you fancy coming on board?' So I was really pleased I had kept up some sort of fitness and stayed in the football fraternity. When Steve asked me to do a little bit for him, I thought he meant just a bit of scouting and so on, but he wanted me to come and look after the reserves.

### What were your first recollections when you joined Blues?
The training ground. It was quite nice at Elmdon but nothing compared to the current facilities. It was incredibly small. You'd have to cram into a tiny team room there would be about 35 players and the groundsman Lionel having a cup of tea.

### What are your memories as a player?
I had a great run, but I was a bit unlucky really, I was at Walsall and I was about 34 and playing quite well and everything was going great guns and then I developed an ache in my foot which developed into a career-threatening injury. I had to have two bones fused and a staple run through my foot and that kind of put paid to being able to play any sort of decent standard football.

**BIRMINGHAM CITY**  MODERN DAY HEROES

# Noel Blake

### Heroic claim to fame
In 2010 he is the coach to the England Under-21 team.

### Vital statistics
*Date of birth:* 12 January 1962
*Place of birth:* Kingston, Jamaica
*Blues career:* 96 – 5 goals
*Blues debut:* 18 September 1982 (h) won 1–0 v Coventry City. Crowd: 11,681
*Team:* Blyth, Langan, Dennis, Stevenson, Blake, Phillips (S) Carrodus, Evans, Whatmore, Curbishley, Handysides
*First Blues goal:* 6 November 1982 (h) won 2–1 v West Bromwich Albion

### Playing Career

| Club | From | To | Fee | Total Appearances incl (subs) | Goals |
| --- | --- | --- | --- | --- | --- |
| Exeter | 1995 | 2001 | Free | 161 | 10 |
| Dundee | 1993 | 1995 | Free | 64 | 2 |
| Bradford | 1992 | 1993 | Free | 51 | 4 |
| Bradford | 1992 | | Loan | 6 | |
| Stoke City | 1990 | 1992 | £175,000 | 90 | 3 |
| Leeds United | 1988 | 1990 | Free | 62 | 4 |
| Portsmouth | 1984 | 1988 | £150,000 | 173 | 13 |
| Birmingham City | 1982 | 1984 | £55,000 | 96 | 5 |
| Shrewsbury Town | 1982 | | Loan | 6 | |
| Aston Villa | 1979 | 1982 | Trainee | 4 | |
| Sutton Coldfield | 1978 | 1979 | | | |

### Career in words
He became player-manager at Exeter City in 2000 leaving after a year to work with the Stoke City Youth set-up. A qualified coach, he holds the UEFA Pro Licence and was appointed in February 2007 as an FA National Coach to work with the England Under-19s in 2008.

He was voted Blues' favourite-ever Black player in 2005 as part of the 'Kick Racism Out Of Football' week of action to celebrate Black History Month. Noel got 24 per cent of the vote, Michael Johnson 16 per cent and Emile Heskey 12 per cent.

He was part of Blues' very own 'Crazy Gang' which featured Mick Harford, Pat Van den Hauwe, Robert Hopkins, Tony Coton, Howard Gayle.

When he was an apprentice at Villa he used to coach a side called Whilminaha in the Birmingham Boys League at the age of 16. He also used to help coach his Dad's pub team and gained lots of other experience along the way to becoming a Pro Licence holder

When he was not working in football he went out and got himself qualified as a teacher with a PGCE. He did not sit around wondering what to do as he already had two degrees in Sports Science and Physical Education. He taught geography and PE as a supply teacher at schools in Stoke on Trent.

Noel was acknowledged as the original 'Zulu Warrior' and when questioned about the antics of the Blues team in the 1980s he responds:

'Look, if that team had done everything it was accused of, we would never had time to play. Did I help lock Julian Dicks in a broom cupboard, arrange a fight after a game at Portsmouth and kick down a dressing-room door at Villa Park?' He asks himself with his facial expression neither denying or accepting the accusations!

His strength of character has been shown at the two clubs he loved best: at Birmingham City he achieved his boyhood ambition as a key part of Ron Saunders's regime in the 1980s in which he brought together one of the toughest teams ever to step out in a royal blue kit. At Portsmouth under Alan Ball away from the industrial Midlands where immigrants were commonplace he had to develop into a man in winning his battle

THE HEROES

with racists from within the club's own fan base, which at one time had him considering whether to quit the game. Now he is one of the most highly qualified coaches in the United Kingdom, one of a small number of black coaches within the Football Association's hierarchy and in charge of the England Under-21 team. In the mid-1980s he was one of the first black central defenders, with a reputation for having a 'take no prisoners' approach. When blood flowed from his head following an injury at Vicarage Road, Watford, the 'Zulu Warrior' shout came from the travelling Bluenoses. In those days, one could only see a bleak future for the Blues with the Trevor Francis £1 million gone and the club on the decline. Ron Saunders bucked that trend by assembling a team of 'bargain basement' buys with a 'never say die' attitude which meant that if we were going to get beaten then it would not be for lack of effort.

## About the man
### What did you think about the mid-80s team so called 'the crazy gang'?
I look back now and think that they do it a disservice. We were meant to have done all sorts. Sure, there were scrapes and incidents, but people attached themselves to us. It was like a badge of honour for them, but we weren't a handful. Not for Ron Saunders, anyway. All this talk and these stories about the so-called 'Birmingham Five'. People forget what good players the other lads were. Mick Harford went on to play for England; if it hadn't been for Tony Coton's knee he would have, too. He was Manchester United's goalkeeping coach for years, so what does that tell you? Pat Van Den Hauwe won a League title with Everton. I ended up playing over 600 games and Robert Hopkins played in the top flight with us, Manchester City and West Bromwich Albion, getting about 500 appearances in his career. There were a few scrapes, I'm not going to deny that. But the way I was brought up, if someone stood in your face, you stood your corner. Perhaps it was what Saunders instilled in us. He was into his boxing. Anyway, we were young and stood together. Birmingham is a big city so there was always someone ready to have a go. As individuals we didn't shy away. But there's no way we could have got up to what people have said we did. And do you notice, not one of us has ever talked about it? Not one.

### When did you first come up against racism?
Growing up in Birmingham it was a truly cosmopolitan city, and therefore I did not encounter racism in a professional sense until I moved to Portsmouth. I had moved for money reasons. I had no idea what moving to Portsmouth would be like. Pompey is like Birmingham, a working-class club, a tough club, but the difference was that on the south coast there was a racist element to it as well. I was racially abused by my own fans. It got so bad I thought about walking out, and I am a resilient sort of bloke. It didn't get to the stage where bananas were being thrown on the pitch. But it wasn't one or two, let's put it like that. What hurt me more than anything else was the fact that it was my own fans. I'd come to expect it away from home, but to get it from your own supporters. I was playing for them! I endured it at Leeds United once – from the home supporters. Ninety minutes of "Shoot that n****r, which f****n' n****r, that f****n' n*****r". Racism was in the game, and I have to say it was not everyone. I've got letters at home now from Portsmouth supporters who were disgusted at the treatment I was receiving.

### In typical style Noel got his own back on the Leeds racist element by signing for the club. Noel takes up the story:
A journalist tried to collar me for some post-match quotes when I was walking out of the dressing-room. The reporter came running down this corridor and was shouting 'Vince, Vince' clearly thinking I was Vince Hilaire. I carried on, but eventually he caught up with me, pulled my arm and said, 'Vince?' I just looked at him and replied, 'Sorry, wrong n****r, man' and walked off. Society has changed. But unless you're on the receiving end, you will never understand it. Politicians don't know what it's like. People are very subtle with their comments. Let me give you an example. I got on a flight to Serbia which was one of my first trips with the Football Association. On the aeroplane there is an atmosphere. You could hear a pin drop. I relieved it by opening my scouting folder and jotting a few things down. When people saw what I was doing it all changed. They realised I was a football person. It changed the whole ambience in an instant. I see and feel that. A white person, on the other hand would not.

### As a spectator what was you biggest Blues disappointment?
The 1975 semi-final replay defeat against Fulham. I was at that semi-final defeat, and I don't think the club has ever truly recovered from that.

### As a player what was your biggest Blues disappointment?
In 1984 against Watford we didn't have our regular full-backs. And I just think it was one of those days when we were fated not to win. John Barnes scored a great goal, but even that sat up nicely for him. That defeat hurt like nothing else.

# Stephen Carr

**Heroic claim to fame**
From retirement to the Premier League.

## Vital statistics
*Date of birth:* 29 August 1976
*Place of birth:* Dublin
*Blues career:* 77 (at end of 2010)
*Blues debut:* 24 February 2009 (a) drew 0–0 v Crystal Palace. Crowd: 12,847
*Team:* Taylor, Carr, Murphy, Larsson, Ridgewell, Jaidi, Fahey, Bowyer, Bent, Costly, Sinclair
*Club honours:* Tottenham Hotspur – League Cup winners 1998–99; Newcastle – 2006 Intertoto Cup; Blues – Promotion from the Championship 2009 – Carling Cup winner 2011
*Representative honours:* PFA Premiership Team of the Season in 2001 and 2003; Republic of Ireland – Schoolboy, Youth, Under-18, Under-21 6 caps and 46 full caps from 1999–2007 retiring from international football on 14 November 2007.

## Playing Career

| Club | From | To | Fee | Total Appearances incl (subs) | Goals |
|---|---|---|---|---|---|
| Birmingham City | 2009 | | Free | 77 | |
| Newcastle | 2004 | 2008 | £2,000,000 | 107 | 1 |
| Tottenham | 1993 | 2004 | Trainee | 270 | 8 |

## Career in words

As a 15-year-old Carr went on trial from Stella Maris FC where he played his schoolboy football to Tottenham Hotspur. He made his Spurs debut on 29 September 1993 at Portman Road against Ipswich Town in the Premier League, although he did not establish himself until 1996–97 when he made 28 appearances in the campaign. He collected a League Cup medal with Spurs in 1999 in a 1–0 win over Leicester City. Steve signed for Newcastle United in August 2004 for a fee of £2 million on a four-year contract. His debut was in a 2–2 draw with Middlesbrough on 14 August 2004, playing 26 League games in that season. With a persistent knee injury he only made 19 League appearances the following campaign (2005–06). His career continued to be blighted by injury which ultimately resulted in Kevin Keegan deciding not to renew his contract. Although there was a lot of interest from senior clubs he failed to find a suitable club and retired on 1 December 2008. In February 2009 he began training with Blues with a view to coming out of retirement and signed a one-month deal on 23 February making his debut the following day. After impressing in the initial month he gained an

# BIRMINGHAM CITY                                                                 MODERN DAY HEROES

extension to the end of the season and signed a two-year deal after the Blues gained promotion to the Premier League.

### About the man
Carr endeared himself to the Blues fans when we played Villa away from home in 2009–10 season when he caused uproar at the end of the game when he ran across the front of the North Stand to the tunnel making a hand gesture. Villa fans complained to the police, who took no action, but he was hauled up before an FA Disciplinary panel and banned for one game after admitting a charge of improper conduct. Emotions ran high at that defeat in April, with Blues furious when Villa were awarded a penalty by referee Martin Atkinson for Roger Johnson's tackle on Gabriel Agbonlahor. James Milner scored what turned out to be the decisive goal. Blues were left fuming and Johnson blasted Atkinson as a 'disgrace' and was fined £7,500 by the FA. The club was also hit with a £10,000 fine for failing to control their players. Carr who also scuffed the penalty spot before Milner was about to take the kick said afterwards that his 'head had gone' as he was so wound up by events. 'I didn't get fines. I just missed a match. I am not going through that again sitting in front of five men talking to me like a child...'

# Simon Thomas Charlton

### Heroic claim to fame
A centre-back in the Premier at 5ft 8in.

### Vital statistics
*Date of birth:* 25 October 1971
*Place of birth:* Huddersfield
*Blues career:* 75 + 3 Substitute
*Blues first appearance as substitute:* 6 December 1997 (a) won 1–0 v Port Vale. Crowd: 7,509
*Blues debut:* 13 December 1997 (h) won 2–1 v Manchester City. Crowd: 21,014
*Team:* Bennett, Bass, Charlton, Bruce, Ablett, O'Connor (M), McCarthy, Robinson, Devlin, Hughes, Ndlovu

### Playing Career

| Club | From | To | Fee | Total Appearances incl (subs) | Goals |
|---|---|---|---|---|---|
| Oldham Athletic | 2006 | 2007 | Free | 39 | 1 |
| Norwich City | 2004 | 2006 | £250,000 | 50 | 2 |
| Bolton Wanderers | 2000 | 2004 | Free | 135 | |
| Birmingham City | 1998 | 2000 | £200,000 | 73 | |
| Birmingham City | 1997 | 1998 | Loan | 5 | |
| Southampton | 1993 | 1998 | £250,000 | 137 | 3 |
| Huddersfield Town | 1989 | 1993 | Trainee | 157 | 2 |

### Career in words
He began his career with his home-town club, Huddersfield Town, where he played over a 100 games before moving to the Premiership with Southampton for £250,000 in 1993. Initially he was loaned to Blues, before making the move permanent in 1998. In 2000 he was transferred to Bolton Wanderers where he was chosen as their Player of the Year for 2001–02 before moving to Norwich City in July 2004. At the end of the 2005–06 season he signed a one-year deal with Oldham Athletic in August 2006. He scored once for Oldham Athletic, scoring a goal from his own half in the 4–1 win over Gillingham. His contract expired in May 2007, and so he retired as a player and returned to Norwich City as a youth coach. He became manager of Mildenhall Town in April 2009 while retaining his player registration.

# THE HEROES

**About the man**
**Who were the best players you have played with and why?'**
Matt Le Tissier at Southampton. He was just something else – an amazing player and a scorer of incredible goals. Steve Bruce; you never appreciated what a good player he was until you played alongside him. He's not 6ft 4in, but he rarely lost a header and there was a real art to the way he would get around a forward so

calmly and just lay the ball off. In fact, he taught me to play centre back, and I played 20 times for Bolton Wanderers in the Premier League in that position and I am only 5ft 8in.

**What are your overriding memories of the Blues?**
Probably the Blues fans themselves. In the nicest possible way they were a bit nuts, and I'm sure they still are! You'd come out to warm up and they'd be singing away merrily or doing the conga or something, not a care in the world. We loved their attitude, the off-beat humour and their passion, and it's those types of things that mean a lot to a player. They were always right behind the lads, and it made coming to work fun.

**Any regrets?**
Yes, the fact that we never managed to get up out of Division One. I'm afraid I blame Trevor Francis for that, I remember one season we were absolutely romping the League, the best passing team by far and in one week he sold Chrissy Marsden and let Frank Barlow go, who was first-team coach. In almost a week we went from being one of the best passing teams to one of the worst. Everything used to go through Mars, and Frank took most of the training, so without them we ended up just hoofing it up the pitch. That was a big regret because that particular season we had more than enough to get promoted and I don't think we recovered afterwards.

**What about off the field?**
I have my daughter Olivia, and I have an events organisation business.

# Aliou Cisse

**Heroic claim to fame**
Sent off in Blues' first game in the Premiership.

**Vital statistics**
*Date of birth:* 24 March 1976
*Place of birth:* Ziguinchor, Senegal
*Blues career:* 38
*Blues debut:* 18 August 2002 (a) lost 0–2 v Arsenal. Crowd: 38,018
*Team:* Vaesen, Kenna, Grainger, Cunningham, Purse, Tebily, Johnson (D), John, Horsfield, Cisse, Hughes
*Representative honours:* Senegal – 28 full caps

**Playing Career**

| Club | From | To | Fee | Total Appearances incl (subs) | Goals |
| --- | --- | --- | --- | --- | --- |
| Nimes Olympique | 2009 | | | 7 | 1 |
| Sedan Ardennes | 2007 | 2009 | | 21 | 1 |
| Portsmouth | 2004 | 2006 | £300,000 | 28 | |
| Birmingham City | 2002 | 2004 | £1,500,000 | 38 | |
| Montpelier Herault SC | 2001 | 2002 | Loan | 17 | 1 |
| Paris Saint-Germain | 2000 | 2001 | | 35 | 1 |
| Sedan Ardennes | 1997 | 1998 | | 0 | |
| Lille | 1994 | 1997 | | 6 | |

**Career in words**
His career began with Lille OSC before moving to CS Sedan and then Paris Saint-Germain. He spent the majority of his time on loan to Montpellier Herault SC. In 2002 he captained the Senegal national side that reached the quarter-finals of the 2002 World Cup, beating the holders France. He was transferred to

# THE HEROES

the Blues for the start of the 2002–03 season which was Blues first-ever in the Premiership. He made his debut at Arsenal on the opening day of the season but was sent off, gaining a red card which was subsequently rescinded. He was an extremely competitive player and with his distinctive hairstyles was impossible to ignore, particularly by game officials. These facts resulted in him gaining five yellow cards in six games, generating a total of 10 before the New Year. He joined Portsmouth for £300,000 on a two-year deal before returning to France with CS Sedan Ardennes, whom he left in September 2009 to join Nimes Olympique.

### About the man
The MV Le Joola was a Senegalese government-owned ferry that capsized off the coast of The Gambia on 26 September 2002. At least 1,863 people lost their lives on that day making the sinking of the ferry the second worst non-military maritime disaster in terms of the number of lives lost, exceeding the death toll of RMS *Titanic* which famously sank in 1912 resulting in 1,503 deaths.

Cissie lost nine family members in the tragedy, but he did not fly back to Senegal until after he had played against West Ham United on 5 October, a game we won 2–1. The fact that he made that gesture in very difficult circumstances touched the hearts of many Blues fans, and they were determined to pay their respects.

At St Andrew's on 26 October 2002 in the match v Manchester City the fans decorated the ground with red, green and yellow cards, the colours of the Senegal flag. Even though the game was lost 0–2, it was a day to remember.

# James Richard Clapham

### Heroic claim to fame
He tackled and worked like a Bluenose.

### Vital statistics
*Date of birth:* 7 December 1975

# BIRMINGHAM CITY

## MODERN DAY HEROES

*Place of birth:* Lincoln
*Blues career:* 97 – 1 goal
*Blues debut:* 12 January 2003 (h) lost 0–4 v Arsenal. Crowd: 29,505
*Team:* Vaesen, Coly, Kenna, Savage, Vickers, Johnson (M), Johnson (D), John, Dugarry, Clemence, Clapham
*First Blues goal:* 28 December 2005 (h) drew 2–2 v Manchester United

## Playing Career

| Club | From | To | Fee | Total Appearances incl (subs) | Goals |
|---|---|---|---|---|---|
| Lincoln City | 2010 | | Free | 3 | |
| Notts County | 2008 | 2010 | Free | 80 | 3 |
| Leicester City | 2008 | 2008 | Free | 11 | |
| Leeds United | 2007 | 2007 | Loan | 15 | |
| Wolverhampton Wanderers | 2006 | 2007 | Free | 29 | |
| Birmingham City | 2003 | 2006 | £1,300,000 | 97 | 1 |
| Ipswich Town | 1998 | 2003 | £300,000 | 240 | 14 |
| Ipswich Town | 1998 | 1998 | Loan | 12 | |
| Bristol Rovers | 1997 | 1997 | Loan | 5 | |
| Leyton Orient | 1997 | 1997 | Loan | 6 | |
| Tottenham Hotspur | 1994 | 1998 | Trainee | 1 | |

## Career in words

He started his career with Tottenham Hotspur, making a single appearance in a 2–1 defeat to Coventry on 11 May 1997. Prior to that he had loan spells at Leyton Orient (six games between 29 January and 22 February 1997) and Bristol Rovers (five games between 27 March and 26 April 1997). He went on loan to Ipswich for two months between 9 January and 12 March 1998 the move becoming permanent for a fee of £300,000 making over 250 appearances in his time at Portman Road. In 1999 he was voted Player of the Year and tasted European football, playing 12 games in two UEFA campaigns in 2001–02 and 2002–03. Ipswich Town were relegated in 2002 and went into administration, resulting in Jamie joining Blues for £1.3 million in 2003. He was released in May 2006, and after a trial at Sheffield United in the summer of 2006 he signed for Wolverhampton Wanderers in August 2006 on a two-year deal. He was loaned to Leeds United in August 2007 for a three-month period before joining Leicester City on 31 January 2008, where he was released five months later in May 2008. He trained with West Bromwich Albion when they were managed by his ex-Ipswich teammate Tony Mowbray, he also had a trial at Sheffield United, then after two weeks' training with Notts County he signed a short-term deal in September 2008 before signing an 18-month contract in January 2009.

## About the man
### How do you relax away from football?
I just try and chill out. I have a PlayStation which I enjoy and a computer. I've got two Boxer dogs and I enjoy golf.

### First pair of football boots?
Hand downs from my brother David. I think they were Hummel.

### First team played for?
Under-9s for St Helen's.

### Football hero?
Paul Gascoigne.

## BIRMINGHAM CITY                                    MODERN DAY HEROES

**First famous person met?**
John Barnes.

**Favourite film star?**
Chevy Chase.

**First car?**
Metro Mayfair.

**First pet?**
An Alsation called Shep.

**First wage?**
It was £3 per week as a YTS at Tottenham Hotspur.

# Ian Stewart Clarkson

**Heroic claim to fame**
Blues captain in Leyland Daf victory at the age of 21.

**Vital statistics**
*Date of birth:* 4 December 1970
*Place of birth:* Solihull
*Blues career:* 159 + 13
*Blues debut:* 27 September 1988 (h) lost 0–2 v Aston Villa. Crowd: 21,177 second round League Cup first leg.
*Team:* Godden, Ranson, Roberts, Atkins, Overson, Clarkson, Morris, Langley, Yates, Robinson (C) Wigley
*Club honours:* Blues – Leyland Daf winners 1991 Division Three champions 1992; Northampton Town – League Two Play-off winners 1997; Kidderminster Harriers – Conference champions 2000.

**Playing Career**

| Club | From | To | Fee | Total Appearances incl (subs) | Goals |
|---|---|---|---|---|---|
| Forest Green | 2003 | 2003 | | | |
| Leamington | 2003 | | | | |
| Stafford Rangers | 2002 | | | | |
| Nuneaton Town | 2002 | 2003 | Free | 12 | |
| Kidderminster Harriers | 1999 | 2002 | Free | 115 | |
| Northampton Town | 1996 | 1999 | Free | 104 | 2 |
| Stoke City | 1993 | 1996 | £40,000 | 97 | |
| Birmingham City | 1988 | 1993 | Trainee | 172 | |

**Career in words**
'Clarky' began as a YTS trainee with Blues in 1987. He made his first-team debut at 17 in the League Cup v Aston Villa in September 1988 and his League debut a few days later. He signed professional terms in December 1988. Former Blues manager Lou Macari signed him for Stoke City in September 1993 for £40,000. He spent three seasons in The Potteries and played in the Championship Play-offs, which they lost to Leicester City in the 1996 semi-final. He joined Northampton Town, where he linked up with ex-Blues players John Gayle, Dean Peer and Ian Atkins, with John Frain joining some time after. In his first season with the Cobblers, he won promotion via the Play-offs and the next year played in the League One Play-off

Final, losing 1–0 to Grimsby Town. In August 1998 he broke his leg, from which he never recovered, and his League career was over at the age of 28. He trained with Kidderminster Harriers becoming club captain, and of his first 30 games he only lost one, at the end of the season they were promoted to the Football League as Conference champions, going on to repay the insurance pay-out Clarky had received on his retirement so that he could play for them in the League. In March 2002 he was assistant to caretaker manager Ian Britton before being released for financial reasons. He joined Nuneaton Borough in the Conference before again being released on financial grounds. He had short periods at Stafford Rangers and Leamington and from March 2003 with Forest Green before finally retiring at the end of the season. Ian is a qualified coach and coach educator and worked for Blues Football in the Community programme. From 2002 he was a football reporter and journalist for the *Birmingham Post* and *Sunday Mercury* and worked for the PFA's website. In 2006 he was project manager for the North Solihull Fusion project which brings football to the youngsters of the northerly communities of the Solihull Metropolitan Borough.

### About the man

Since leaving his role as a sports journalist with *The Birmingham Post*, 'Clarky' has found a renewed enthusiasm for football, having recently completed a four-game tour of Tenerife! (OK so it was only a daily game at 4.30pm between the staff and guests of his holiday hotel – but the man loves his football.)

As well as his full-time job and looking after his family, Ian also finds time to write for the Professional Football Association's website, attend Blues' home games to entertain guests in the Blues' corporate hospitality areas, be a freelance Boxing journalist and, of course, play football for the Birmingham City All-Stars (which is organised by Tom Ross of BRMB/Capital Gold).

### Middle name Stewart?

My Dad has a number of Scottish relatives, so it was inevitable that I got a Scottish name – I guess if I was playing now I would qualify for Scotland's International squad!

### Born in December? What star sign are you and are you superstitious?

Sagittarius – not really superstitious, but I had three things which I felt helped my performance: As a youngster I liked to prepare my own chicken and pasta on a Friday night. I liked to run out onto the pitch in a sweat top while the rest of the lads were in their shirts. I always preferred long-sleeved shirts as they felt like proper shirts.

### How did you get spotted by Blues?

I was playing for North Star in the Central Warwickshire League when I was invited to Blues by their scout Norman Bodell. After being signed under the Youth Training Scheme I did not kick a football for two weeks. I got paid £28.50 a week plus a Bus Pass with a £4 win bonus and a £2 draw bonus for Youth and Reserve games. In those days we could play two games in five hours, a reserve game in the afternoon and a Midweek Floodlit game in the evening.

### Being born in Solihull, does that make you a Bluenose?

Yes, my first introduction was as a five-year-old during season 1976–77. I had the same initial experience that every Bluenose gets – Loss, Loss, Loss, Loss! My childhood heroes were most definitely Colin Todd and Frank Worthington.

### Why do you think the atmosphere has been lost at St Andrew's in recent times?

I think seating has made a difference, but there are other social factors. Supporters reflect the way people are these days – impatient and very much 'me' orientated – it makes a difference to how fans see the game.

### Who were the characters during your time at the Blues?

There were a number of funny guys – Steve Whitton, Paul Fitzpatrick [remember him? Seven appearances between January–March 1993] and Darren Rowbotham. David Rennie was the complete opposite – very serious.

# BIRMINGHAM CITY

## MODERN DAY HEROES

### You captained the Blues – how did that happen?

Trevor Matthewson was skipper at the time, and he got injured in the first match of the season against Bury at home on 17 August 1991. Terry Cooper threw me the armband, and that was that, when Trevor came back at the end of September, the lads had a vote and I kept the captaincy. I guess I was chosen because I am 'gobby', but I do get on with people, and if someone isn't pulling their weight then I will tell them!

### How many managers did you serve under?

Four – Garry Pendrey, Dave Mackay, Lou Macari and Terry Cooper. Oh and for about three games Bill Caldwell in his caretaking role.

I got on with them all, but Lou introduced me to fitness, he was a fitness nut – one day he got us to run down to the Aston Villa Leisure Centre on the pretext that there would be transport to get us back – no transport was there so we had to run all the way back to St Andrew's. He would organise five-a-side games with no boundaries so the game would just go on and on. I liked him – he had no favourites!

Garry was fine, and I suppose you always look up to the manager who gives you your first opportunity. He was always bright and bubbly, an honest fella and what you saw was what you got. But I think some of the older players let him down. He was a little unlucky that things were so bad at the time we had to queue for our wages on a Friday afternoon. I remember one of my first pre-seasons, when we went back early in June we had to cut the grass at Elmdon ourselves. We didn't have a proper sit-on mower so we had to use scythes and shears, anything we could get hold of.

Dave Mackay came in and stabilised things a bit, although his input was more on matchdays, and he did not want us to play pure football and he wanted his players to be 'real men' That was his favourite quote: he wanted everyone to be tough but to play football as well. Dave used to give Bobby Ferguson carte blanche to do what he wanted, and he was like chalk to cheese compared to Dave. Dave was old school; honest and one of those who wanted you to get up after tackles or he'd bring you off, whereas Bobby was a good coach, but he'd come from Ipswich where he had been working with better players and he could never work it out why we couldn't do the same. He got very frustrated with us!

### Who are your favourite six best Blues players?
Wayne Clarke – Tony Coton – Dave Langan – Kevin Dillon and, of course Todd and Worthington.

### What's bad about the current game?
Diving and all-seater stadiums.

## THE HEROES

**What was the best and worst thing about playing for Blues?**
The best thing was playing for the club I supported and the worst thing was the Triton strip of 1992–93.

**How did you career develop after leaving Blues?**
They signed Scott Hiley from Terry Cooper's previous cub Exeter City for £100,000 in March 1993 and TC wanted me to go to Exeter, but I said no. So I was on a weekly deal and missed a pre-season tour to Italy, I trained with Peterborough for a while, then on 1 September 1993 we played at Stoke in an Anglo-Italian preliminary round, losing 2–0. Lou Macari was managing them, and I moved to Stoke City for a fee of £50,000. My first three games at Stoke were against Middlesbrough, Nottingham Forest and Manchester United. We won all three games. In the United game I was marking Lee Sharpe, who was released by Blues as a 16-year-old.

When Joe Jordan and Jez Moxey came to the Potteries I was signed by Ian Atkins to join Northampton Town. I stayed with the Cobblers for four years before suffering an injury that forced me to retire from the game. I trained with Nuneaton Borough and Kidderminster and got a contract with the Harriers after they had repaid my insurance payout of £15,000. Jan Molby was the manager, and we went onto to win the Conference thanks to an incredible run when we only lost one game in 28!

**You have an impressive list of football qualifications?**
FA Coaching Certificate, Emergency Aid Course, FA Coaching Licence (UEFA 'B' Award), SAQ Preliminary Award, FA Coach Educator Level 1.

**Author's note:** I received a text message from Clarky at 23:46 hours on 1 December 2010 after Blues had beaten Aston Villa 2–1 to reach the semi-finals of the Carling Cup. It read: 'Are you listening Tony Barton, Peter Withe, Bernie Gallagher, Steve Sims, Pongo Waring, Billy Mac, Kevin Gage, Andy Gray, Black and White Frank Carrodus, Dr Jo Peter Murphy, Gordon Cowans, Turn Coat Heskey, Brendan & Chris Price, Steve Hunt, Simon Stainrod, Gary Barry, Gabby Agbonlahor, your boys took one hell of a beating…'

# Stephen Neal Clemence

### Heroic claim to fame
Son of Ray Clemence Liverpool, Spurs and England goalkeeper.

### Vital statistics
*Date of birth:* 31 March 1978
*Place of birth:* Liverpool
*Blues career:* 135 – 9 goals
*Blues debut:* 12 January 2003 (h) lost 0–4 v Arsenal. Crowd: 29,505 (**Author's note:** The same debut match for Coly, Dugarry and Clapham)
*Team:* Vaesen, Coly, Kenna, Savage, Vickers, Johnson (M), Johnson (D), John, Dugarry, Clemence, Clapham
*First goal:* 23 February 2003 (h) won 2–1 v Liverpool
*Club honours:* Promotion to Premier League 2006–07
*Representative honours:* England Under-21

### Playing Career

| Club | From | To | Fee | Total Appearances incl (subs) | Goals |
|---|---|---|---|---|---|
| Leicester City | 2007 | 2010 | £1,000,000 | 34 | 3 |
| Birmingham City | 2003 | 2007 | £250,000 | 135 | 9 |
| Tottenham Hotspur | 1994 | 2003 | Trainee | 108 | 3 |

# BIRMINGHAM CITY                     MODERN DAY HEROES

## Career in words
'Clems' first club was Tottenham Hotspur, for whom he made his debut v Manchester United on 10 August 1997 in a 2–0 defeat. He joined Blues in January 2003 after an injury had blighted career at White Hart Lane. The fee was £250,000 and he helped Blues win promotion to the Premier League in season 2006–07. On 13 July 2007 he signed for Leicester City on a three year contract for an initial £750,000 with options for the fee to reach £1 million. He was appointed club captain on 28 July, scoring his first goal for the Foxes in a 3–2 League Cup win over Forest on 18 September. His injury bad luck returned and he was sidelined as Leicester were relegated eventually playing no part in the 2008–09 campaign due to complications arising after achilles heel surgery. He eventually returned to action in a 3–1 win over Derby County Reserves on 8 September 2009 playing only 30 minutes.

## About the man
### Tell me about your actress wife?
Angela (Saunders) was born in May 1977 in Bromley, Kent and as a young girl she trained in tap and ballet. She was a hospital worker and part-time model but after appearing in the Scottish 'soap opera' *McCallum* she worked on the cruise ships as a dancer. After that she became a full-time model and then grid-girl for three years in Formula One. She also worked on Ant and Dec's children's show *SMTV Live*. Ironically, she played Tash Parker in Sky One's football soap opera *Dream Team* in 2002. We got married in 2003, even though she was an Arsenal fan, and have two children aged five and three.

### Which sporting event would you like to attend?
The Masters.

### Which football stadium would you like to play in?
Bernabeu or Neu Camp.

### Sporting Hero?
Paul Gascoigne.

### Favourite sports Programme?
*Match of the Day*.

### Best player played against?
Steven Gerrard.

### First pair of football boots?
Patrick Laudrup.

### First team played for?
Broxbourne Sports.

### Favourite TV Programme?
*24*.

### Favourite Stadium?
Old Trafford.

### Favourite Sports Commentator?
Martin Tyler.

### Favourite Newspaper?
*The Sun*.

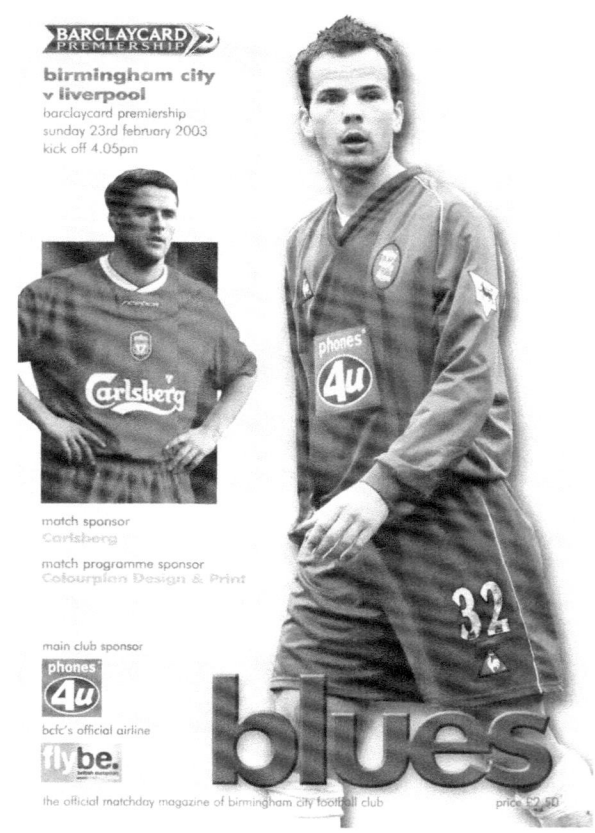

## THE HEROES

**Favourite Food?**
Chicken Pasta.

**Favourite Drink?**
Coke.

**Favourite Film?**
*Gladiator.*

**Favourite holiday destination?**
Anywhere hot with a pool and a beach.

**Favourite Pizza topping?**
Ham and Mushroom.

**Favourite sport after football?**
Golf.

**Favourite City**
London.

# Gary J. Cooper

**Heroic claim to fame**
His problems brought Barry Fry and Karren Brady together.

**Vital statistics**
*Date of birth:* 20 November 1965
*Place of birth:* Hammersmith, London
*Blues career:* 83 – 4 goals
*Blues debut:* 18 December 1993 (h) won 1–0 v Charlton Athletic. Crowd: 13,714
*Team:* Miller, Fenwick, Cooper, Lowe, Dryden, Whyte, McMinn, Wallace, Peschisolido, Saville, Harding
*First goal:* 11 January 1994 (a) lost 1–2 v Notts County
*Club honours:* Fisher Athletic – Southern Football League Premier Division champions 1987; Blues – Division Two champions 1994–95, Auto Windscreens Shield winners 1995

### Playing Career

| Club | From | To | Fee | Total Appearances incl (subs) | Goals |
| --- | --- | --- | --- | --- | --- |
| Welling United | 1996 | | | 62 | 2 |
| Birmingham City | 1993 | 1996 | Free | 83 | 4 |
| Peterborough United | 1991 | 1993 | £200,000 | 116 | 14 |
| Maidstone United | 1989 | 1991 | | 77 | 8 |
| Fisher Athletic | 1986 | 1989 | Free | | |
| Brentford | 1985 | | Loan | 10 | |
| Queen's Park Rangers | 1983 | 1986 | Apprentice | 3 | |

**Career in words**
Edwin Stein was an integral part of the Barry Fry regime that won the Division Two Championship in 1994–95 season. He had this to say about Gary Cooper's contribution to the triumph:

# BIRMINGHAM CITY                                    MODERN DAY HEROES

'Coops was our unsung hero, without a doubt. He wasn't in the frame at all until the start of the New Year for various reasons. He missed training and reserve games, and we had our rows with him. When he was called upon, credit to him for taking his chance and staying in the side.'

Colin Tatum reported on Monday 1 May 1995:
'MR. CONSISTENT TURNS IT ROUND'

Gary Cooper was facing up to being given the boot in October after Blues had lost patience with him. He had skipped training and reserve matches so he could be with his baby daughter, who was ill with liver problems. It didn't please managing director Karren Brady and Cooper was fined and put on the transfer list. But by the time the Huddersfield crunch game came around Cooper had long been back in the fold and arguably had been Blues' most consistent player in 1995. 'I missed the start of the season through injury and then with the team playing so well I couldn't get back in' he said. 'I then had my problems with Karren and went on the list. I didn't expect to figure again. Barry stuck by me and I had a few good games in the reserves and when I got a chance I managed to do Okay. That's what spurred me on. You know that if you don't impress when you are in the side there is someone to take your place. I kept out last season's player of the year, John Frain, and things went well.'

### About the man
**Extract from *Brady Plays the Blues* by Karren Brady published by Pavilion Books in 1995**
'But his [Barry Fry] treatment of Gary Cooper was an important proving ground in our relationship. (**Author's note:** On 15 September 1994 the club sold Harry Willis and Dave Regis to Southend in exchange for Gary Cooper and Johnathan Hunt.)

It was 18 October and two and half hours before we were due to play Walsall in an Autoglass Windshields Cup game, when Barry came into my office. 'Bloody Gary Cooper hasn't turned up again' 'What do you mean?' 'He hasn't been in for about four or five weeks because his kid's not well' he said 'Now he's rung in tonight to say she's been taken into hospital again and he can't come to the game. I don't know who I'm going to play instead because we've got so many injuries'.

I was surprised because only the week before Gary had told me his baby daughter had been given the all-clear and this seemed to me one sick-day too many. Barry had told me before about Gary's absences – a virus one week, a British Rail suicide the next, and plenty more time off for his sickly daughter. I decided to ring him and to no surprise, Gary himself answered. 'It's Karren Brady, Gary' I announced 'I thought you were in hospital with your daughter?'

'Oh, er I was just on my way back there' he said, hesitantly. 'Well could you kindly tell me the name of the hospital, the name of the ward and the name of your daughter.' I said 'because this has been going on for too long' The phone went down with a click by way of reply, I knew I was on firm ground. The phone remained engaged for hours after, but, by sheer luck my dad Terry's printing business was in the same street in North London as Gary's house. I faxed a letter down for him to deliver, detailing the serious nature of our complaint against him and summoning him to a meeting at St Andrew's the next day. Barry was even more upset than me, feeling rightly that he had been misled. When we got Gary's file out all we saw was a long list of club fines for absenteeism – and it appeared that if we wanted to fire him tomorrow we would have right on our side.

The chance to see Gary, let alone sack him, would have been welcome. At eight o'clock the next morning my phone rang at home and Gary announced he could not make our meeting as his girlfriend had to go to work and he had to stay at home to babysit. At that time in the morning I was not at my best and immediately lost it. 'You had this letter yesterday, in plenty of time to find a babysitter. You are a professional footballer and well rewarded for playing for us, not sitting at home minding babies. I want you in the office as soon as you can' And this time it was my turn to abruptly hang up. Gary arrived at St Andrew's at 11.30am but not with the explanation we had been waiting to hear. 'I've been lying about my kid ' he admitted, 'she was ill, but she's over the worst now and is out of hospital. It's just that I don't like the travelling and my girlfriend wants me in London. I don't know if I can come to any more games. I'll just have to keep you informed as and when the games come.'

'Gary, you've got two choices,' I told him 'You can carry on earning a lot of money, I'll go down and have a word with your girlfriend and we can try to get something sorted out. Or you can be sacked and go on the dole for £40 per week. It's up to you.'

He looked at me straight in the face, 'I'll think about it.' He said.

'Look, this is a joke, give me one good reason why we should give you another chance, because I can't think of any? You've lied to me, you've lied to the manager, you've made us all look bloody stupid. There are kids out there who would give their right arms to be professional footballers and we are saying if you show you are committed to Birmingham City we'll do all we can to help you. Problems we can deal with, lies we will not tolerate. You've got to think seriously about your future, because a stable job has got to be better than just walking away and living on nothing.'

'I'll think about it,' he echoed, and the meeting ended.

A week later Barry told me Gary had not travelled with the team or played in our match at Brentford on Saturday as requested – luckily for him we won 2–1 – but, for me, that was the final straw. 'He is taking the piss out of us all,' I told Barry. 'Contact the Professional Footballers' Association and tell Brendon Batson we are terminating his contract. He's been fined so many times he probably owes us money.'

We sorted out all the papers to end our association and Brendon came down to sit in on the final negotiations. What annoyed me most about Gary's behaviour was that we could not have tried harder to be fair and understanding. We hadn't fined him for not travelling to the Brentford game in case he had money worries and both myself and Barry had made ourselves available to help out with any problems. But it seemed no use – all our attempts to prevent this day happening had been rejected. Reluctantly, I told Barry: 'The decision is yours, but I don't think we have any option but to get rid of him. His career has hung by a thread for so long and if he won't abide by your decisions, then he has to go. If he stays he undermines your authority. He doesn't take his career seriously and nothing we tell him seems to sink in.

He has even asked to be released and handle his own registration and I think we should no longer stand in his way' Barry agreed. As far as I was concerned, the matter was over.

So it came as a bit of a surprise on 29 November, when Gary's name turned up on the team-sheet for an Autoglass Cup match against Gillingham. 'One more chance, Karren,' said Barry, 'I'll give him one more chance'

All I can say is thank God Barry did. Gary has been steadily improving these last few weeks, and last night he got into the team and scored. I'm not saying I understand Barry's methods, but after his patient handling of this affair I am at last beginning to appreciate them.

There have been times during our first 12 months together when I thought we would never click – never. I could not comprehend his style, he could not get to grips with mine. We are both from such different backgrounds I think we were on a war footing from day one and his handling of Gary Cooper proves our different outlooks. If I had been solely in charge, Gary would have been history. I don't think I was ever hard on him, but at the end when even the PFA seemed to be failing, that would have been his lot. Barry thought he could get something out of him, he listened to me, ignored everything I had said and followed his own hunch. And he was right. Barry Fry was right and I was wrong.

# Anthony Philip Coton

**Heroic claim to fame**
Saved John Hawley's penalty after 50 seconds of his debut.

**Vital statistics**
*Date of birth:* 19 May 1961
*Place of birth:* Tamworth, Staffordshire
*Blues career:* 114

# BIRMINGHAM CITY                                    MODERN DAY HEROES

*Blues debut:* 27 December 1980 (h) won 3–2 v Sunderland. Crowd: 19,005
*Team:* Coton, Langan, Lees, Curbishley, Gallagher, Todd, Ainscow, Bertschin, Worthington, Gemmill, Dillon
*Club honours:* Blues – Division Two runners-up 1984–85
*Representative honours:* England B

## Playing Career

| Club | From | To | Fee | Total Appearances incl (subs) | Goals |
|---|---|---|---|---|---|
| Hereford United | 2003 | 2004 | Free | | |
| Sunderland | 1996 | 1999 | £600,000 | | 10 |
| Manchester United | 1996 | 1996 | £500,000 | | 0 |
| Manchester City | 1990 | 1996 | £1,000,000 | | 195 |
| Watford | 1984 | 1990 | £300,000 | | 291 |
| Hereford United | 1979 | | Loan | | 0 |
| Birmingham City | 1978 | 1984 | | | 114 |
| Mile Oak Rovers | 1977 | 1978 | | | |

### Career in words
He started his career at Mile Oak Rovers in his home town of Tamworth, signing for Blues in 1977 as an amateur before agreeing professional terms in 1978. He made his League debut as a 19-year-old against Sunderland, and his first touch was saving a penalty! By 1982–83 he was Blues' number-one goalkeeper and when they were relegated at the end of the 1983–84 season. He returned to the top flight by joining Watford for £300,000 and at the end of his second full season was the Hornets' Player of the Season.

He went on to become Player of the Season for an unprecedented third time in 1989–90. Before the start of 1990–91 campaign he joined Manchester City for £1 million and once again showed his popularity by winning their Player of the Year in 1991–92 and 1993–94 season. His time at Maine Road was cut short through injury in 1995 but not before he won an England B Cap. In 1996 he joined Manchester United for £500,000, a record fee at the time between the Red and Blue halves of Manchester, regrettably he never played a first-team game and joined Sunderland after six months for £300,000. He broke his leg in five places in a League game v Southampton which marked the end of his career although in April 2004 he was bought in as emergency goalkeeping cover by Hereford United in the Conference. He was goalkeeping coach at Old Trafford for a number of years, but a knee injury forced him to step down in December 2007. He finally left Manchester United at the end of his contract in June 2008 to become a player's agent.

# Kenneth Edward Cunningham

### Heroic claim to fame
Drove a 'W' registration Ford Mondeo while playing in the Premier.

### Vital statistics
*Date of birth:* 28 June 1971
*Place of birth:* Dublin, Ireland
*Blues career:* 144
*Blues debut:* 18 August 2002 (a) lost 0–2 v Arsenal. Crowd: 38,018

*Team:* Vaesen, Kenna, Grainger, Cunningham, Purse, Tebily, Johnson (D), John, Horsfield, Cisse, Hughes
*Club honours:* Sunderland – Championship champions 2006–07
*Representative honours:* Republic of Ireland – 79 full caps, also B cap in 1994

## Playing Career

| Club | From | To | Fee | Total Appearances incl (subs) | Goals |
|---|---|---|---|---|---|
| Sunderland | 2006 | 2007 | Free | 12 | |
| Birmingham City | 2002 | 2006 | Free | 144 | |
| Wimbledon | 1994 | 2002 | £650,000 | 306 | |
| Millwall | 1989 | 1994 | | 153 | 2 |
| Tolka Rovers | 1988 | 1989 | | | |

## Career in words

He started his career at Tolka Rovers (1 August 1988 to 18 September 1989) before signing for Millwall. In his five-year stay he made over 150 League appearances, scoring twice. He moved to Wimbledon in November 1994 with Jon Goodman for a joint fee of £1.3 million. Kenny made over 300 appearances for the Dons. He moved to Blues in 2002 and was named Player of the Year in his first season. He joined Sunderland on 19 July 2006 helping them to win the Championship but he was released by the then manager Roy Keane at the end of 2006–07. He was unable to find a new club and retired as a player. Recently worked as a radio pundit on RTE and Sky Sports.

He was a Republic of Ireland international, captaining their 2002 World Cup campaign. He retired after the ROI failed to qualify for 2006 World Cup drawing 0–0 with Switzerland on 12 October 2005

## About the man

'An outstanding buy and a superb skipper' David Gold in *Pure Gold* published in 2006 by Highdown.

When Blues were relegated at the end of 2005–06 he was released, together with seven other first-team players, on 11 May 2006 and he launched a scathing attack on the Blues Board, likening the club to a 'stiff corpse' that has 'no heartbeat and, more worryingly, no soul'.

While his colleagues arrived at the ground in their Chryslers, Bentleys, Range Rovers and Porsches, Kenny turned up for much of his time at the Blues in a W-registered Mondeo!

BIRMINGHAM CITY                                              MODERN DAY HEROES

# Liam Sean Daish

**Heroic claim to fame**
He created Blues history by captaining them to two major trophies in one season.

## Vital statistics
*Date of birth:* 23 September 1968
*Place of birth:* Portsmouth
*Blues career:* 98 – 6 goals
*Blues debut:* 11 January 1994 (a) lost 1–2 v Notts County. Crowd: 7,212
*Team:* Bennett, Hiley, Cooper, Daish, Dryden, Whyte, Lowe, Claridge, Saville, McGavin, Harding (**Author's note:** This game was also the debut for Claridge and McGavin.)
*First goal:* 10 December 1994 (a) won 4–0 v Chester City
*Club honours:* Cambridge United – Division Four promotion 1990 Division Three champions 1991; Blues – Division Two champions 1995, Auto Windscreens Shield winners 1995; Havant & Waterlooville – FA Trophy semi-finalist 2003; – Ebbsfleet: FA Trophy winners 2008.
*Representative honours:* Republic of Ireland – 5 full caps 1992–95, B cap 1994

## Playing Career

| Club | From | To | Fee | Total Appearances incl (subs) | Goals |
| --- | --- | --- | --- | --- | --- |
| Havant & W | 2000 | 2004 |  | 157 | 15 |
| Coventry City | 1996 | 1999 | £1,500,000 | 34 | 3 |
| Birmingham City | 1994 | 1996 | £500,000 | 98 | 6 |
| Cambridge United | 1988 | 1994 | Free | 181 | 7 |
| Portsmouth | 1986 | 1988 | Apprentice | 1 |  |

## Career in words
Liam began his career with his home-town club but made only one appearance in the first team before being released in 1988. He joined Cambridge United, helping them to successive promotions from the Fourth to the Second Division. He made his international debut for the Republic of Ireland, qualifying on the basis of his Irish Ancestry on 19 February 1992 at home to Wales. He joined Blues in January 1994 for £50,000, and he captained the side to the Division Two Championship in 1994–95 and the Auto Windscreens Shield triumph in the same season. In February 1996 Daish joined Coventry City for a fee of £1.5 million; however, during the four seasons he was there he was never a regular in the first team, playing only 34 games for the Sky Blues mainly due to a severed knee ligament injury which eventually resulted in his retirement from the professional game. He joined Havant & Waterlooville in 1999, making 157 appearances and scoring 15 goals, before his playing career was finally ended by a further injury to a knee in October 2002. In April 2000 he was appointed joint manager at Havant & Waterloo with Mick Jenkins. He spent three and a half years in that role before being sacked in January 2004. He joined Welling United FC as a coach, serving as caretaker manager for four games before leaving in February 2005 to become manager of Gravesend & Northfleet FC which in May 2007 was renamed Ebbsfleet United. He oversaw the club's move to a full-time playing squad, leading them to a 1–0 win in the FA Trophy Final on 10 May 2008.

Edwin Stein was an integral part of the Barry Fry regime that won the Division Two Championship in 1994–95 season, and he had this to say about Liam Daish's contribution to the triumph:

'The rock on which our defence was built. Daishy was such a good organiser, such a good leader. An inspirational figure. I think he has really enjoyed playing for a club as big as Birmingham City. He rose to the challenge. His presence at set pieces has been vital to us as well. He's scored powerful goals and also had many assists. Fancied himself as a natty dresser, but the lads questioned that throughout the year because of some of the gear he wore.'

# THE HEROES

### About the man
'If a jumbo jet was coming towards our area, he'd try and head it clear' Barry Fry.

### *Big Fry* by Barry Fry published in 2000 by CollinsWillow
'In the second half of the season I got a call from Ron Atkinson, who said he was desperate for a centre-half. I told him there was no one better than Daish, but Ron felt he was too slow. I could not have disagreed more "No one gets past him, Ron," I said. "He's brilliant." Sensing an imminent deal, I agreed to leave him out of the first team at Stoke and field him instead in a reserve game in which Ron plotted to play Peter Ndlovu among a few other talented players and to throw the kitchen sink at Daish who, at this stage, was thoroughly disaffected. He had had several run-ins over all kinds of issues, such as his views that the club's ambitions did not match his own as club captain, and just wanted away. He was the salt of the earth in my book. He would head away 707s and 747s. We played this match at St Andrew's on the Saturday morning, with me already having marked Daish's card that he was being watched. Big Ron stood next to me on the touchline and every time Ndlovu got the ball his manager screamed: 'Go on, Peter. Piss all over him!' He was to be disappointed in one respect and delighted in another. Every time Ndlovu made to go by him, Daish would kick him a mile in the air and emerge with the ball. By lunchtime Coventry's chairman Brian Richardson, Big Ron and I were huddled over a contract in the boot room...'

*Big Fry* – 'The captain Liam Daish – they don't make players like him any more – was stunned to discover that Karren (Brady) was going to make us pay for sporting club ties, having forked out for very smart blazers and trousers. He made a stand and said that, as a matter of principle, the players were going to go along to Marks & Spencer and buy 20 of the same ties. Again more petty squabbling. We were going to make a quarter of a million by going to Wembley (Auto Windscreens Trophy) and here there's a dispute about 20 £5 notes for ties. Stupid.'

# Kevin Paul Dillon

### Heroic claim to fame
Scored the goal which clinched promotion for Blues in 1979–80.

### Vital statistics
*Date of birth:* 18 December 1959
*Place of birth:* Sunderland
*Blues career:* 212 – 19 goals
*Blues debut:* 19 November 1977 (h) drew 1–1 v Leicester City. Crowd: 21,208
*Team:* Montgomery, Calderwood, Pendrey, Towers, Sbragia, Want, Page, Francis, Bertschin, Hibbitt, Dillon

# BIRMINGHAM CITY — MODERN DAY HEROES

*First goal:* 2 January 1978 (a) won 2–1 v Manchester United
*Club honours:* Blues – Division Two promotion 1980; Portsmouth – Division Three promotion, Division Two runners-up 1986–87; Reading – Division Two champions 1993–94
*Representative honours:* England Under-21 v Romania in 1980–81

## Playing Career

| Club | From | To | Fee | Total Appearances incl (subs) | Goals |
| --- | --- | --- | --- | --- | --- |
| Reading | 1991 | 1993 | | 101 | 4 |
| Newcastle United | 1989 | 1991 | | 62 | |
| Portsmouth | 1983 | 1989 | | 215 | 45 |
| Birmingham City | 1977 | 1983 | Apprentice | 212 | 19 |

## Career in words

He began as an apprentice with Blues before signing professional forms in July 1977. His selection for his debut was significant as he was the last player to be given his debut by Sir Alf Ramsey. He joined Portsmouth in March 1983 and was involved in their promotion from Division Three. In 1986–87 Pompey were promoted to Division One as runners-up to Derby County. He made 215 appearances before leaving on 1 July 1989 to join Newcastle United. In the summer of 1991 he joined Reading on a free transfer and spent three years at Elm Park helping them to win the Division Two title in 1993–94.

He moved into football management initially joining Stevenage Borough where he acted as youth and reserve team manger, he moved to Yeovil Town and then had a brief spell at Fareham Town at the end of 1996–1997. Kevin returned to Reading in 1995 and held a number of roles within their academy set up. He was reserve team manager before he became Alan Pardew's assistant in November 2001. When Pardew resigned in September 2003 he got the caretaker role until Steve Coppell was appointed in October 2003 at which time he became his number two.

He passed his UEFA Pro Licence in 2004 and in 2005–06 Reading won the Championship with a record 106 points. He left in May 2009 along with Coppell when after returning to the Championship after one season in the Premier they failed to return to the top flight. On 9 November 2009 he was appointed manager of Aldershot Town where he has a contract until the end of 2010–11. His appointment was announced on the Aldershot web site as follows:

'Aldershot has confirmed the appointment of Kevin Dillon as their new manager. The club has been managerless since Gary Waddock left to take over at Wycombe Wanderers a month ago and have handed Dillon, 49 a two-year contract.' The former Southampton full-back Jason Dodd was in caretaker charge for four games, but the Shots moved for Dillon after Dodd accepted a job within Southampton's Academy. Dillon was assistant manager to both Alan Pardew and Steve Coppell at Reading until he left at the end of last season. The club's acting chairman, John Leppard, said ' We went through the interview process last week and were impressed with the quality of applicants. Kevin's organisational qualities and professionalism was head and shoulders above the rest. He has done extensive research regarding the club and has watched the team play on a number of occasions. The whole appointment is a progressive move for the club, and we are delighted to have Kevin on board as our new manager.'

**About the man**
**What car did you drive when first at Blues?**
Daf Automatic.

**Nickname?**
Dill.

**Favourite player?**
Kenny Dalglish.

**Favourite foreign player and why?**
Rudi Krol because he leads by example and has excellent vision.

**Most difficult opponent?**
Bristol Rover's Gerry Sweeney.

**Favourite other sports?**
Golf, Pool and Badminton.

**Likes?**
Cinema and dog walking.

**Dislikes?**
Smoking and people who talk behind your back.

**Favourite TV shows?**
*Fawlty Towers*, *Dallas* and *Family Fortunes*.

**TV show you switch off?**
*Crossroads*.

**Favourite singers?**
George Benson, David Bowie and Donna Summer.

**Favourite food?**
Pate followed by Steak Diane.

**Favourite drink?**
Ginger beer.

**Favourite actors?**
James Dean and Peter Sellers
**Favourite actress?**
Linda Gray.

**Best films?**
*Midnight Express* and *Fame*.

**Pre-match meal?**
Steak and toast.
The above Q&A session featured in *Match Weekly* in the 1980s.

**What is your current job?**
I was manager of Aldershot prior to being sacked in January 2011. Prior to that I had 18 years at Reading, ending up as assistant manager before getting sacked after Blues had beaten us in the last match of 2008–09 season to get promotion.

**Who was your favourite player as a boy? And why?**
Jim Montgomery because he was at Sunderland when I was there on schoolboy forms. He was also with me at Blues.

**Which game in your career stands out in your memory?**
The 3–3 draw against Notts County which saw Blues promoted, and I scored. It was a goal I came to regret because 20 years later I was informed by Jim Smith that if Blues had not got promotion then Mark Dennis and I would have been sold to Brian Clough's Nottingham Forest. I could have won League Championships and European Cups if I had not scored that goal!

(**Author's note:** 3 May 1980 at home in front of 33,863 spectators. The other goals were scored by Bertschin and Curbishley)

**What's your best football experience?**
Playing for England Under-21s – I had just signed a contract which had a clause in it that said I would get a £100 rise if I got selected for the Under-21s. It was a short time after signing the contract that I got selected. £100 was a lot of money in those days.

**Who was the best player you played with and why?**
Trevor Francis is the best player I've played with. He was brilliant and clever and loved getting on the end of my diagonal passes.

**If you could go back to your days at Blues what one thing would you do differently?**
I should not have left when I did. The club had some financial problems, and Ron Saunders did not want to sell me. But Portsmouth was top of the Third Division and Blues look certain to be relegated. In those days you got no advice, and as it was a good package I accepted. Blues stayed up and I should have stayed, but having said that my time at Fratton Park was the best of my career.

**What was your best moment while at St Andrew's?**
Scoring that goal against Notts County.

**If you hadn't chosen football as a career what would you be?**
A welder at Sunderland Ship Builders. Sunderland only offered me a six-month contract when two years was the normal length. Don Dorman heard about it and asked me down to Blues for a trial. It took me five hours on the train, but I did alright and got a two-year apprenticeship deal.

**What is your opinion of football today?**
It's faster and the players are more powerful, although I do not think they are as tactically clever like they were in my day. Today everything's done for them so they don't have to think for themselves.

**If you could be one of today's Premier League stars who would you want to be and why?**
There's nobody I would want to be. I am not like anybody else.

# Jose Manuel Martins Dominguez

### Heroic claim to fame
One of the smallest Blues players and the only Portuguese international to wear the Royal Blue.

### Vital statistics
*Date of birth:* 16 February 1974
*Place of birth:* Lisbon, Portugal
*Blues career:* 45 – 4 goals
*Blues debut:* 12 March 1994 (a) lost 0–1 v Grimsby Town. Crowd: 5,405
*Team:* Bennett, Huxford, Frain, Cooper (G), Daish, Whyte, Shutt, Claridge, Marsden, Harding, Dominguez
*First goal:* 18 September 1994 (h) won 4–0 v Peterborough United
*Club honours:* Blues – Division Two champions 1994–95; Tottenham Hotspur – League Cup winners 1999
*Representative honours:* Portugal – 2 full caps

### Playing Career

| Club | From | To | Fee | Total Appearances incl (subs) | Goals |
|---|---|---|---|---|---|
| Vasco DA Gama | 2005 | | | | |
| Al-Ahli Doha | 2004 | 2005 | | 7 | |
| FC Kaiserslautern | 2000 | 2004 | | 24 | 3 |
| Tottenham Hotspur | 1997 | 2000 | £1,600,000 | 58 | 5 |
| Sporting Lisbon | 1996 | 1997 | | 62 | 4 |
| Birmingham City | 1994 | 1996 | £180,000 | 45 | 4 |
| Benfica | 1993 | 1994 | | | |

### Career in words
Jose played as a youth for SL Benfica and then as an amateur with SU Sintrense. In March 1994 he joined Blues enduring relegation in his first season. In June 1995 he returned to the Sporting Club of Lisbon as a replacement for Luis Figo, after two seasons he was signed by Tottenham Hotspur in August 1997 for £1.6 million. He made his Spurs debut v Derby County winning a penalty after coming on as a substitute. During his stay at White Hart Lane he won the League Cup with Spurs in 1999 as an unused sub. He moved to German club FC Kaiserslautern in November 2000 for £250,000 scoring three in 24 matches. After a brief spell in Qatar with Al-ahli(Doha) he moved to Brazil in 2005 to play for CR Vasco da Gama. As he never received his playing licence from the Portuguese Football Association he officially retired at the age of 31. He helped the Portugal Olympic team to finish fourth in the 1998 Olympics in Atlanta.

# BIRMINGHAM CITY                                                    MODERN DAY HEROES

Edwin Stein was an integral part of the Barry Fry regime that won the Division Two Championship in 1994–95 season he had this to say about Jose Dominguez's contribution to the triumph:

' The little fella has got frightening skill and potential. The crowd loved him and it was easy to see why. No one fancied marking him as he could beat people at the drop of a hat. Jose improved considerably since he came here in March 1994. He adapted to the English style and added work rate to his high level of skill. When he did play he excited the crowd and made us a dangerous attacking force with his dribbling.'

### About the man
*Big Fry* by Barry Fry published in 2000 by Collins Willows

'There are occasions on which my football business brain ticks into overdrive, too, and I manage to achieve something which is benefical to all parties. This was never better demonstrated than my signing for Birmingham of the diminutive Portuguese winger Jose Dominguez. My chief scout, Lil Fuchillo, told me that one of his acquaintances, David Hodgson, the former Liverpool player, was the agent for a foreign kid whom he had seen on tape and was deeply impressed by. He wanted me to view the tape, but I have never done business that way and I told him to tell Hodgson to get the player over to Birmingham, where I could see him in the flesh among all the muck and bullets. At the time Dominguez was with Benfica and out on loan to Faro. Benfica were looking for £80,000, with a further £80,000 after a number of appearances, and when I first told Karren that I wanted to get him over she said that no more players were to be signed. She refused to pay his flight and accommodation. I told Hodgson of the situation and he said: "Baz, if you see this bloke you will sign him. He is your type of player." I went to David Sullivan who, again, demonstrated his fairness by promising to meet these expenses if a transfer was concluded. Hodgie was so confident that he forked out for the boy, so this little dwarf, speaking broken English, arrived on the scene. We got him set up for training and when he started to play I rubbed my eyes in disbelief. He was brilliant…so quick, so agile, so deceptive. And that was in spite of Birmingham having the single worst training facilities it has been my misfortune to encounter in a lifetime of football. We didn't even have a training ground in the first 12 months that I was there, and everywhere we turned to corporation pitches and the like – it was too wet or churned up. I would spend all morning seeking out a suitable place to train and it became a hugely frustrating exercise. The club had sold off its training ground and during my first six months we had seven different centres. There was no stability and no pattern and this must have contributed to our downfall. Dominguez, however, conjured such tricks that you would have thought he had trained in such circumstances all his life. I had to have him. I told Sullivan that I could obtain international clearance for him to play in the reserves the day after he arrived and he agreed that I should proceed. There were only 500 people at this reserve game, but how privileged they were to have seen such a performance. He was excitement personified and they gave him a standing ovation. I was really sold on him and I told Karren we must sign him. "He's money in the bank," I said. Both Karren and David were loathed to take action. I turned to David. "If I said to you that if you gave me £100,000 now and in 12 months' time I would give you back £1 million, what would you do?" He said he would give me £100,000. "Well, f**king give me £80,000 now!"

'I received a call from Karren (Brady), who said that we had received an offer of £500,000 for Jose Dominguez from Sporting Lisbon. She thought this a good price but I disagreed and said: "Karren, there's no way we are selling a player like Dominguez for half a million." In the summer I had negotiated for him a new three-year contract, but while I was away Sporting told Karren that the player was homesick and craved a move home to Portugal. I told Karren to do nothing until I returned; that I was in Portugal anyway and would go to see him. I told the player that I had gone to the ends of the earth to sign him, what a great player he was and how highly I valued him. He said much of his problem was down to his girlfriend, who could never settle in Birmingham. "Then don't change your club," I told him. "Change your bloody girlfriend." I related to him that at one of the forums a couple of weeks previously, one fan had said that if he returned from the pub one night to find Jose in bed with his wife, he would simply turn round, go back to the pub and allow Jose to finish the job he had started. "That's how much they love you in Birmingham," I told the little fellow. It didn't work. "Barry," he said, "I am not coming back. I am staying here." "This makes me look a right c**t. You have no sooner signed a contract than you are walking out on it." His response negated every aspect of my argument. "At Birmingham, I am to get £500 per week," he said. "At Sporting I will get £25,000 a month in my hand, an apartment and a Mercedes sports car." "I understand," I said. "But please don't tell me lies. It's nothing to do with your girlfriend and everything to do with the f**king money."

# Brian Louie Donowa

**Heroic claim to fame**
The first Blues substitute to be substituted.

**Vital statistics**
*Date of birth:* 24 September 1964
*Place of birth:* Ipswich
*Blues career:* 168 – 19 goals
*Blues debut:* 31 August 1991 (h) won 1–0 v Darlington. Crowd: 8,768
*Team:* Thomas, Clarkson, Frain, Donowa, Hicks, Mardon, Rodgerson, Gayle (J), Peer, Gleghorn, Sturridge
*First goal:* 12 October 1991 (h) won 3–0 v Stockport County
*Club honours:* Norwich City – Youth Cup winners 1983, League Cup winners 1985; Blues – Division Two champions 1994–95, Auto Windscreens winners 1995
*Representative honours:* England Under-21 – 3 caps

## Playing Career

| Club | From | To | Fee | Total Appearances incl (subs) | Goals |
| --- | --- | --- | --- | --- | --- |
| Tamworth | 2000 | | | | |
| Boston United | 1999 | 2000 | | 1 | |
| FC Inter Turku | 1998 | | | 4 | 1 |
| Ayr United | 1997 | 1998 | | 9 | |
| Walsall | 1997 | 1997 | Free | 7 | |
| Peterborough United | 1997 | 1997 | Free | 17 | |
| Peterborough United | 1996 | 1997 | Loan | 6 | 1 |
| Walsall | 1996 | 1996 | Loan | 6 | 1 |
| Shrewsbury Town | 1994 | | Loan | 4 | |
| Crystal Palace | 1993 | | Loan | 0 | |
| Burnley | 1993 | | Loan | 4 | |
| Birmingham City | 1990 | 1997 | £60,000 | 168 | 19 |
| Bristol City | 1990 | 1991 | £55,000 | 26 | 3 |
| Ipswich Town | 1989 | 1990 | Free | 30 | 2 |
| Willen II Tilburg | 1989 | 1989 | | 13 | 4 |
| Deportivo | 1986 | | £400,000 | 85 | 20 |
| Stoke | 1985 | | Loan | 5 | 1 |
| Norwich City | 1982 | 1986 | Apprentice | 80 | 15 |

BIRMINGHAM CITY                                  MODERN DAY HEROES

### Career in words
Although a native of Ipswich Louie began his career with arch-rivals Norwich City as a 16-year-old in 1980. He turned professional in September 1982 becoming a member of the youth team that won the FA Youth Cup in 1983 by which time he had already played for the first team, making his debut against Sunderland in the then Milk Cup in 1982, eventually winning the League Cup in 1985. Shortly into the 1986–87 season he signed for Spanish club Deportivo La Coruna for a fee of £50,000. He spent three years in Spain before joining his hometown club, Ipswich Town although he had had trials with Sheffield United and the Dutch side Willem 11 Tilburg before putting pen to paper. He moved to Bristol City in July 1990. The following summer he signed for Blues scoring 18 goals in 116 League appearances although while at St Andrew's he was sent out on loan on four occasions to Burnley, Crystal Palace, Shrewsbury Town and Walsall. Barry Fry re-connected with Louie taking him to Peterborough United in the summer of 1996. In July 1997 he went to Walsall before moving to Scotland with Ayr United. In July 1998 he trialled with Cambridge United and trained with Northampton Town but although he was expected to get a short-term contract with United he began the 1998–99 season playing for King's Lynn in a friendly against Borehamwood. He then signed for Finnish side TPS Turku. In March 1999 he joined Boston United in the Dr Marten's League but only played one game (and he was substituted). On the transfer deadline day of 2000 he joined Tamworth.

# Nicholas Jeremy Eaden

### Heroic claim to fame
Gained promotion to the top division with three sides.

### Vital statistics
*Date of birth:* 12 December 1972
*Place of birth:* Sheffield
*Blues career:* 90 – 5 goals
*Blues debut:* 12 August 2000 (a) drew 0–0 v Queen's Park Rangers. Crowd: 13,926
*Team:* Bennett, Eaden, Johnson (M), Hughes, Holdsworth, Purse, Lazaridis, Grainger, Horsfield, Sonner, Ndlovu
*First goal:* 26 August 2000 (a) won 2–1 v Nottingham Forest
*Club honours:* Barnsley – Division One runners-up 1996–97, Play-off finalists 1999–2000; Blues – League Cup runners-up 01, Division One Play-off winners 2001–02; Wigan – Division Two winners 2002–03, Championship runners-up 2004–05; Kettering – Blue Square North champions 2007–08;

### Playing Career

| Club | From | To | Fee | Total Appearances incl (subs) | Goals |
| --- | --- | --- | --- | --- | --- |
| Kettering | 2007 | | | 29 | |
| Solihull Moors | 2007 | | | 1 | |
| Halesowen | 2007 | | | 1 | |
| Lincoln City | 2007 | 2007 | Loan | 18 | |
| Lincoln City | 2006 | 2007 | Loan | 17 | |
| Nottingham Forest | 2005 | 2007 | Free | 30 | |
| Wigan Athletic | 2002 | 2005 | Free | 129 | |
| Wigan Athletic | 2002 | 2002 | Loan | 6 | |
| Birmingham City | 2001 | 2002 | Free | 90 | 5 |
| Barnsley | 1991 | 2000 | Junior | 339 | 13 |

### Career in words
He started at Barnsley contributing to their promotion to the Premiership before joining Blues. He also had a successful spell at Wigan Athletic winning promotion from Division Two and then into the

Grainger is mobbed Nicky Eaden, Jerry Gill and Geoff Horsfield.

Premiership. In 2005 he joined Nottingham Forest on a free transfer. On 31 August 2006 he joined Lincoln City on loan from Nottingham Forest initially for a month which was later extended to the maximum 93 days loan total. He then returned to the City Ground but was again loaned to Lincoln in January 2007 this time for the remainder of the season. Eventually released by Forest he signed for Halesowen Town, making just one appearance in September 2007. He joined Solihull Moors and again made a single appearance before signing for Kettering Town. He made his debut in a 1–1 draw at Nuneaton Borough on 20 October 2007 initially as a player–coach before eventually becoming Mark Cooper's assistant during the 2008–09 season. In November 2009 Cooper was appointed manager of Peterborough United and Eaden joined him once again as his assistant.

### About the man

In the 2003 book *Broken Dreams – vanity, greed and the souring of British football* by Tom Bowers there is reference to Birmingham City and the transfer of Nicky Eaden: 'That month, May 2002, the Smith brothers were fearful of failing to produce the profits promised to the City banks which had invested in First Artist. At their offices in Wembley, Phil Smith, a robust trader who justified his frequent use of expletives as a manifestation of 'wearing my heart on my sleeve' was setting his staff high targets to sign new players. During their regular Monday morning conference, the young recruits claimed to have heard Phil Smith urge them to "get alongside the club managers", bend the truth to obtain business and even boast that some managers required bribes. Smith would vigorously deny those claims but his aggressive demands caused several of the agency's younger staff concern. They were especially worried that Phil Smith was expecting them to breach the FA's code of conduct. Rule 12.4. of the FA's professional code in the "Players' Agents Regulations" stated that the contract between a player and a club should explicitly identify who was paying the agent's fee. A second rule stipulated that an agent could only be paid by one party in a transaction – either the club or the player – but not both."Paying at both ends" was forbidden. Two transfers completed by First Artist concerned some employees. The first involved the transfer in June 2002 of Steve Robinson (**Author's note:** Not the Steve Robinson featured in this book), a 28-year-old midfielder from Preston North End to Luton Town. First Artist obtained £5,000 in commission from Luton Town and subsequently asked Robinson to also pay £5,000 commission, although he only paid £1,000. The second transfer raising concern was Nicky Eaden's from Barnsley to Birmingham City. Eaden, a defender, had signed a contract with First Artist in 1997. In 2000, he became a "free" player under the Bosman rules. Phil Smith finalized Eaden's employment by Birmingham City and invoiced the club on 10 July 2000 for a commission of £50,000. Eight weeks later, after the contract was finalized and the club had paid the commission. First Artist asked Eaden to pay £15,000 commission over three years for negotiating the transfer. "We are not earning enough money on these deals," Eaden recalled Smith saying. Unaware that First Artist had received as much as £50,000 from the club, Eaden paid the first instalment but later protested, firstly, after he was told about Birmingham City's payment to First Artist by the club's chief executive; and secondly, in early 2002, after he was actually shown First Artist's invoice by Steve Bruce, the club's manager. Eaden's complaint of the double payment only became known to First Artist's young employees during 2002, after a heated argument between Eaden and Phil Smith. According to Eaden, Smith had said that Birmingham City had only paid £20–25,000 in commission for his transfer and the remainder was for other work. Furthermore, Phil Smith allegedly told Eaden that the agency had "done a favour" to the player by not recording the fee, which would have otherwise have attracted income tax. Eaden received advice from an accountant contradicting Smith's suggestion. Their bitter argument about illegal double payments became known to everyone in First Artist's headquarters. In the opinion of First Artist's disgruntled employees, their agency was breaking the FA's rules. Eaden's transfer to Birmingham could only be completed after the player's own contract was finalized. Therefore, approaching Eaden for a commission for work completed eight weeks earlier, and taking fees from both sides simultaneously broke the FA's rules. The Smiths disagreed. They believed that they were innocent of any wrongdoing. They vehemently argued that Eaden's transfer was two separate transactions. The first transaction was the transfer between clubs, in which First Artist was acting for Birmingham City, and the second transaction was the negotiation of the player's contract with the club. That arrangement, they argued, was accepted in the football industry. The Smiths argued that Eaden was not contracted to First Artist at the time the agency was negotiating his transfer, but only after the agency obtained its commission from the club. Hence, they insisted, the FA's rules had not been breached. That explanation was rejected by the agency's dissatisfied employees. The letter and the spirit of the FA's rules, requiring an agency to possess a written contract with either the club or the player during the negotiations, had, they argued, been broken. The combination of the Smiths' aggressive pursuit of profits and the disquiet within the Wembley headquarters about the agency's treatment of several other players transformed the increasing antagonism into a crisis in July 2002.' (**Author's note:** First Artist's General Manager, Neil Miller resigned together with Steve Wicks an employee and ex-professional footballer for Chelsea and Queen's Park Rangers and six other members of staff who went on to form Grassroots a rival agency which took several of First Artist's clients. First Artist sought an injunction against Grassroots and many hoped that the subsequent trial would resolve the 'Paying at both ends' issue, but unfortunately the case was settled out of court and the matter was never resolved in court.)

# Mikael Kaj Forssell

### Heroic claim to fame
Scored the perfect hat-trick against Spurs: left foot, right foot and a header.

### Vital statistics
*Date of birth:* 15 March 1981
*Place of birth:* Steinfurt, Germany
*Blues career:* 119 – 37 goals
*Blues debut:* 14 September 2003 (h) drew 2–2 v Fulham and he scored both goals. Crowd: 27,280
*Team:* Taylor, Kenna, Clapham, Savage, Purse, Upson, Johnson (D) John, Forssell, Clemence, Dunn
*Club honours:* Championship runners-up 2006–07
*Representative honours:* He was regular in the Finland national team in the 2000s his debut being on 9 June 1999 v Moldova with his first international goal on 28 February 2001 v Luxembourg. He played for Finland in the 2001 FIFA World Youth Championships

### Playing Career

| Club | From | To | Fee | Total Appearances incl (subs) | Goals |
| --- | --- | --- | --- | --- | --- |
| Hannover | 2008 | | Free | | |
| Birmingham City | 2005 | 2008 | £3,000,000 | 77 | 18 |
| Birmingham City | 2004 | 2005 | Loan | 4 | |
| Birmingham City | 2003 | 2004 | Loan | 38 | 19 |
| Borussia Munchengladbach | 2003 | 2003 | Loan | 12 | 7 |
| Crystal Palace | 2000 | 2001 | Loan | 49 | 15 |
| Crystal Palace | 2000 | 2000 | Loan | 13 | 3 |
| Chelsea | 1998 | 2005 | Free | 53 | 12 |
| HJK Helsinki | 1997 | 1998 | Youth | 17 | 1 |

### Career in words

He made his Veikkausliiga (Finland) debut for HJK Helsinki at the age of 16. In 1998 at the age of 17 he joined Chelsea in the Premier League where he found it hard to find a place in the first team and therefore was loaned to Crystal Palace (twice), Borussia Monchengladbach and Blues (twice) during the first five years of the 21st century. During his second loan period at Blues he suffered a second serious knee injury which ruined his season. In the summer of 2005 he joined Blues on a three-year deal for £3 million but he struggled in a side that was relegated in 2005–06. The decision to take him on a permanent transfer was considered to be a risky one and this doubt re-emerged when he suffered another knee injury in October 2006. He endured surgery on both knees which kept him sidelined until February 2007. In 2007–08 he returned to his goal scoring ways culminating in him scoring his first hat-trick on 1 March 2008 in a 4–1 win over Tottenham Hotspur. In May 2008 after Blues' second relegation from the Premier League he signed a pre-contract agreement to join Hannover 96 in the Bundesliga on a free when his Blues contract expired at the end of June. His contract with Hannover terminates at the end of 2010–11 season.

### About the man
**Who has been your most difficult opponent?**
Cannavaro and Nesta for Italy when I played as a lone striker for Finland.

**Who has been your most difficult opponent in the Premiership?**
Jaap Stam when he was with Manchester United.

**Who is the best player in your position?**
Ronaldo.

**Who is the best player in your position in the Premiership?**
Thierry Henry with Van Nistelrooy a close second.

**What is your favourite ground?**
Helsinki Olympia Stadium.

# Kevin Derek Michael Francis

**Heroic claim to fame**
Heaviest player to play for Blues at 16st 10lb.

## Vital statistics
*Date of birth:* 6 December 1967
*Place of birth:* Birmingham
*Blues career:* 83 – 21 goals
*Blues debut:* 4 February 1995 (h) won 1–0 v Stockport County. Crowd: 17,160
*Team:* Bennett, Whyte, Cooper (G), Ward, Barnett, Bodley, Donowa, Claridge, Francis, Otto, Tait
*First goal:* 18 February 1995 (a) won 4–2 v York City – scored twice!
*Club honours:* Stockport County – Division Four runners-up 1991, Division Three Play-off Final runners-up 1992; Blues – Auto Windscreens Shield winners 1994, Division Two runners-up 1994–95.
*Representative honours:* 1998 Saint Kitts & Nevis 2 caps qualified as both his parents come from the tiny Caribbean island. The games were in the Caribbean Cup.

## Playing Career

| Club | From | To | Fee | Total Appearances incl (subs) | Goals |
| --- | --- | --- | --- | --- | --- |
| Studley | 2005 | | | | |
| Redditch United | 2005 | | | | |
| Hednesford | 2001 | | Free | 41 | 9 |
| Hull City | 2000 | 2001 | Free | 24 | 5 |
| Exeter City | 2000 | 2000 | Non-Contract | 9 | 1 |
| Stockport County | 2000 | 2000 | Free | 4 | |
| Oxford United | 1998 | 2000 | £100,000 | 40 | 8 |
| Birmingham City | 1995 | 1998 | £800,000 | 83 | 21 |
| Stockport County | 1991 | 1995 | £45,000 | 198 | 117 |
| Derby County | 1989 | 1991 | Free | 17 | 1 |
| Mile Oak Rovers | 1988 | 1989 | | | |

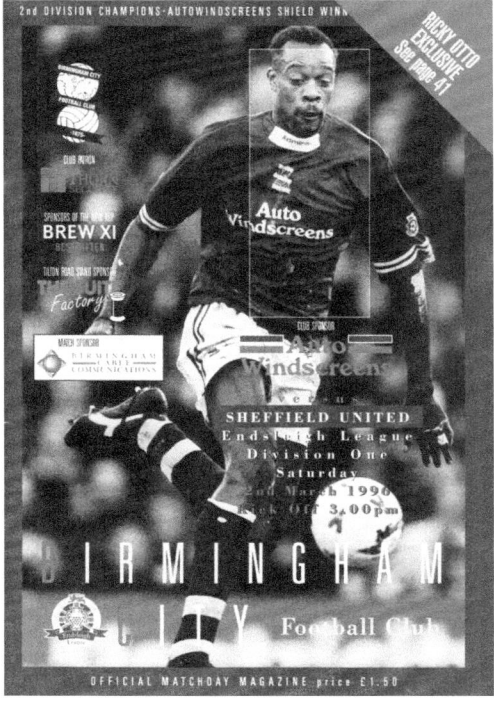

## Career in words
In 198 appearances for Stockport County 'Big Kev' scored 117 goals, achieving the remarkable feat of scoring 28 League goals in consecutive seasons in 1992–93 and 1993–94.

The Small Heath lad emigrated to Canada in 2005 to become a trucker, but a couple of years later he switched to working for the Calgary Police Service. Kevin, his wife Sharron and daughter Keisha made the transatlantic move while their other daughter Stacey stayed in England to pursue her academic and sporting career. She is an England netball star. He is still keen on football and coaches the Foothills Soccer Club who produced Owen Hargreaves.

Edwin Stein had this to say about Kevin Francis's contribution to the Division Two Championship triumph in 1994–95:

'He was tremendous after arriving from Stockport County in January 1995. A lot of people raised their eyebrows when we went for him but we knew his worth. He surprised a lot of people. Nicknamed Snoop Doggy Dog because of his hairstyle when he first signed, big Kev was the option we had been lacking. I don't think he was suited to our passing game at first so we changed the style a little bit and he profited. He scored nine goals in 18 games – a great ratio – and he also worked hard on his game to improve. A genuine lad, his attitude and will to win was exceptional.'

### About the man
Liam Daish recalls 'But the big game was against Brentford at St Andrew's three days after Wembley, because they were flying at the time. But we just went out there, got about them and ended up comfortable winners. Big Kev had done his cruciates at Wembley but he was determined to play against Brentford. He basically played without a cruciate ligament in his knee, but he scored and that summed up the spirit in the side. Everyone wanted to be out there and anyone not in the team was gutted. I got the second to make it 2–0 – I nearly did two laps of honour after it! – and that was that.'

### In her book *Brady Plays the Blues* published in 1995 by Pavilion Books Limited, she talks about the transfer of Big Kev:
I think the most constructive event in our relationship [**Author's note:** Barry Fry and Karren Brady] was our attempt to sign Kevin Francis from Stockport when David Sullivan was away on holiday in St Lucia. When David left for St Lucia it was on the understanding that Francis was to become a Birmingham player. The day David flew out, Barry phoned us to say the deal had changed and Stockport wanted £800,000 plus instalments. I immediately put a stop on the transfer until I had spoken to David. What is the most you will pay for Francis, I asked. '£600,000' he said, so that was the bid we put into Stockport. What I didn't realise was Francis had already been told the fee had been agreed and was on his way down to St Andrew's to sign. In the meantime, Stockport were not budging from £800,000 as the asking price and were now accusing us of welshing on the deal and upsetting their player. Upset was putting it mildly. When Francs heard he was returning to Edgeley Park he was devastated, which left myself and Barry sitting in the office discussing how to resolve the situation.

'David told me we could go to £800,000,' said Barry. 'He told me £600,000,' I insisted, 'and I can't change that without his authority.' So we rang David. 'OK go to £800,000,' he said.

Back we went to Stockport. Now the extras were the sticking point, money down after certain games, money after international appearances and other bits and pieces. So no deal. Finally we settled on £400,000 down and four instalments of £100,000 over a period of time. And then Francis failed his medical because of a dodgy knee. So now we were left trying to rework the deal based on the risk he could suffer a career-threatening injury. We settled on £200,000 down and then three instalments of the same after certain games had been played. But David said 'No'. Then he phoned Stockport direct. Now Stockport said 'No'. But all the time Barry and I were coming closer together because we were getting a greater understanding of each other as people and professionals. It helped to realise the real power behind Birmingham City was not Barry Fry or Karren Brady, it is David Sullivan. Even going second in the League didn't do us as much good as our trials in signing Kevin Francis.

# Howard Gayle

### Heroic claim to fame
The first black player to play for Liverpool.

### Vital statistics
*Date of birth:* 18 May 1958
*Place of birth:* Toxteth, Liverpool
*Blues career:* 59 – 11 goals
*Blues debut:* First appearance was as a substitute on 10 September 1987 (a) drew 1–1 v Wolverhampton Wanderers
*First start:* 17 September 1987 (h) won 1–0 v Ipswich Town and he scored. Crowd: 13,159
*Team:* Coton, Mumford, Van Den Hauwe, Blake, Wright, Broadhurst, Gayle, Phillips, Harford, Halsall, Rees

# THE HEROES

*Club honours:* Liverpool – European Cup winners 1980–81; Sunderland – Milk (League) Cup runners-up 1985
*Representative honours:* England Under-21 – 3 caps. He helped England win the 1984 UEFA European Under-21 Championship scoring a goal in the Final v Spain.

## Playing Career

| Club | From | To | Fee | Total Appearances incl (subs) | Goals |
| --- | --- | --- | --- | --- | --- |
| Halifax | 1992 | 1993 | | 5 | |
| Blackburn Rovers | 1987 | 1992 | £5,000 | 121 | 29 |
| Stoke City | 1987 | | £125,000 | 6 | 2 |
| Dallas Sidekicks (Indoor) | 1986 | 1987 | | 30 | 6 |
| Sunderland | 1984 | 1985 | £75,000 | 48 | 4 |
| Birmingham City | 1983 | 1984 | | 59 | 11 |
| Newcastle United | 1982 | 1983 | Loan | 8 | 2 |
| Fulham | 1980 | | Loan | 14 | |
| Liverpool | 1977 | 1983 | | 4 | 1 |

## Career in words

Howard was at Anfield for six years but only made five first-team appearances. Having said this, he won a European Cup-winners' medal in 1980–81 as a non-playing substitute. Howard was a pioneer in Merseyside football, being the first black player to pull on a Liverpool shirt in 1980, paving the way for

likes of John Barnes, Mark Walters and Michael Thomas. Born in Toxteth and raised in Norris Green, he went from playing on the fields of Sefton Park to running out in a European Cup semi-final against Bayern Munich inside three years. But his journey to the top and his battle to stay there was tough and painful as he suffered at the hand of the racists who were endemic in the 1970s and 1980s. Howard's chance came in August 1977 when as a 19-year-old he was invited for a trial by Liverpool. 'I beat three or four players and then had a shot which came back off the bar, before it bounced I volleyed it in from the edge of the box and as I turned I could see the coaches watching. I turned my ankle and was in a lot of pain but carried on playing. I showed them just how much it meant to me.' A month later Gayle broke into the reserves and in November boss Bob Paisley offered him a professional deal. His first-team debut came when he replaced David Fairclough at Manchester City in October 1980. But it was six months before he appeared again –

in the second leg of the European Cup semi-final at Bayern Munich in April 1981. Gayle's reward for his performance in the Semi was a first start three days later when he scored in a 1–1 draw at Tottenham Hotspur. He played the final two home games and was on the bench when the Reds lifted the European Cup in Paris. But rather than it being the start of something special it was the end. The following season Gayle, who scored 62 goals in 156 League games for the reserves, realised he was surplus to requirements. He went out on three loan deals: Fulham in January 1980, Newcastle United in November 1982 and Blues in January 1983 before leaving for good in June 1983. He was about to sign for Newcastle United before Blues stepped in, and he proved something of a mystery in terms of his performances: one minute – fast, aggressive and a match-winner and in the next moment – sluggish and disinterested. He was transferred to Sunderland following an off-field misdemeanour for £75,000 in the summer of 1984. (**Author's note:** It is alleged that his 'crime' was to be romantically attached to Ron Saunder's daughter. It is part of the Blues' folklore that Saunders kept his dogs at the training ground to dissuade potential suitors for his daughter.) After retiring in 1993 he became involved in a charity trust funding the £3.5 million development of a Sporting Centre of Excellence in Toxteth.

## About the man
### How did you react when you knew about the European Cup game?
I had scored a hat-trick for the reserves on the Saturday and came in Monday ready to train. But then I saw Roy Evans who said 'go home and get your stuff because you are travelling with the first team'. I was buzzing. I got my chance when Kenny Dalglish limped off after just nine minutes, and it proved to be my finest hour as I ran the Germans ragged. I didn't have time to think about the magnitude of what was happening. I was determined I was not going to let myself or my teammates down. That game went so quickly and it was exhausting playing at a different level. The Germans didn't know anything about me, and my pace gave them problems. To be thrown in at the deep end in a game of such significance showed me how far I had come. I came in for some rough treatment, and Bob Paisley was worried I might retaliate and get sent off so I became the first Liverpool substitute ever to be subbed when I made way for Jimmy Case with 20 minutes to go. I was gutted because I felt I still had more to offer. But first and foremost I was a Liverpool fan and the most important thing was we progressed to the Final.

### What was it like being a black man in those days?
One thing that was constantly levelled at my community was that we were under-achievers and not very good for much. There were so many stereotypes of black people we had to overcome, and we always had to work harder than our white counterparts. When I played for Liverpool I think that it helped dispel those myths. It showed people we can achieve at the highest level as long as we're given the opportunity.

### How were you accepted when you signed for the Reds?
As a kid I used to go to bed each night dreaming of scoring the winner at Anfield, so to sign for the club was very special. But I would not say I was welcomed with open arms by everyone. You always get the old school who are pig headed and ignorant. But those people were compromised by the likes of Emlyn Hughes, Ian Callaghan, Phil Thompson and Graeme Souness, who saw you for what you were.

### What made you want to join the Blues?
I hoped I had made an impact at Anfield, but I found myself going backwards. It was often commented that I had a chip on my shoulder. But in all my time I've never had a black person tell me I've got a chip on my shoulder.

### What about racism?
I have never turned my back on racism, and I always face it whether that is to comment on it or correct it when needs be. I have had banana skins thrown at me, I have been spat at and had to endure verbal abuse from the terraces. But times have changed, and I am proud of the progress that has been made to combat the racists. Football has probably done more than any authority or government to eradicate racism. By educating people of the values of different cultures, we have slowly but surely changed views on black players.

# David Geddis

**Heroic claim to fame**
Scored two goals on his Blues debut.

## Vital statistics
*Date of birth:* 12 March 1959
*Place of birth:* Carlisle
*Blues career:* 56 – 21 goals
*Blues debut:* 22 December 1984 (a) won 2–1 v Wimbledon and he scored both goals. Crowd: 3,674
*Team:* Seaman, Ranson, Roberts, Wright, Armstrong, Daly, Platnauer, Clarke (W), Bremner, Geddis, Hopkins
*Club honours:* Ipswich Town – FA Cup winners 1978; Aston Villa – League champions 1980–81, European Cup (unused substitute) 1981–82; Blues – Division Two Promotion 1984–85
*Representative honours:* England – 2 Youth caps, 1 B cap

## Playing Career

| Club | From | To | Fee | Total Appearances incl (subs) | Goals |
| --- | --- | --- | --- | --- | --- |
| Darlington | 1990 | | Free | 9 | 3 |
| Swindon Town | 1988 | 1990 | £25,000 | | |
| Shrewsbury Town | 1987 | 1988 | £25,000 | | |
| Brentford | 1986 | | Loan | | |
| Birmingham City | 1984 | 1987 | £80,000 | 56 | 21 |
| Barnsley | 1983 | 1984 | £50,000 | 50 | 24 |
| Luton Town | 1982 | | Loan | | |
| Aston Villa | 1979 | 1983 | £300,000 | | |
| Luton Town | 1977 | | Loan | | |
| Ipswich Town | 1973 | 1979 | Apprentice | | |

## Career in words
On Boxing Day 1977 Trevor Whymark, Ipswich Town's leading goalscorer was injured for the derby game against Norwich City 'Geddo' replaced him and remained in the side to become one of the youngest players to make an appearance in the FA Cup Final. It was Geddis that delivered the cross that led to Roger Osborne's winning goal. He commanded a fee of £300,000 when he moved to Villa Park in 1979 and his role was to stand in for either Gary Shaw or Peter Withe when they were injured or suspended. He is well remembered by both Blues and Villa fans when he scored two goals in a 3–0 defeat of the Blues! His limited first-team appearances led to his transfer to Second Division Barnsley in September 1983 where he scored 24 goals in 45 starts before attracting interest from his ex-Villa boss Ron Saunders who was then in charge of promotion-chasing Blues. He joined just before Christmas 1984 for £80,000 and quickly became a fans' favourite due to his contribution to the Blues promotion to the top flight at the end of 1984–85 season. In January 2002 Bobby Robson brought him in to work as coach alongside John Carver at Newcastle United. He was released from the position in September 2004 when Graeme Souness took over as manager and brought his own backroom staff from Blackburn Rovers. He spent some time scouting for the England set up under Sven Goran Eriksson at the 2006 World Cup before joining Leeds United as reserve-team coach. He coached the English celebrity side in the Soccer Aid charity match alongside Terry Venables. He left Elland Road on 19 December 2006.

## About the man
### What do you recall of your early days in Ipswich?
Most of us who were in the youth programme were given opportunities by the Bobby Robson regime very early on in our careers if we showed good progress and ability. For example if the first-team striker

# BIRMINGHAM CITY                                    MODERN DAY HEROES

was injured he was replaced by the reserve team striker, there was no shuffling players around. You always knew that if you were doing well then you would be given a chance and that is important to a young player.

**Was the FA Cup Final win over Arsenal your career highlight?**
Yes, it was an incredible experience to play in an FA Cup Final at such a young age. The problem is that often with Cup Finals the day simply passes you by and then you have little to recollect. I made sure that I savoured every moment.

**What happened to end your time at Ipswich?**
Keith Bertschin had been sold to Blues on the strength of my development, and the same thing happened to me two years later. I was sold to Aston Villa because Alan Brazil had come through the ranks.

**What are your best memories of the Villa?**
At the time I was disappointed by my non-selection at times, but now I can look back and realise that I was part of a very tight-knit group of players that won the Championship and the European Cup – there were just 15 players used. It was a great experience, and I am very proud that I was involved in everything that Villa did at that time.

### Did things go well for you at Blues?
Well, it did after a great start to my career with Blues at Wimbledon. Funnily enough, I had played at Plough Lane two weeks before for Barnsley and scored twice in a 3–3 draw. When I went back with Birmingham the bloke on the tannoy system said 'we hope Birmingham's number 10 has left his shooting boots at home this week' Well, 20 minutes into the game I had scored another two goals. I enjoyed it at Birmingham and we went up that season. However, we went down 12 months later, mainly because we did not have the financial resources to improve and stabilise our position in that League.

### What about life at Barnsley?
Norman Hunter was the main reason for me moving there. I was a Leeds United fan when I was younger, so to go and work for someone like that was very special for me.

# Jeremy Morley Gill

### Heroic claim to fame
Ever-present in 2001 Worthington Cup games but missed out on the Final.

### Vital statistics
*Date of birth:* 8 September 1970
*Place of birth:* Clevedon, Somerset
*Blues career:* 74
*Blues debut:* 18 April 1998 (h) won 3–0 v Swindon Town. Crowd: 17,016
*Team:* Bennett, Gill, Charlton, Bruce, Johnson (M), Marsden, McCarthy, O'Connor, Adebola, Hughes, Furlong
*Club honours:* Bath – Somerset Premier Cup winners 1994 and 1995; Yeovil – Isthmian League Premier Division champions 1996–97; Blues – Birmingham Senior Cup winners 1999 and 2000, Blues Clubman of the Year 2000–01, League Cup runner-up 2001, Championship Promotion 2001–02; Cheltenham Town – Division Two Play-off winners 2005–06
*Representative honours:* He was selected for the England National Game XI – England's representative side for semi-professional players.

### Playing Career

| Club | From | To | Fee | Total Appearances incl (subs) | Goals |
|---|---|---|---|---|---|
| Redditch United | 2009 | 2010 | | | |
| Forest Green Rovers | 2009 | 2009 | Loan | 20 | |
| Cheltenham Town | 2004 | 2009 | | 180 | |
| Northampton Town | 2002 | 2004 | | 25 | |
| Northampton Town | 2002 | | Loan | 16 | |
| Birmingham City | 1997 | 2002 | | 74 | |
| Yeovil Town | 1996 | 1997 | | 41 | 10 |
| Bath City | 1990 | 1996 | | | |
| Weston Super Mare | 1990 | | | | |
| Leyton Orient | 1988 | 1990 | | 0 | |
| Trowbridge | 1987 | 1988 | | | |

### Career in words
Jerry attended Backwell School as a schoolboy where he played football for Parkway Youth club alongside Marcus Stewart and for Backwell United. He was invited to join Bristol Rovers youth team for a tournament in Germany. He was a late starter in the game making his Football League debut at the age of 27. Jerry began his career as a 16-year-old with non-League Trowbridge Town. After a one-game trial

he signed for Orient on an 18-month contract in 1988. He found it difficult to settle but stuck it out for the full 18 months in London without playing for the Leyton Orient first team. He returned to become a semi-professional with Weston-Super-Mare, followed by six seasons with Bath City who were newly promoted to the Conference during which time he played part-time combining his football with his role as a salesman for a supplier of pitch care products finally making 218 appearances in all competitions and scoring 14 goals. Jerry finally established himself in the first team in 1992–93 season. In 1993–94 he helped the club reach the third round of the FA Cup where they held First Division Stoke City to a 1–1 draw before losing 4–1 in the replay. He joined Yeovil in 1996–97 for a fee of £9,500. He scored 16 goals in all competitions helping them to gain promotion to the Conference League. His cap for the England semi-professional team was against Ireland B in Dublin in 2002. In 2002 the FA selected an 'all-time' team of players capped at semi-professional level 'representing the very best of this level over the years' Jerry occupied the right back spot in this team which included players such as Alan Smith and Steve Guppy who had become full internationals. His representative selection brought him to the attention of Blues who invited him to take part in trial matches, halfway through the season Yeovil signed Howard Forinton from Oxford City and his 23 goals in 21 matches did much to secure Yeovil's promotion to the Conference and attract the attention of Trevor Francis. A deal was struck which saw Gill and Forinton join the Blues in August 1997 for a combined fee of £100,000 with Jerry valued at £30.000 plus an additional £10,000 when he played 10 first-team matches. He spent nearly a full season at St Andrew's before he finally made his League debut. His second game away to Oxford United was eventful. With the score 0–0 the referee first failed to award a penalty when Gill handled the ball in the penalty area, then disallowed the goal scored when Gill deflected an opponent's cross into his own net; a few minutes later Gill was substituted. He captained the Blues Reserves to victory in the Birmingham Senior Cup in 1999 and 2000.

Francis was quoted on Jerry: 'Jerry knows what the situation is. I think he's done very well for us, considering we plucked him out of non-League football at Yeovil. But he is aware that I have been looking for a right-back and I will continue looking for one. That doesn't mean I don't appreciate what Jerry has done for me since I signed him three-and-a-half years ago. There isn't a more reliable player at the club than Jerry Gill. He captains my reserve team, his fitness is of a very high standard and he has endless enthusiasm. When I put him in the first team, he never lets me down. I value Jerry's professionalism and for as long as I remain manager of Birmingham, there will always be a place for him here.' He signed a two and a half year contract in January 2001 having taken part in most of the games in Blues' League Cup run he was left out of the first leg of the semi-final at Ipswich in favour of a loan player Steve Jenkins. When Jenkins returned to his parent club Gary Rowett said that Gill should be given a run of games in the Blues First team saying 'if anything he's too nice. He doesn't complain a lot and its easy for people not to take notice of you. Perhaps if he moaned a bit more he'd get a start'. Recalled for the second leg, he produced an excellent performance, making a goalline clearance from a header which would have left Blues two goals adrift had it crossed the line. Yet when it came to the Final Francis could not find a place for him even amongst the substitutes, preferring Eaden and McCarthy, making only his second start after recovering from a broken leg, in the starting line up. David Holdsworth a defender unavailable since the previous November due to serious illness was on the bench. Gill was devastated by the decision describing it as 'the biggest disappointment of my whole life'. He played in almost every game after the Final until Francis left the club the following October but then lost his place due to injury. Though he did receive a League Cup runners'-up medal, Alan Jones the secretary had kept one back and presented it to Jerry after Francis had left.

At the start of 2002–03 season he joined Northampton Town on a month's loan where the manager Kevan Broadhurst praised his qualities of leadership and determination: 'Jerry will lead at the back by example. He does not pull out of anything and if there is a tackle to be won he will win it.' The loan was twice extended by a further month and on 11 November 2002 he left Blues permanently signing for the Cobblers until the end of the season. With the promise of a two-year contract in sight with two games remaining, he damaged his anterior cruciate ligament. Northampton Town gave him a six-month contract on reduced wages to allow him time to recover and prove his fitness, and Blues allowed him to use their facilities for his rehabilitation. He recovered enough to play a few reserve games for Northampton but the new manager Colin Calderwood did not offer him a further contract. Following a trial he signed for Cheltenham Town on 25 February 2004 on a non-contract basis until the end of the season. He was given

# THE HEROES

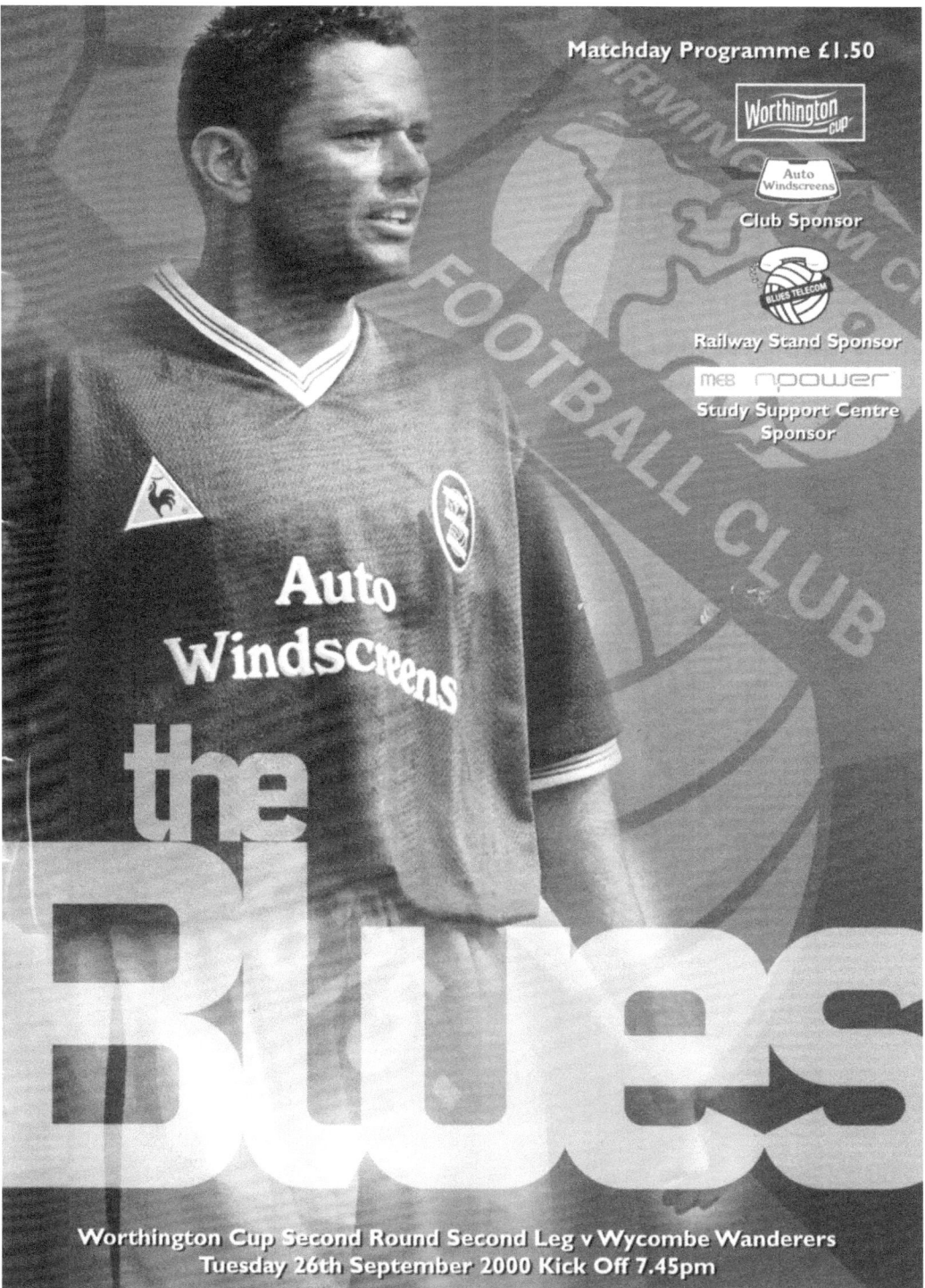

a one-year contract for 2004–05 season, and at the age of 34 played in all 46 League games. The following season he was given another one-year contract with an option for 2006–07 if he played 20 games during the season. Not only did he start twice that number, he helped them reach the League Two Play-off Final at the Millennium Stadium, where he was given a starting place and a winner's medal. By Christmas 2006 he had reached his target of 25 games which triggered the offer of another year's contract. He missed only three games in all competitions in the 2007–08 season. He was appointed captain in October 2007 and at the end of the season signed another year's contract with the club. Manager Keith Downing said 'Jerry's form has been impressively consistent over the past few seasons, he has maintained excellent fitness levels and will once again be a very valuable player for us next season. He is a very good professional who is always on the training field. That is why his career has lasted as long as it has. Jerry is a very good influence in the dressing room as well and I'm delighted that he will be staying with us.'

He made his 200th start for the club in August 2008 but was transfer-listed in September 2008 by new manager Martin Allen. He was involved in coaching at Cheltenham Town but wanted to continue playing so saw a player-coach role at Forest Green Rovers too good to turn down, joining on 1 October 2008 initially on loan with the expectation of making the move permanent in January 2009 when the transfer window opened. He made his debut three days later in a 3–2 home defeat to Wrexham. When January arrived the loan was not made permanent but extended until the end of 2008–09. During a match against Oxford United in March 2009 he suffered a triple fracture to his cheekbone and eye socket resulting in a titanium plate being inserted into his face following his collision with a steel bar after a 'nudge' from an opponent sent him through the perimeter advertising boards. The remainder of the season he acted as a coach gaining his UEFA 'B' Licence. He left in June 2009. In the summer of 2009 he worked as a coach with the Blues youth system before being shortlisted for the manager's job at Cambridge United in which he lost out to Martin Ling and also failed to secure the Forest Green Rovers role. In September 2009 he joined Redditch United where he became a first-team regular in the Blue Square North side. In January 2010 he was appointed manager at Weymouth then bottom of Blue Square South but budget restrictions meant he lost players which he was unable to replace so he resigned after 44 days feeling his position had become untenable.

Cheltenham manager John Ward said of him: 'We played Birmingham City in a pre-season game and he got a lovely ovation from their supporters and it was the same at Yeovil last year. He got a lovely clap at Northampton a few weeks ago when he was taken off. I don't think that happened by coincidence. And I've got a feeling that if he leaves Cheltenham he will get a similar reception if he comes back with another club. Supporters recognise him and they see the whole-heartedness and the commitment and the ability that he has got.' When Gill did leave Cheltenham, chairman Paul Baker confirmed Ward's feeling: 'Jerry has been a fantastic ambassador for the club following his arrival from Northampton some four years ago. He quickly established himself in the first team and became one of the fans' favourites with his consistent performances, cheery smile and friendly manner. Without question he has played a very important part in the club's success in achieving promotion and subsequently retaining our Coca-Cola League One status'

Gill is married to Victoria and they have a son. He is a director of sports marketing and retail company Protech Sport and is a keen golfer.

### About the man
### What is your current job?
Bristol Rovers youth-team coach-manager Under-18s.

### Who was your favourite player as a boy? And why?
Kevin Keegan…growing up in late '70s, Liverpool were the team I supported, and I idolised his professional attitude, work rate and talent.

### Which game in your career stands out in your memory?
Winning the League Two Play-off Final with Cheltenham in 2006 at the Millenium Stadium at the age of 36! And Blues' 3–1 win away at Spurs in the Worthington Cup.

### What's your best football experience?
Playing for my country, albeit the England Non-League team, in 1997 against the Republic of Ireland. Meeting Trevor Francis at his house at Wentworth Golf Club to discuss and agree my first contract for Birmingham City.

### Who was the best player you played with and why?
Steve Bruce…made my debut alongside him, and the information he gave me was invaluable…he read the game so well even in his later years and made sure I did all his running that day and covered him…a true gentleman and legend. My career owes a lot to him because when I left Blues for Northampton I ruptured my anterior cruciate ligament, yet he told me to come back, have the Blues surgeon and rehab at the club at no cost, even though I was no longer an employee…at 32 I then went on to play another 200+ League games that I would not have done if I hadn't got the best surgeon and rehab etc.

### If you could go back to your days at Blues what one thing would you do differently?
I would do a lot more strength and conditioning work if I had the knowledge I do now…the game has moved on sports science wise so much and those programmes are a vital part of modern game.

### What was your best moment while at St Andrew's?
Without doubt the semi-final second leg against Ipswich Town in the Worthington Cup 4–1 win to get us to the Final. St Andrews was physically rocking that night and is still spoken about as one of the best nights ever. And hearing the Blues fans chanting the infamous 'Jerry Jerry Jerry' anytime I stepped on the field, I had such a good rapport with the Zulus!!

### If you hadn't chosen football as a career what would you be?
I was a sales representative until turning professional and playing semi professional football so probably still doing that.

### What is your opinion of football today?
Being a coach at the moment in football I think the game is really interesting and moving on, coaches are trying different shapes and systems, you never come up against the same one and its important to be adaptable in the modern game. I also think this country has a serious problem with the lack of real first-team game time for our young 18 to 21 professionals because of the foreign influx. In years gone by the best young pros were given a chance.

### If you could be one of today's Premier League stars who would you want to be and why?
Jamie Carragher…he is the ultimate professional and a real club man! He has made the best of his talent and had to work hard to get to the very top. I had to be at my best everyday to stay in the game at the top level. He is a true role model to any young aspiring footballer.

# Martin Grainger

### Heroic claim to fame
His final kick in a Blues shirt was a scoring free-kick against Manchester United.

### Vital statistics
*Date of birth:* 23 August 1972
*Place of birth:* Enfield, Middlesex
*Blues career:* 266 – 28 goals
*Blues debut:* 30 March 1996 (a) lost 1–2 v Grimsby Town. Crowd: 5,773
*Team:* Griemink, Frain, Grainger, Samways, Breen, Johnson (M), Hunt, Devlin, Barnes, Cornforth, Legg
*First goal:* 29 March 1997 (a) won 1–0 v Crystal Palace
*Club honours:* Blues – 2000–01 League Cup runner-up 2001, Championship promotion 2001–02

# BIRMINGHAM CITY

## MODERN DAY HEROES

### Playing Career

| Club | From | To | Fee | Total Appearances incl (subs) | Goals |
|---|---|---|---|---|---|
| Coventry City | 2004 | 2004 | Loan | 7 | |
| Birmingham City | 1996 | 2005 | £400,000 | 266 | 28 |
| Brentford | 1993 | 1996 | £60,000 | 124 | 16 |
| Colchester United | 1992 | 1993 | Trainee | 57 | 8 |

### Career in words

He started his career in 1992 with Colchester United signing as a trainee in July 1992. He stayed at Layer Road until October 1993 making 37 League starts. 'Grainge' moved to Brentford on 21 October for a fee of £60,000 making 100 League starts and scoring 12 goals. He joined Blues on 25 March 1996. In February 2004 he went on loan to Coventry City for whom he made seven League appearances. On 10 April 2004 he was recalled to the Blues first team due to an injury crisis; his final kick was a goal from a free kick v Manchester United at St Andrew's but he was injured in doing so and never played again for the Blues. He retired on 1 January 2005 after 13 years as a player, currently working as a VIP chauffeur. On 10 January 2008 he was announced as manager of Cheshunt FC but on 12 January 2008 the club issued a statement saying he had left the club due to family and personal reasons.

### About the man

The respect shown to Martin by the Blues fans and his colleagues was never better demonstrated than at his testimonial match. A Blues side beat Martin Grainger's XI 6–2 on 9 November 2005. A crowd of 4,428 braved the elements to pay their respects to a great career, and top-class referee Alan Wiley volunteered to officiate. After the event, a rumour circulated that the Blues Board had charged Martin £20,000 for the hire of St Andrew's.

The Blues line up was: Colin Doyle (Andy Bagnall 70), Mario Melchiot (Chris Cottrill 58), Martin Taylor (Sam Oji 46), Matt Upson (Alex Bruce 46), Marcos Painter (Carl Motteram 58), Nick Wright (Njazi Kuqi 58), Neil Kilkenny (David Howland 46), Nicky Butt (Asa Hall 58), Jamie Clapham (Mat Sadler 46), Jermaine Pennant (Sone Aluko 46), Walter Pandiani (Oliver Allen 46).

THE HEROES

The Martin Grainger XI was: Kevin Poole, Jerry Gill (Jon Bass 46, Ian Danter 70), Martin G. (Tom Ross 80), Gary Ablett (Ian Clarkson 46), Dave Busst (Michael Johnson 46), Jon McCarthy (Steve Robinson 46, Mick Flaherty 70), Nicky Eaden (Paul Devlin 46), Danny Sonner (Dougie Brown 46), Tommy Mooney (Jeff Kenna 46), Nicky Forster (Dean Gaffney 46, Trevor Francis 65), Dele Adebola (Paul Furlong 46). Scorers: Blues: Pennant (2) Pandiani (2) Wright and Kuqi. Martin Grainger XI: Grainger (pen) Kenna

Before leaving St Andrew's, Martin had to reject a job with the Blues Academy as he had relocated his family to Hertfordshire several months before the offer. On reflection 'I can say I've played and scored in every Division, even the Conference.'

# Julian Raymond Gray

**Heroic claim to fame**
Appeared in the soap opera, *EastEnders*.

**Vital statistics**
*Date of birth:* 21 September 1979
*Place of birth:* Lewisham, London
*Blues career:* 76 – 5 goals
*Blues first appearance:* As a substitute v Portsmouth on 14 August 2004 (a) drew 1–1. Crowd: 20,021
*Blues full debut:* 21 August 2004 (h) lost 0–1 v Chelsea. Crowd: 28,557
*Team:* Taylor (Maik), Melchiot, Lazadridis, Savage, Upson, Taylor (Martin), Johnson (D), Gray, Heskey, Izzet, Gronkjaer
*First goal:* 12 February 2005 (h) won 2–0 v Liverpool
*Club honours:* Championship runners-up 2006–07

## Playing Career

| Club | From | To | Fee | Total Appearances incl (subs) | Goals |
| --- | --- | --- | --- | --- | --- |
| Walsall | 2010 | | Free | 24 | 5 |
| Barnsley | 2009 | 2009 | Free | 7 | |
| Fulham | 2009 | 2009 | | 2 | |
| Fulham | 2008 | 2009 | Loan | 1 | |
| Coventry City | 2007 | 2009 | Free | 33 | 4 |
| Birmingham City | 2004 | 2007 | Free | 76 | 5 |
| Cardiff City | 2003 | 2003 | Loan | 9 | |
| Crystal Palace | 2000 | 2004 | £500,000 | 138 | 14 |
| Arsenal | 1996 | 2000 | Trainee | 1 | |

**Career in words**
Julian began his career as a trainee with Arsenal but after a few seasons he joined Crystal Palace in 2000 for £500,000, a significant sum based on a single appearance for The Gunners. The Eagles spent the money based on his 'potential' which was a description he bore throughout his career and he never realised that 'potential. He spent a month on loan at Cardiff City in 2003–04 When his contract expired in June 2004 he signed for Blues on a free before being released by the Blues in May 2007. He joined Coventry City on 10 July 2007, then signed for Fulham on a season-long loan on 1 September 2008, despite not making a single League appearance the move was made permanent on 2 February 2009, after making one appearance as a substitute he was released at the end 2008–09 season with his potential still unrealised! In July 2009 he went on Sheffield United's pre-season tour of Malta on trial which was followed by a trial for Cardiff City in August 2009. On 15 September 2009 he joined Barnsley on a free initially on a monthly contract, but he was let go after two months during which he made seven appearances in all competitions. Julian joined Walsall in February 2010.

### About the man
**Tell me about your appearance in *EastEnders*.**
I didn't have a massive part to play. In fact, all the director asked me to do was ride a bicycle in the background. I made sure I rode that bike as slowly as I possible could to make sure my friends would recognise me.

**Favourite film?**
My favourite film of all-time is *Scarface*.

**Favourite TV programme?**
*EastEnders* and *Question of Sport*.

**Favourite drink?**
Pineapple and Cranberry.

**Any superstitions?**
I am superstitious; I always put my shorts on first.

**Favourite holiday destinations?**
New York and Jamaica.

**Favourite actress?**
Halle Berry.

**Favourite actor?**
Al Pacino and Robert de Niro.

**Which sporting event would you like to attend?**
NBA Finals.

**Which football stadium you would love to play in?**
Nou Camp.

**Sporting heroes**
Pele and Maradona.

**First pair of football boots?**
Adidas.

**Favourite Stadium?**
Highbury.

**Favourite newspaper?**
*Voice*.

**Favourite food?**
Steak with rice.

**Favourite sport after football?**
Table tennis.

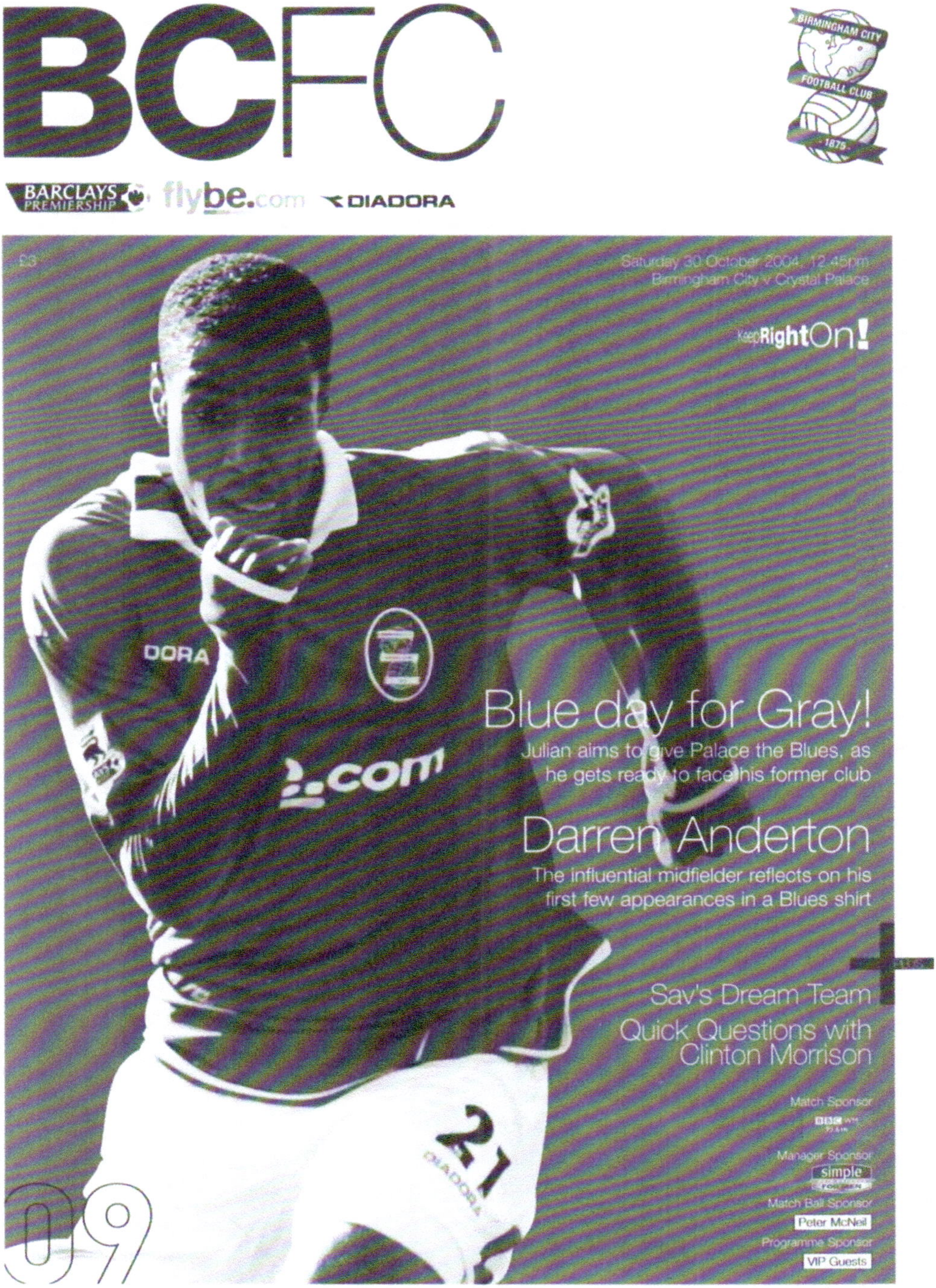

THE HEROES

# BCFC

Saturday 30 October 2004, 12.45pm
Birmingham City v Crystal Palace

keep Right On!

## Blue day for Gray!
Julian aims to give Palace the Blues, as he gets ready to face his former club

## Darren Anderton
The influential midfielder reflects on his first few appearances in a Blues shirt

Sav's Dream Team
Quick Questions with Clinton Morrison

Match Sponsor
BBC
Manager Sponsor
simple
Match Ball Sponsor
Peter McNeil
Programme Sponsor
VIP Guests

09

73

BIRMINGHAM CITY

MODERN DAY HEROES

# Jim Hagan

**Heroic claim to fame**
Voted Ulster's Young Footballer of the Year in 1976.

**Vital statistics**
*Date of birth:* 10 August 1956
*Place of birth:* Monkstown, Northern Ireland
*Blues career:* 167
*Blues first appearance:* As a substitute v Liverpool on 31 August 1982 (h) drew 0–0. Crowd: 20,976
*Blues full debut:* 11 September 1982 (a) lost 0–5 v West Ham United. Crowd: 18,754
*Team:* Blyth, Hagan, Dennis, Hawker, Van Den Hauwe, Phillips, Van Mierlo, Dillon, Harford, Curbishley, Carrodus
*Club honours:* Blues – Division Two runners-up 1994–95; Seiko – Hong Kong League Cup and Senior Cup

**Playing Career**

| Club | From | To | Fee | Total Appearances incl (subs) | Goals |
|---|---|---|---|---|---|
| Coleraine | 1995 | | | 2 | |
| Crusaders | 1995 | | | 3 | |
| Larne | 1994 | | | 16 | |
| Carrick Rangers | 1994 | | | 10 | |
| Ballymena | 1991 | 1994 | | 41 | |
| IK Oddevold (Sweden) | 1990 | 1991 | | | |
| Larne | 1990 | | | 5 | |
| Colchester United | 1989 | 1990 | | 2 | |
| Larne | 1989 | | | 3 | |
| Celta de Vigo (Spain) | 1987 | 1989 | | 60 | |
| Birmingham City | 1982 | 1987 | | 167 | |
| Seiko (Hong Kong) | 1980 | 1981 | Loan | | |
| Torquay United | 1979 | | Loan | 7 | |
| Coventry City | 1977 | 1982 | £25,000 | 16 | |
| Larne | 1974 | 1977 | | | |

**Career in words**
Jim began his career with Larne, where he was voted Ulster Young Player of the Year in 1975–76 season. He was only part-time also working as a booking clerk for the ferries between Larne and Stranraer. Although he played for Northern Ireland in a testimonial game v Glentoran in May 1977 he never made a full international appearance. He joined Coventry City in November 1977 for £25,000 making 13 appearances in his first season. He struggled to establish himself and joined Torquay United on loan in September 1979 and experienced football in the Far East with the Hong King side Seiko in October 1980 on an extended loan. During his time there the club won two

senior trophies. He returned to Coventry in July 1981 but was released at the end on 1981–82 season and in May 1982 he joined Blues. In 1987 he joined Celta de Vigo in the Spanish Primera Liga and he was named Overseas Player of the Year. He returned to Larne in August 1989 moving to Colchester United in the November of the same year. He only played twice and returned to Larne before joining Swedish side IK Oddevold in May 1990. In May 1991 he was appointed player-manager of Ballymena United on leaving he played briefly for Carrick Rangers and had a short unsuccessful spell in charge of Larne in 1994. He subsequently played for Crusaders before ending his playing career with Coleraine in December 1995. In 2001–01 he was Youth Development Officer (YDO) at Sunderland but he went back to Larne yet again, this time as their YDO before becoming assistant manager to Kenny Shiels in October 2005, he was appointed manager in May 2006 only to be sacked in the November. He went on to manage the Larne amateur side Wellington Recreation.

# Ian Robert Handysides

**Heroic claim to fame**
Everyone predicted he was the next Trevor Francis.

**Vital statistics**
*Date of birth:* 14 December 1962
*Place of birth:* Jarrow, Northumberland
*Date of death:* 17 August 1990, Solihull
*Blues career:* 133 – 6 goals
*Blues first appearance:* As a substitute 17 January 1981(h) lost 0–3 v Southampton. Crowd: 16491
*Blues full debut:* 14 February 1981 (a) drew 2–2 v Liverpool. Crowd: 32,199
*Team:* Wealands, Langan, Broadhurst, Dillon, Gallagher, Todd, Ainscow, Handysides, Worthington, Gemmill, Evans
*First goal:* 5 October 1982 (a) drew 1–1 v Shrewsbury League Cup second round first leg
*Club honours:* Blues: Division Two promotion 1980
*Representative honours:* England – Schoolboy & Youth

**Playing Career**

| Club | From | To | Fee | Total Appearances incl (subs) | Goals |
|---|---|---|---|---|---|
| Wolverhampton Wanderers | 1986 | | Loan | 11 | 2 |
| Birmingham City | 1986 | 1988 | | 56 | 4 |
| Walsall | 1984 | 1986 | | 66 | 11 |
| Birmingham City | 1980 | 1984 | | 77 | 2 |
| Birmingham City | 1979 | 1980 | Apprentice | | |

**Career in words**
He signed Associate Schoolboy forms for Blues on 16 February 1979 and then as an apprentice the following summer, after turning down interest from a number of clubs including Tottenham Hotspur and Manchester United. He signed professional terms in January 1980 and made his first-team debut at the age of 18, coming on as a substitute for Archie Gemmill. Four weeks later he wore the number-11 shirt at Anfield for his first starting appearance. When Ron Saunders replaced Jim Smith he did not rate Handysides, and he was placed on the transfer list towards the start of the 1982–83 season, but he knuckled down to his work and made 32 appearances which is pretty good for a player unwanted by the manager. After a period at Walsall he was re-signed to the Blues by John Bond in March 1986. He scored in the 1–1 draw against Manchester United at St Andrew's, which turned out to be the last point Blues earned in that season and they were relegated back into the second tier of English football. A loan period with Wolverhampton Wanderers enabled him to establish a record of playing in all four Leagues.

BIRMINGHAM CITY                                          MODERN DAY HEROES

# BLUESNEWS

FOOTBALL LEAGUE DIVISION TWO—SEASON 1986-87 • OFFICIAL PROGRAMME—PRICE 60p

**BIRMINGHAM CITY**
**v**
**BRADFORD CITY**
MONDAY 25th AUGUST 1986

● **INSIDE TODAY...**
● FULL COLOUR TEAM PHOTOGRAPH
● ANOTHER BALL GAME—Page 16

### About the man

Don Dorman, Blues' legendary scout, recommended him to the then manager Jim Smith describing him as 'the next Trevor Francis'.

Jim Smith recalls 'Ian was an exciting young lad, full of bounce and life and ideas. At Youth level, he was one of the best players in the country and you felt then that he could reach the highest level. We don't always make that sort of progress, perhaps the lack of height told against him in the end, but he had two great feet and was a tremendous striker of the ball.'

In the summer of 1988 he was diagnosed with a brain tumour which resulted soon after in his retirement from the game before embarking on his treatment. The cancer spread to his spine, resulting in his death at the age of 27. A testimonial match was played in November 1988 against a full-strength Manchester United team which attracted a crowd of 8,993, which does not sound a lot but it was 2,000 above the average League attendances for that season. United won 5–2, but the real result was the raising of almost £50,000 to his benefit fund.

# Michael Gordon Harford

### Heroic claim to fame
Steve Bruce considers him to be his most difficult opponent – Mike Wiseman.

### Vital statistics
*Date of birth:* 12 February 1959
*Place of birth:* Sunderland
*Blues career:* 109 – 33 goals
*Blues debut:* 27 March 1982 (h) won 1–0 v Brighton & Hove Albion and he scored. Crowd: 13,234
*Team:* Wealands, Langan, Hawker, Stevenson, Scott, Curbishley, Dillon, Evans, Harford, Broadhurst, Van Mierlo
*Club honours:* Blues – Division Two runners-up 1984–85; Luton – League Cup winner 1988, manager Luton Trophy winner 2009
*Representative honours:* England – Full

### Playing Career

| Club | From | To | Fee | Total Appearances incl (subs) | Goals |
| --- | --- | --- | --- | --- | --- |
| Wimbledon | 1994 | 1998 | £50,000 | 82 | 11 |
| Coventry City | 1993 | 1994 | £200,000 | 1 | 1 |
| Sunderland | 1993 | 1993 | £250,000 | 11 | 2 |
| Chelsea | 1992 | 1993 | £300,000 | 36 | 9 |
| Luton Town | 1991 | 1992 | £325,000 | 31 | 12 |
| Derby County | 1990 | 1991 | £450,000 | 68 | 18 |
| Luton Town | 1984 | 1990 | £250,000 | 186 | 81 |
| Birmingham City | 1982 | 1984 | £100,000 | 109 | 33 |
| Bristol City | 1981 | 1982 | £160,000 | 40 | 14 |
| Newcastle United | 1980 | 1981 | £180,000 | 19 | 4 |
| Lincoln City | 1977 | 1980 | Free | 131 | 41 |

### Career in words
He joined Lincoln City in 1977, spending three years at Sincil Bank before moving to Newcastle United in a £180,000 transfer. He was at St James's Park for eight months before joining Bristol City for £160,000 in August 1981. In March 1982 he signed for Blues for £100,000. In December 1984 he joined Luton Town for £250,000 which represented great business for the Blues. While at Kenilworth Road he won his two England caps, making his international debut v Israel in February 1988. (Note: His other game was v Denmark in November 1988.) He won the League Cup in 1988 when the Hatters beat Arsenal, he appeared in the 1989 Final scoring for Luton in their defeat at the hands of Nottingham Forest. He joined Derby County in January 1990 for £450,000, bringing his aggregate fees to date to over £1.1 million. He rejoined Luton Town in September 1991 for £325,000, following their relegation despite his 12 goals in 29 League games, he went to Chelsea in August 1992 for £300,000.

BIRMINGHAM CITY                                            MODERN DAY HEROES

He joined his home-town club of Sunderland in March 1993 for £250,000, where he lasted just four months before moving to Coventry City for £200,000 in July 1993 although, there for over a year, he only made one League appearance as a substitute. In August 1994 he joined Wimbledon for £50,000, going on to make 60 appearances before he moved to a coaching role with the club. At the end of his playing career he had commanded transfer fees in excess of £2.25 million. When Joe Kinnear moved to Luton Town Mick went with him and together they got Luton promoted in 2001–02 season to Division Two regrettably he left after falling out with the new owners of the time, but when they were forced out he returned as Director of Football as well as being first-team coach. In November 2004 he joined Kinnear again this time at Nottingham Forest, Kinnear lasted only a few weeks and Mick was given the caretaker role before leaving the club in January 2005 when Gary Megson was appointed. Mick went to Swindon Town in February 2005 to assist Andy King then he was appointed manager at Rotherham United at the end of 2004–05 but was sacked in the December after a run of 17 games without a win. He finished the season as striker coach at Millwall. In the summer of 2006 he assisted Geraint Williams at Colchester United. He became assistant manager of Queen's Park Rangers in June 2007 before becoming their caretaker-manager. In January 2008 he was the new manager of Luton Town and stayed with the club after the docking of 30 points prior to the 2008–09 season. He led them to victory in the Football League Trophy v Scunthorpe on 5 April 2009 winning 3–2 after extra time. The Hatters were also relegated to the Conference on 1 October resulting in Mick leaving by mutual consent. In December 2009 he was appointed assistant manager at Queen's Park Rangers eventually becoming their manager.

THE HEROES

**About the man**
**Favourite food?**
Roast beef.

**Favourite Drink?**
Guinness.

**Favourite other sports?**
Cricket & Snooker.

**What is your current job?**
I am a part-time scout for the England Under-21s.

**Who was your favourite player as a boy?**
For Sunderland it was Colin Todd, but my all-time favourite is Bobby Charlton.

**What game stands out in your memory?**
That would be Luton Town beating the mighty Arsenal 3–2 in the 1998 League Cup Final.

**What's your best football experience?**
Standing in the centre circle at Wembley with Peter Beardsley just prior to making my debut for England.

**Who was the best player you played with?**
Steve Foster – he was also a great captain and leader.

**If you could go back to your days at Blues what one thing would you do differently?**
I would keep away from Mark Dennis.

**What was your best moment while at St Andrew's?**
My debut winning goal against Brighton. Funnily enough, I was being marked by Steve Foster. Also the passion of the fans was incredible.

**If you had not chosen football as a career what would you be?**
A plumber – I served my time for two years – I would have been a good plumber.

**What is your opinion of football today?**
I do not believe that the current crop of players are fitter or stronger than in my day. I also believe that the players were better technically in the past. The new back pass rule has been good for the game. It is a quicker game, the pitches are better and the ball moves easier.

**If you could be one of today's Premier League stars who would you want to be and why?**
It would be Andy Carroll. If he gets it right he will have a great future.

# Martin Hicks

**Heroic claim to fame**
England Over-35 International.

**Vital statistics**
*Date of birth:* 27 February 1957
*Place of birth:* Stratford-upon-Avon

# BIRMINGHAM CITY                                                MODERN DAY HEROES

*Blues career:* 73 – 2 goals
*Blues debut:* 17 August 1991 (h) won 3–2 v Bury. Crowd: 9,033
*Team:* Thomas, Clarkson, Matthewson, Frain, Hicks, Mardon, Rodgerson, Gayle (J) Peer, Gleghorn, Sturridge
*First Blues goal:* 27 August 1991 (h) won 4–0 v Exeter City League Cup round one second leg
*Club honours:* Blues – Division Three runners-up 1991–92; Reading – Division Four champions 1986, Simod Cup winners 1988
*Representative honours:* England Over-35

## Playing Career

| Club | From | To | Fee | Total Appearances incl (subs) | Goals |
|---|---|---|---|---|---|
| Birmingham City | 1991 | 1993 | | 73 | 2 |
| Reading | 1978 | 1991 | | 500 | 23 |
| Charlton Athletic | 1977 | 1978 | | 0 | |

## Career in words

Martin holds the record for the highest number of first-team appearances by a Reading player, making a total of 603 first-team outings, scoring 26 goals. Hicks signed for Reading from non-League Stratford Town in 1976 but was released and allowed to join Charlton Athletic on the understanding that he returned to Elm Park in February 1978. He won a Division Four Championship medal in 1985–86 season and captained Reading to a Simod Cup win over Luton Town at Wembley in March 1988. He joined Blues in 1991 and later played for Newbury Town, Worcester City as a semi-professional.

In 1985–86 season he was the captain of the Reading side that won their opening 13 matches beating the 25-year-old record set by Tottenham Hotspur in 1960–61 strangely enough his testimonial game was v a Spurs XI.

He was a regular with the England Over-35 team. In 1994 at the Pele Cup in Italy he marked Paolo Rossi and John Neeskens in a veterans match preventing both former internationals from scoring. On retiring from professional football he returned to his birthplace, Stratford-upon-Avon to work in a post office.

Along with Paul Tait, and Simon Potter he had the ignominity of playing in both of the Anglo-Italian Cup ties that attracted all-time low attendances: 16 December 1993 v Lucchese (a) Lost 0–3. Crowd: 139 and 14 September 1994 v Wolverhampton Wanderers (h) lost 2–3. Crowd: 2,710

THE HEROES

# Scott Patrick Hiley

### Heroic claim to fame
Broke his ankle in three places and still came back to play.

### Vital statistics
*Date of birth:* 27 September 1968
*Place of birth:* Plymouth
*Blues career:* 58
*Blues debut:* 13 March 1993 (h) lost 0–1 v Bristol City. Crowd: 15,611
*Team:* Catlin, Hiley, Frain, Parris, Mardon, Matthewson, Moulden, Gayle (J), Peschisolido, Tait, Smith (D)
*Club honours:* Blues – Division Two champions 1994–95; Exeter – Division Four champions 1989–90

### Playing Career

| Club | From | To | Fee | Total Appearances incl (subs) | Goals |
| --- | --- | --- | --- | --- | --- |
| Crawley | 2006 | 2007 | Free | 44 | |
| Exeter | 2002 | 2006 | Free | 141 | 1 |
| Exeter | 2002 | 2002 | Loan | 12 | |
| Portsmouth | 1999 | 2002 | £200,000 | 80 | |
| Southampton | 1998 | 1999 | Free | 32 | |
| Southampton | 1998 | 1998 | Loan | 1 | |
| Manchester City | 1996 | 1998 | £250,000 | 3 | |
| Manchester City | 1996 | | Loan | 6 | |
| Birmingham City | 1993 | 1996 | £100,000 | 58 | |
| Exeter | 1986 | 1993 | Trainee | 259 | 12 |

### Career in words
Scott joined Exeter City at the age of 11 and came through their youth system, eventually playing in the side which won Exeter's only honour; the Fourth Division title in 1989–90 season. In 1993 he followed manager Terry Cooper to Blues. He spent three injury prone years at St Andrew's before in February 1996 he was the subject of a surprise loan signing to Premiership side Manchester City, two months later the move became permanent but first-team chances were limited, and he spent most of his time playing mainly for the reserves for two years as Manchester City slid down the Leagues. In August 1998 he returned to the Premiership with Southampton and spent 18 months there before joining Portsmouth in December 1999. He was made captain and won Player of the Year in his first full season with Pompey. In November 2002 he rejoined Exeter City but could not stop them losing their Football League status at the end of 2002–03 season. Scott remained with Exeter after relegation and in 2003 joined the coaching staff as well as continuing to be a first-team regular until October 2005. He left the club in February 2006 by mutual consent having spent over 10 years at St James Park, during his two spells with the Grecians he started almost 400 games. In August 2006 he signed for Crawley Town leaving after 12 months. In September 2008 he signed for Tiverton Town. He also featured a few times for Cullompton Rangers during 2008–09 season.

### About the man
Scott ran a Bed & Breakfast establishment with his wife Tina in Clyst St Mary just outside of Exeter and he turns out for the Exeter City Legends team.

Edwin Stein was an integral part of the Barry Fry regime that won the Division Two Championship in 1994–95 season he had this to say about Scott Hiley's contribution to the triumph: 'Arguably our most consistent player before he got injured, doing his knee ligaments in September 1994. He worked hard to get back after seven months and when we played him he did remarkably well. I think he expected a little too much of himself after being sidelined for so long. No question that Jungle has got exceptional talent.'

BIRMINGHAM CITY                                   MODERN DAY HEROES

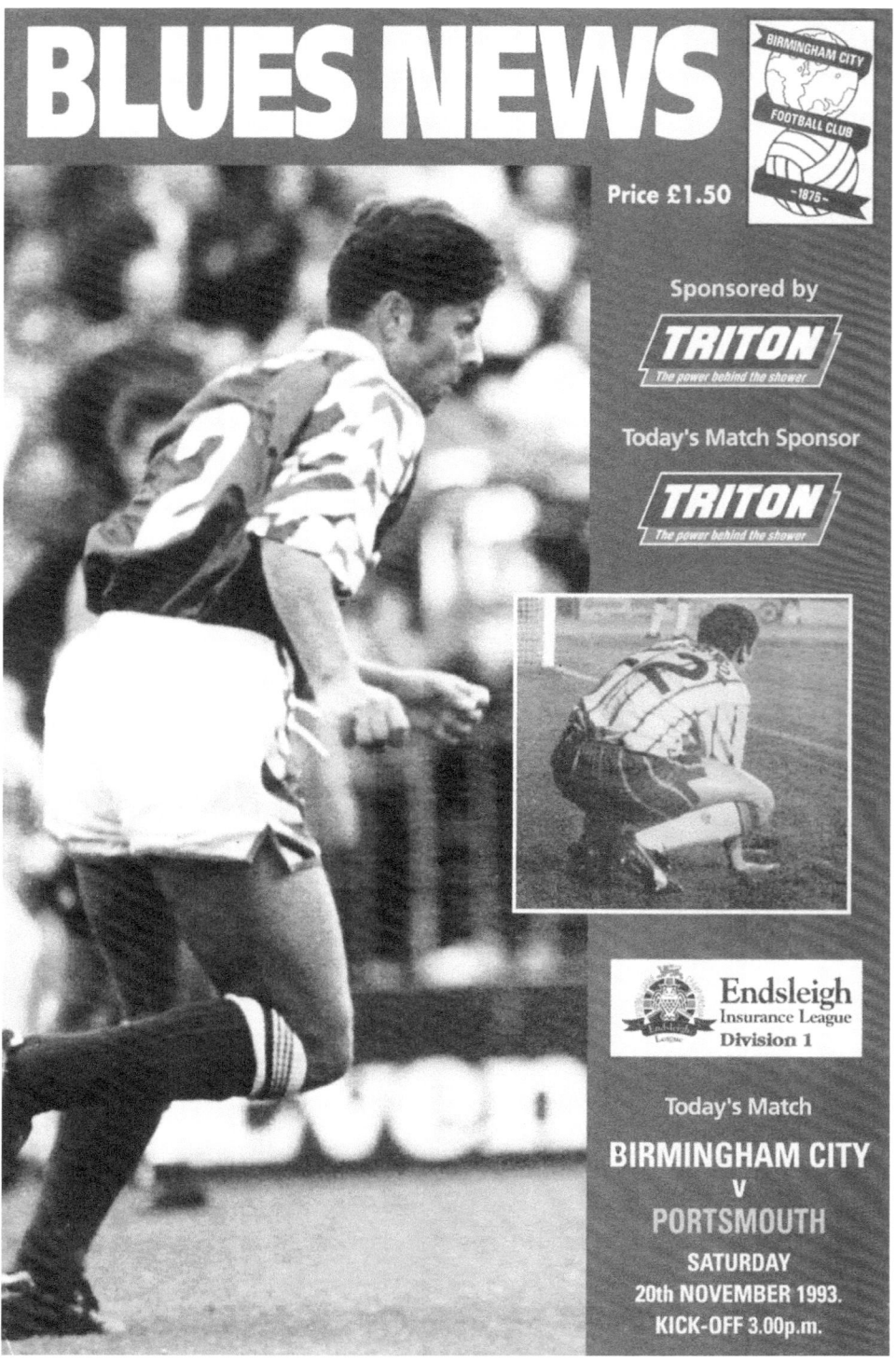

**What do you recall of the Barry Fry days?**
In 1996 I was one of the many fringe players at Barry Fry's overstaffed Blues. We did not have five-a-sides we had 15-a-sides.

**What about your time at Manchester City?**
I was signed by Alan Ball who had been my manager at Exeter but had moved to Maine Road. I was just establishing myself when I broke my ankle in three places at Bolton Wanderers. By the time I was fit to play again the club had been relegated and Ball had left. I got back in under caretaker manager Asa Hartford, but then I suffered a ruptured tendon so I was out for another 14 months, during which time City had several managers. By the time I came back Joe Royle was in charge and it was very difficult to force my way in… I wanted to prove myself on that stage and I was at a great club with great fans. But I only played nine games in two and a half years. Being told it will be an awful long time before you come back, if you come back at all, really knocks you for six. It was a long road. You don't travel or train with the team. I was on my own for almost two seasons and that was difficult.

**So what happened then?**
I have to thank Terry Cooper, who had given me my debut at Exeter and signed me for Blues. He recommended me to Dave Jones at Southampton. I played for a season, but then Jones decided he wanted to bring in younger players. By then Alan Ball was back in management, at Portsmouth. He wanted a right-back, but I wasn't sure. There is such a rivalry between Southampton and Portsmouth, Bally said 'If you show what you can do they'll take to you.' Two days later he was sacked. My first match was Sunderland away. It was a long way by bus and I remember sitting there thinking 'maybe this was the wrong move'. Then a few weeks later David Jones left Southampton and I began to wonder what would have happened if I had stayed.' By then I was in the Portsmouth reserves. Those were the good days. On the bad ones I was in the first team. Tony Pullis came in and didn't fancy me so I didn't play much, but when I did I was getting booed because of the Southampton connection. It was quite stressful at the time. Every time I had the ball I was booed, whatever I did. That's hard to take when you are playing at home. And they make a lot of noise at Fratton Park. When they are booing you can hear it. Then Steve Claridge, a Pompey legend, came in and put me straight in the side. With him being so respected the fans thought they would give me a chance. Steve told me he would give me a run of games regardless, and gradually I won them over. I ended up the fans' Player of the Year which was a big turnaround.

Steve Claridge writes in his book *Beyond The Boot Camps* published by Orion in 2009 'In reality I had little scope to bring people in, though I did get the former flying Manchester United winger Lee Sharpe on loan for a month, and he did all right for me. Instead, I recalled people like Jason Crowe and Scott Hiley, who Pullis had let go out on loan and they also came back to do decent jobs for me.'

# Christopher James Holland

**Heroic claim to fame**
Three games at Newcastle United valued him at £600,000.

**Vital statistics**
*Date of birth:* 11th September 1975
*Place of birth:* Whalley, Lancashire
*Blues career:* 87
*Blues first appearance:* As a substitute 7 September 1996 (a) lost 0–1 v Tranmere Rovers. Crowd: 8,548
*Blues full debut:* 18 September 1996 (h) drew 0–0 v Oldham Athletic. Crowd: 17,228
*Team:* Bennett, Poole, Ablett, Bruce, Breen, Holland, Devlin, Newell, Furlong, Horne, Tait
*Representative honours:* England Youth – Under-21 10 caps the first of his caps while at St James's Park

# BIRMINGHAM CITY                                               MODERN DAY HEROES

## Playing Career

| Club | From | To | Fee | Total Appearances incl (subs) | Goals |
|---|---|---|---|---|---|
| Southport | 2007 | 2009 | Free | 17 | |
| Boston United | 2004 | 2007 | Free | 99 | |
| Huddersfield Town | 2000 | 2004 | £100,000 | 138 | 3 |
| Birmingham City | 1996 | 2000 | £600,000 | 78 | |
| Birmingham City | 1996 | 1996 | Loan | 9 | |
| Newcastle United | 1994 | 1996 | £100,000 | 3 | |
| Preston North End | 1993 | 1994 | Trainee | 2 | |

## Career in words

He started his career as a trainee with Preston North End in 1993 making just one League appearance as a substitute before signing for Newcastle United on 20 January 1994 for a fee £100,000. He sustained an eye injury during an ammonia attack before joining Blues on loan on 3 September 1996 a move that was made permanent in October 1996 for £600,000. He joined Huddersfield Town on 3 February 2000 for £100,000 where he scored the first goal of his professional career a winner v Nottingham Forest on 21 March 2000. He played regular first-team football for three seasons before joining Boston United in League Two in March 2004. After two years he signed an 18-month contract with Conference side Southport on 31 January 2007 on a free transfer. Despite their relegation to Conference North at the end of the 2006–07 season he signed a new contract and was appointed club captain. In July 2008 he joined Leigh Genesis on a free making his debut on the opening day of the 2008–09 season in a 2–0 defeat v Eastwood Town. On 14 November 2008 he joined Fleetwood Town making his debut on 15 November in a 2–1 win at Stafford Rangers. In March 2009 he joined Burscough.

## About the man

*Pure Gold* by David Gold, published in 2006 by Highdown: 'Trevor [Francis] brought in too many players who didn't enhance the squad or improve the team. We couldn't see the difference they would make, and sometimes players actually made the situation worse. Trevor's pride made him stick with a player. Chris Holland was a classic example. When Trevor bought him he'd played just three League games for Newcastle, and even those had been a few years earlier, as a teenager. Trevor played him, and while we were saying he was not good enough, he stuck with him. I'm the first man to admire loyalty and promote it as a virtue, but this wasn't loyalty, I felt, it was more an error of judgement. I can only believe that Trevor had seen Chris on occasions when he had played above himself, and he was waiting to see if he could reproduce the same form. But if it can't be done after a dozen games, or if a player does it only for only half a game, what good is he to the team?'

… THE HEROES

# Robert Arthur Hopkins

### Heroic claim to fame
His last selection for Blues was at Wembley in the Leyland Daf Final of 1991.

### Vital statistics
*Date of birth:* 25 October 1961
*Place of birth:* Hall Green, Birmingham
*Blues career:* 205 – 33 goals
*Blues debut:* 26 March 1983 (h) won 3–0 v Notts County. Crowd: 11,744
*Team:* Coton, Hagan, Dennis, Stevenson, Blake, Van den Hauwe, Gayle (H), Ferguson, Harford, Halsall, Hopkins
*First Blues goal:* 12 April 1983 (a) lost 1–3 v Luton Town
*Club honours:* Aston Villa – Southern Junior Floodlit Cup winner 1980; Blues– Division Two champions 1985, Leyland Daf Cup winner 1991

### Playing Career

| Club | From | To | Fee | Total Appearances incl (subs) | Goals |
| --- | --- | --- | --- | --- | --- |
| Solihull Borough | 1994 | 1995 | | | |
| Colchester United | 1993 | | | 14 | 1 |
| Solihull Borough | 1992 | | | | |
| Instant-Dictionary FC (Hong Kong) | 1992 | | | | |
| Shrewsbury Town | 1991 | 1992 | Free | 27 | 3 |
| Birmingham City | 1989 | 1991 | £25,000 | 58 | 9 |
| West Bromwich Albion | 1987 | 1989 | £60,000 | 83 | 11 |
| Manchester City | 1986 | 1987 | £130,000 | 7 | 1 |
| Birmingham City | 1983 | 1986 | | 147 | 24 |
| Aston Villa | 1979 | 1983 | | 3 | 1 |
| Aston Villa | 1977 | 1979 | Youth | | |

### Career in words
Hoppy is as big a Bluenose as any fan, and therefore you can imagine how he must have felt when he started his playing career at Aston Villa. During his six years at Villa Park he trained and played every time wearing his Blues medallion. After playing for South Birmingham Schools and West Midlands County Boys it was inevitable that he would be a footballer but there was only one club he wanted to play for and that was the Blues. His dream came true when Ron Saunders signed in March 1983 off-loading Alan Curbishley in exchange. He did not want to leave the Blues recalling 'I left the Blues because John Bond wanted to get rid of me. I went to Manchester City. I think it was for £160,000 that equates to about three or four million in current times. Basically, it was the management at the club. I never wanted to leave, but if a club wants you to leave you have to leave really' He only had one season at Maine Road before moving to The Hawthorns in March 1987 for £60,000 in a deal involving Imre Varadi moving in the opposite direction. He enjoyed two good seasons at West Bromwich Albion as virtually ever-present, he recalls his move back to St Andrew's in March 1989 for £25,000: 'I must be the only player in the world to move from West Brom to Birmingham for less money. My heart ruled my head. I had a two-year contract at West Brom, I didn't have to go anywhere but Garry Pendrey said "come and sign". We were on our way down. Blues were going to get relegated, and no one was going to help us, but it was a chance to sign back. I thought it would be like it was before, but it wasn't, regrettably so. My first day's training was on the car park! Can you believe it? As soon as I saw that I thought "what have I done?" They say never go back.'

BIRMINGHAM CITY                                         MODERN DAY HEROES

**About the man**
**Which Villa Blues derbies do you remember?**
The first Villa-Blues derby I remember watching was in 1969 when Villa beat us 2–0 at home in front of 40,000 fans. They got relegated that year to the old Third Division. The best derby was when we beat them 2–1 at Villa Park at the beginning of the 1976–77 season when John Connolly and Kenny Burns scored.

**What about when you played in those derbies?**
The first Blues Villa derby I played in was October 1983. Kevan Broadhurst got stretchered off after an appalling tackle from Steve McMahon. 'Broads' was never the same player after that tackle. Villa won 1–0, it was pouring down with rain and Peter Withe scored for them. Someone sent a pass back to Tony Coton, but it got stuck in the mud and he nicked it. It was a niggly game, and I remember going up the steps in the tunnel afterwards and following the Villa players into their dressing room. They had to lock the door because we were so incensed about what had happened to 'Broads'. McMahon's tackles were horrendous – he'd be out of the game today. He'd have been banned for six months at least for that one.

**What is the best goal you have scored during your career?**
We drew 2–2 with Manchester United at home and I scored a header passed Jeff Wealands.

THE HEROES

**And your worst goal?**
My bizarre own-goal at home to Altrincham in the FA Cup on 14 January 1986. In making a tackle I sent the ball into my own net to give the non-League side a 2–1 win.

**Who was the best manager you played under?**
Ron Saunders. He always said as long as you train hard, you play hard, as long as you give your best on a Saturday you could have a drink. Having said that there was always a 48-hour rule, and you could not go out less than 48 hours before a game.

**Who is the best player you have played with during your career?**
Mick Harford.

**What do you remember about your time at Blues?**
What I can remember is we had a proper team, there were no individuals – we had your Mick Harfords, Tony Cotons, Howard Gayles and Noel Blakes. We were all really good mates. After a game 11 of us, or 12 of us, would be down the pub and having a drink, or a few, because there were no individuals. We were drinking with the supporters in the local pubs – that's what I always remember, it was a proper team, a team spirit. I never found that spirit at any of my other clubs: West Brom was a nice friendly club, but at the Blues it was a special thing because everybody just seemed to get on. Ron Saunders was in charge, but he knew we would go out and have a drink, and that was all part of it.

# Geoffrey Malcolm Horsfield

**Heroic claim to fame**
Blues' first £2 million plus transfer fee.

**Vital statistics**
*Date of birth:* 1 November 1973
*Place of birth:* Barnsley
*Blues career:* 126 – 28 goals
*Blues debut:* 12 August 2000 (a) drew 0–0 v Queen's Park Rangers. Crowd: 13,926
*Team:* Bennett, Eaden, Johnson (M), Hughes, Holdsworth, Purse, Lazaridis, Grainger, Horsfield, Sonner, Ndlovu
*First Blues goal:* 17 September 2000 (a) drew 1–1 West Bromwich Albion
*Club honours:* Fulham – Division One champions 1998–99; Blues – Worthington League Cup finalist 2001, Division One Play-off winners 2002

**Playing Career**

| Club | From | To | Fee | Total Appearances incl (subs) | Goals |
|---|---|---|---|---|---|
| Port Vale | 2009 | 2010 | Free | 11 | |
| Lincoln City | 2009 | 2009 | Free | 17 | 1 |
| Scunthorpe United | 2008 | 2008 | Loan | 12 | |
| Leicester City | 2007 | 2007 | Loan | 13 | 2 |
| Leeds United | 2006 | 2007 | Loan | 15 | 2 |
| Sheffield United | 2006 | 2009 | £1,200,000 | 2 | 1 |
| Sheffield United | 2006 | 2006 | Loan | 3 | |
| West Bromwich Albion | 2003 | 2006 | £1,000,000 | 72 | 15 |
| Wigan Athletic | 2003 | 2003 | £1,000,000 | 17 | 7 |
| Birmingham City | 2000 | 2003 | £2,250,000 | 126 | 28 |
| Fulham | 1998 | 2000 | £300,000 | 74 | 31 |
| Halifax Town | 1997 | 1998 | | 34 | 38 |

## Career in words
Geoff began his adult life as a bricklayer in Barnsley and worked his way up through amateur football, won promotion from the Vauxhall Conference with Halifax Town at the age of 24 and was an early member of Mohamed Al Fayed's revolution at Fulham before Trevor Francis broke the then club record transfer fee by paying £2.25 million in the summer of 2000. His first season in the top flight was certainly eventful aside from the Villa goals; he scored match-sealing goals in both derby triumphs, he endured two red cards, against Bolton Wanderers and Charlton Athletic, plus a double hernia operation. He left Scarborough as a 17-year-old and played part-time for non-League Guiseley and Witton Albion before joining Halifax, where he scored 38 goals in 34 games.

The son and grandson of a coal miner, he started playing for a local men's team Athersley Recreation FC in the Barnsley Sunday League while still at school. While there he had an unsuccessful trial with Barnsley. On leaving school he took a college course in bricklaying continuing to play part-time for Athersley and Worsbrough Bridge in the Northern Counties East League. He turned professional with Scarborough in July 1992 making his debut in March 1993 but he was released after playing 12 League games and he returned to part-time football with Halifax Town. He played nine games before in 1994 he joined Guiseley where his 36 goals helped the club reach third place in the Premier Division of the Northern Premier League in 1994–95 season. He moved to Witton Albion, where he sustained a potentially career-threatening knee injury; however, after a full recovery he returned for a second spell with Halifax for a fee of £4,000. He made his second debut at The Shay in October 1996, the following season saw the club regain its Football League status winning the Conference title by a nine point margin. Geoff scored 30 goals in 40 League games making him the Conference Top scorer which resulted in him being selected for England Semi-Professional representative team v Holland but injury prevented him from playing. He turned professional once again and seven goals in his first 10 games in the Third Division attracted a bid from Fulham in the Second Division of £300,000 plus an additional £50,000 depending on appearances, the deal was done in October 1998 with Halifax benefitting from any profit on future transfer dealings. The season 1998–99 Fulham achieved promotion to the First Division, winning the Second Division title by 14 clear points, and although less prolific in the top flight his 14 goals in all competitions made the club's top scorer in 1999–2000 season. In July 2000 he signed a five-year contract with Blues for a club record fee at the time of £2.25 million (of which £350,000 went to Halifax). He was top scorer in his first season with 12 goals and played in the 2001 Worthington Cup Final, gaining promotion to the Premier League in 2002. His first Premier League goal came in September 2002, beating Aston Villa. He played three games at the start of 2003–04, and with Steve Bruce unable to guarantee him a first-team place he joined Wigan Athletic on a three-year deal in September 2003. He scored on his Wigan debut in a 4–2 win v Wimbledon on 13 September 2003. After just three months with Wigan he joined West Bromwich Albion for £1 million, making his Baggies debut in a 1–0 defeat away to Coventry City on 20 December 2003. The following month he scored his first goal for the club in a 2–0 win v Walsall. In 2003–04 as he again won promotion to the Premier League. In February 2006 he joined Sheffield United on loan but appeared in just three games under Neil Warnock. Geoff and Warnock wanted to end the deal but the Blades had agreed to sign Geoff on a permanent basis at the end of the season and the Albion refused to change the arrangements therefore the deal went through in May 2006 for a fee of £1.2 million. On 3 August 2006 he signed for Leeds United on loan which ended in January 2007 at which time he joined Leicester on loan for the rest of the season making his debut in a 1–1 draw with Luton Town on 3 February 2007. Back at Sheffield Warnock had been replaced by Brian Robson but Geoff remained out of the side making a solitary appearance in the League Cup. On 31 January 2008 he moved to Scunthorpe United on loan but after playing 12 games he was released from his contract by The Blades at the end of the season. He had a trial with Chesterfield during the summer of 2008 but rejected a move because he wanted a club nearer to his home in the Midlands. He had trials with Kettering Town and in September began training with Walsall. On 10 October 2008 he announced he had been diagnosed with testicular cancer but after treatment he signed a six-month contract for Lincoln City to run from 2 January 2009 until the end of the 2008–09 season. In July 2009 he was appointed player-assistant manager with Port Vale under Micky Adams.

## About the man
He is married to Tina and they have four children Chris, Chloe, Leah and Lexie-Brooke. He played as an emergency centre-half against Manchester United and Leeds United in the Premiership in season 2002–03

On Sunday 5 September 2010 he was named Player of the Tournament in the Masters Cup Grand Final at the LG Arena in which Blues Over 35s squad triumphed.

Sponsored by Peter's Pies the squad was Kevin Dearden, Jeff Kenna, Martin O'Connor, Jerry Gill, Graham Hyde, Geoff and captain Paul Devlin.

The other teams in the competition were Aston Villa, Nottingham Forest, Tranmere Rovers, Sunderland, Manchester City, Queen's Park Rangers and Barnsley.

In the quarter-finals Manchester City defeated Sunderland, Tranmere disposed of Aston Villa, Barnsley beat Queen's Park Rangers while Blues trounced Nottingham Forest 3–0 with goals from Devlin, Gill and Horsfield.

The semi-final ties saw Tranmere demolish Manchester City 6–1 while Blues beat Barnsley on penalties after a 2–2 draw (Mooney and Devlin).

In the Final Blues drew 3–3 against Tranmere with goals from O'Connor, Devlin and Horsfield. Blues triumphed in the penalty shoot out 4–2, Jerry Gill firing in the winning penalty just three days before his 40th birthday.

Typical of Blues they won a tournament that they did not qualify for through their efforts in the Regional Heats, but as the final was being held in Birmingham the organisers decided that both Birmingham sides should be handed an automatic place.

**What are your favourite sports outside of football?**
Snooker and golf.

**What outside interests do you have?**
In 2001 I set up a company that buys plots of land or old houses and renovates them.

**Tell us about your generosity?**
I had promised a donation to my first club, Athersley Red if I ever reached the Premiership; a few days after the Play-off victory I gave them £25,000 towards improving their facilities.

# Bryan Hughes

**Heroic claim to fame**
Won Two Championship Play-off Finals.

**Vital statistics**
*Date of birth:* 19 June 1976
*Place of birth:* Liverpool
*Blues career:* 293 – 42 goals
*First Blues appearance:* As a substitute 16 March 1997 (a) lost 0–2 v West Bromwich Albion. Crowd: 15,972
*Blues full debut:* 22 March 1997 (h) drew 1–1 v Sheffield United. Crowd: 14,969
*Team:* Bennett, Bass, Grainger, Legg, Ablett, Barnett, Devlin, Tait, Furlong, Hughes, O'Connor
*First Blues goal:* 2 September 1997 (a) won 3–0 v Tranmere Rovers
*Club honours:* Blues: Worthington League Cup finalist 2001 – Division One Play-off winner 2002 Hull City: Championship Play-off winner 2008

**Playing Career**

| Club | From | To | Fee | Total Appearances incl (subs) | Goals |
|---|---|---|---|---|---|
| Derby County | 2009 | 2009 | Loan | 3 | |
| Hull City | 2007 | 2010 | Free | 47 | 1 |
| Charlton Athletic | 2004 | 2007 | Free | 89 | 10 |
| Birmingham City | 1997 | 2004 | £800,000 | 293 | 42 |
| Wrexham | 1994 | 1997 | Trainee | 127 | 24 |

## THE HEROES

### Career in words
He originally made his name at Wrexham guiding them to the FA Cup quarter-finals in 1996–97, with the goals he scored on that cup run he attracted the attention of Blues. He eventually made 293 appearances for Blues, scoring 42 goals, and was a part of the Play-off-winning team in 2002. He also appeared as a substitute in the 2001 Worthington Cup Final. He was signed by Trevor Francis for the sum of £800,000. Unable to agree terms with Blues in July 2004 he joined Charlton Athletic on a three-year contract, quitting St Andrew's on a Bosman free transfer. He made his debut for The Addicks v Bolton as a substitute after only five minutes. He scored twice (his first goals for the Addicks) in the 4–1 FA Cup win over Rochdale in January 2005. After making only 10 starts all season, Hughes went to Hull City on a free on a three-year deal on 29 June 2007 and scored on his home debut in a 1–0 friendly win over Newcastle United. He scored his first League goal for the Tigers in a 5–0 win over Southampton. He had a month's loan with Derby County on 22 Oct 2009.

At Hull City he helped them win promotion to the Barclays Premier League as part of the side that beat Bristol City at Wembley in the 2008 Play-off Final.

He only managed six top-flight appearances for the KC Stadium-based team, and his contract was subsequently terminated in January 2010. In the summer of 2010 was been looking for a new contract and had had unsuccessful trials at Cardiff City and Huddersfield Town. In September 2010 he was on trial at Walsall when he suffered a hamstring injury.

### About the man
**Which famous person gets on your nerves?**
John Fashanu.

**What would be your specialist subject on Mastermind?**
Childcare.

**Tell me about your family?**
Wife: Lyndsey. Children: Holly and Flynn.

Player Comment - Bryan Hughes

BRYAN HUGHES has revealed that the arrival of Wimbledon midfielder Michael Hughes has given him the licence to get

The Northern Ireland captain is one of eight new players brought in by Steve Bruce since he took over at the helm.

the play-offs, I think we can go on and win it."

Blues now prepare for two home games in the space of four days

BIRMINGHAM CITY                                              MODERN DAY HEROES

# Jonathan Richard Hunt

### Heroic claim to fame
Blues' top goalscorer in 1995–96 with 15 goals.

### Vital statistics
*Date of birth:* 2 November 1971
*Place of birth:* Camden, London
*Blues career:* 102 – 25 goals
*Blues debut:* 18 September 1994 (h) won 4–0 v Peterborough United. Crowd: 10,600
*Team:* Bennett, Poole, Small, Ward, Whyte, Dryden, Hunt, Claridge, Bull, Tait, Wallace
*First Blues goal:* 5 November 1994 (a) won 2–0 v Shrewsbury Town
*Club honours:* Barnet – Division Three promotion; Blues – Division Two champions 1995, Auto Windscreen Shield winner 1995

### Playing Career

| Club | From | To | Fee | Total Appearances incl (subs) | Goals |
| --- | --- | --- | --- | --- | --- |
| Wimbledon | 2000 | 2004 | Free | 88 | 1 |
| Cambridge United | 2000 | 2000 | Loan | 7 | 1 |
| Sheffield United | 1999 | 2000 | Swap | 29 | 1 |
| Ipswich Town | 1998 | 1998 | Loan | 6 | |
| Sheffield United | 1998 | 1998 | Loan | 5 | 1 |
| Derby County | 1997 | 1999 | £500,000 | 34 | 2 |
| Birmingham City | 1994 | 1997 | £500,000 | 102 | 25 |
| Southend United | 1993 | 1994 | Free | 61 | 6 |
| Barnet | 1992 | 1993 | Junior | 43 | |

### Career in words
In his first full season he won promotion to Division Two with Barnet. He joined Blues from Southend United in September 1994 for a fee of £500,000 after one season at the South Coast club. After three years at St Andrew's where his strike rate had been 1 in 4 – not bad for a midfielder, he joined Derby County for £500,000 but he only made seven starts for the Rams in the Premier League. He had loan spells with Sheffield United and Ipswich Town before joining The Blades on a permanent basis when Neil Warnock was appointed manager. After a trial with Norwich proved unsuccessful Hunt made another loan move to Cambridge United. At the end of the 1999–2000 season Sheffield United paid up the remaining two years of his contract thereby allowing him to join Wimbledon in September 2000. He joined Peterborough United in September 2002 on a non-contract basis but made no appearances. Having been out of the game for five years in February 2008 he signed a short-term contract until the end of the season for St Albans City of the Conference South who were managed by Steve Castle a former colleague at Blues and The Posh.

### About the man
Edwin Stein was an integral part of the Barry Fry regime that won the Division Two Championship in 1994–95 season. He had this to say about Jonathan Hunt's contribution to the triumph:

'Hunty or Boy Blunder was absolutely superb. He has an exceptional talent and when he was in the team it took us onto a different plain. He scored eight goals before he suffered knee ligament damage in the November after netting against Stockport County. I honestly feel that had he not got injured we would have walked away with the League. The balance Hunty gave us with Wardy, Donowa and Shearer was perfect. The good thing about him is he can get even better. He can reach the top without a shadow of a doubt.'

# THE HEROES

**What is your current job?**
I am a Hanna Somatic Educator & Equine Hanna Somatic Educator. I retired from the pro game in 2002 with a persistent lower back problem. The technique Somatics resolved my long-standing back issue, and I remain pain free to this day. I also returned to playing football at semi-pro level. I currently play for AFC Hornchurch in the Ryman Premier. My website, if you are interested, is somaticliving.com

**BIRMINGHAM CITY**  **MODERN DAY HEROES**

**Who was your favourite player as a boy? And why?**
Glenn Hoddle. I was a Spurs fan as a boy, and he was the reason why. Two footed and a scorer of amazing goals, he could do things other players could only dream of.

**Which game in your career stands out in your memory?**
Auto Windscreens Final at Wembley. A full house with something like 40,000 Blue Noses.

**What's your best football experience?**
Again playing at Wembley, my Premiership debut for Derby and my hat-tricks for Birmingham.

**Who was the best player you played with and why?**
Stefano Eranio. He was great to play with, always would find space and never gave the ball away. I learnt a lot from him.

**If you could go back to your days at Blues what one thing would you do differently?**
Injuries are the hardest thing to stomach as a footballer. Although I am not the person who lives with regrets, I would have changed the timing of my second knee injury.

**What was your best moment while at St Andrew's?**
Wembley Final and hat-tricks.

**I you hadn't chosen football as a career what would you be?**
That's a tough one as I only ever wanted to be a footballer. My other great passion s horse racing, so a career in that industry would have suited me.

**What is your opinion of football today?**
Its very exciting to watch and the coverage is fantastic. I would change one thing. I think too many foreign players have crept into our game. I think there should be a maximum of six in each starting line up.

**If you could be one of today's Premier League stars who would you want to be and why?**
Cesc Fabregas. I love his cavalier approach to the game. He is my favourite player right now.

**Author's note:** He scored two hat-tricks: 1 November 1994 v Crewe Alexandra (h) won 5–0 and 26 August 1995 v Norwich City (h) won 3–1.

# Graham Hyde

**Heroic claim to fame**
Lost two Wembley Finals in the same season.

**Vital statistics**
*Date of birth:* 10 November 1970
*Place of birth:* Doncaster
*Blues career:* 59 – 2 goals
*Blues debut:* 21 February 1999 (h) drew 0–0 v Bolton Wanderers. Crowd: 26,051
*Team:* Poole, Bass, Charlton, Purse, Rowett, Grainger, Hyde, O'Connor, Furlong, Hughes, Ndlovu
*First Blues goal:* 23 November 1999 (h) won 3–1 v Tranmere Rovers
*Club honours:* Sheffield Wednesday – FA Cup runners-up 1993, Coca-Cola Cup runners-up 1993; Blues – Championship Play-off winners 2001–02

## Playing Career

| Club | From | To | Fee | Total Appearances incl (subs) | Goals |
|---|---|---|---|---|---|
| Hereford United | 2004 | 2005 | Free | 38 | |
| Bristol Rovers | 2002 | 2004 | Free | 62 | 3 |
| Peterborough United | 2002 | 2002 | Loan | 9 | |
| Chesterfield | 2001 | 2001 | Loan | 9 | 1 |
| Birmingham City | 1999 | 2002 | Free | 59 | 2 |
| Sheffield Wednesday | 1988 | 1999 | Trainee | 218 | 16 |

## Career in words

Graham joined Sheffield Wednesday as a 17-year-old trainee and stayed at Hillsborough for 11 years, making over 200 appearances for The Owls. He joined Blues on 4 February 1999 on a free transfer and helped them get promotion to the Premiership in 2001–2002. After two loan periods with Chesterfield and Peterborough United he joined Bristol Rovers on a free transfer at the end of 2002 and stayed two years before joining non-League Hereford United for the 2004–05 season. The following season he stayed in non-League football with Worcester City, Hednesford Town and Fleet Town respectively. In November 2006 he became player-assistant manager to Martin O'Connor at Halesowen Town, and 11 months later he signed for Fleet Town who were then managed by an old Sheffield Wednesday teammate, Andy Sinton.

## About the man
### What is your current job?

I work full-time with other ex-Blues favourites, Tommy Mooney, Kevan Broadhurst and Kevin Poole for Dean Holtham who runs Blues' Community Programme, but more of that later.

### What brought about your move from Sheffield Wednesday?

I had played with and been managed by Trevor Francis during his time at Hillsborough so he knew me, and what I could do pretty well. It was the early stages of the Bosman ruling and my contract had run out, so I was available on a free transfer, and the rest is history. I moved straight down from Yorkshire with my then girlfriend Emma and, after three months in the Arden Hotel on the A45, we rented a place before buying our current home in Dickens Heath.

### Who were the characters at Blues?

It was a crazy dressing room with so many great personalities, Martin O'Connor, Michael Johnson, Dele Adebola, Paul Furlong and then later on Geoff Horsfield, and Paul Devlin came back. It was tremendous!

### What do you remember of your debut?

My debut for Blues was also my most memorable game for the Blues, it was 'live' on Sky Sports, a full house and it was the opening of the new stand at the Railway End. The atmosphere was electric just like a packed Hillsborough, fabulous. It was against Bolton Wanderers and we drew 0–0. My League debut for Sheffield Wednesday was against Manchester City on 14 September 1991. I was 20 and we won 1–0.

### What was your most memorable goal?

Of the two you mean. I really admire midfielders like Frank Lampard who can score their fair share of goals – that was never my game. Both of my Blues goals are memorable to me, the first was a free-kick against Tranmere Rovers and the second against West Ham in the League Cup.

### What was your funniest moment?

With the dressing room we had there was never a dull moment, but I do remember rooming with Robbie Savage for a week in Scotland one pre-season. 'Sav' is a very funny man but very down to earth, outwardly it is all about the long blonde hair and the flash cars but deep down he's just a lad from Wrexham. He's great company.

# BIRMINGHAM CITY  MODERN DAY HEROES

**Tell me about your injuries?**
One major injury to my right leg was a ruptured medial ligament that kept me out of action for five months, a long time at that stage of my career. I missed the Division One Play-offs and the Worthington

THE HEROES

Cup Final. By the time I reached match fitness the team had moved on and I was surplus to requirements, and my two loan periods followed.

### How did you career end at Blues?
I joined Bristol Rovers on 28 November 2002 on a free transfer and had two good seasons there, scoring three goals in 62 appearances.

### What happened after that?
I achieved my B and A licences for coaching and went onto the non-League scene initially joining Hereford United who were managed by Graham Turner and John Trewick. We played some good football and got to the Conference Play-offs.

### Any career highlights?
I played over 150 times for Sheffield Wednesday and appeared in two Wembley Finals: I got a runners'-up medal in the 1993 FA Cup when we lost to Arsenal 2–1 after extra-time and in the same season we lost in the Coca-Cola League Cup Final again to Arsenal 2–1. At least I have a medal each for my two children, a boy aged two and a daughter aged six! My senior debut was as a 20-year-old in front of 30,000 at Maine Road competing in midfield against Gary Megson and Peter Reid. I think it was fair to say I had the legs on them!

### How do you spend your time these days?
I still play for the Birmingham City All-Stars with Tom Ross, which is about as good as it gets these days. Every day I am Wast Hills working with the lads helping to run the scheme set up by the Community Department in partnership with City College Birmingham. Our students train in the morning then head to St Andrew's in the afternoons to study for a BTEC First Diploma in Sport or a BTEC National Diploma in Sport and Level One and Level Two certificates in football coaching. The scheme is for youngsters aged 16–18 and has never before been run by a Premiership Club. It is designed to nurture local footballers who may have drifted out of the game or failed to land a scholarship at an Academy without compromising their education. We run four teams. I look after the third team, and there are a few lads who could make a career of it.

### What do you think of how youngsters are developed these days?
Firstly, the facilities they enjoy are second to none but they have it easier than their predecessors. I was scouted into Wednesday as a 13-year-old and as part of my YTS scheme my first job in the morning was to make Howard Wilkinson's (the manager) lemon tea and take it to his office. Imagine one of the academy lads today being asked to do that! It has definitely changed.

# Stern John

### Heroic claim to fame
Scored Blues first goal in the Premiership.

### Vital statistics
*Date of birth:* 30 October 1976
*Place of birth:* Trincity, Trinidad and Tobago
*Blues career:* 85 – 21 goals
*Blues debut:* 16 February 2002 (h) won 1–0 v Barnsley and he scored. Crowd: 19,208
*Team:* Bennett, Kenna, Grainger, Hughes, Purse, Vickers, Devlin, John, Horsfield, Carter, Mooney
*Club honours:* Columbus Crew – 1998 MLS Scoring Champion, 1998 MLS Golden Boot, 1998 MLS Best XI; Blues – 2002 Division One Play-off winners medal; Sunderland – Championship winners 2007
*Representative honours:* Trinidad & Tobago – 109 caps 69 goals

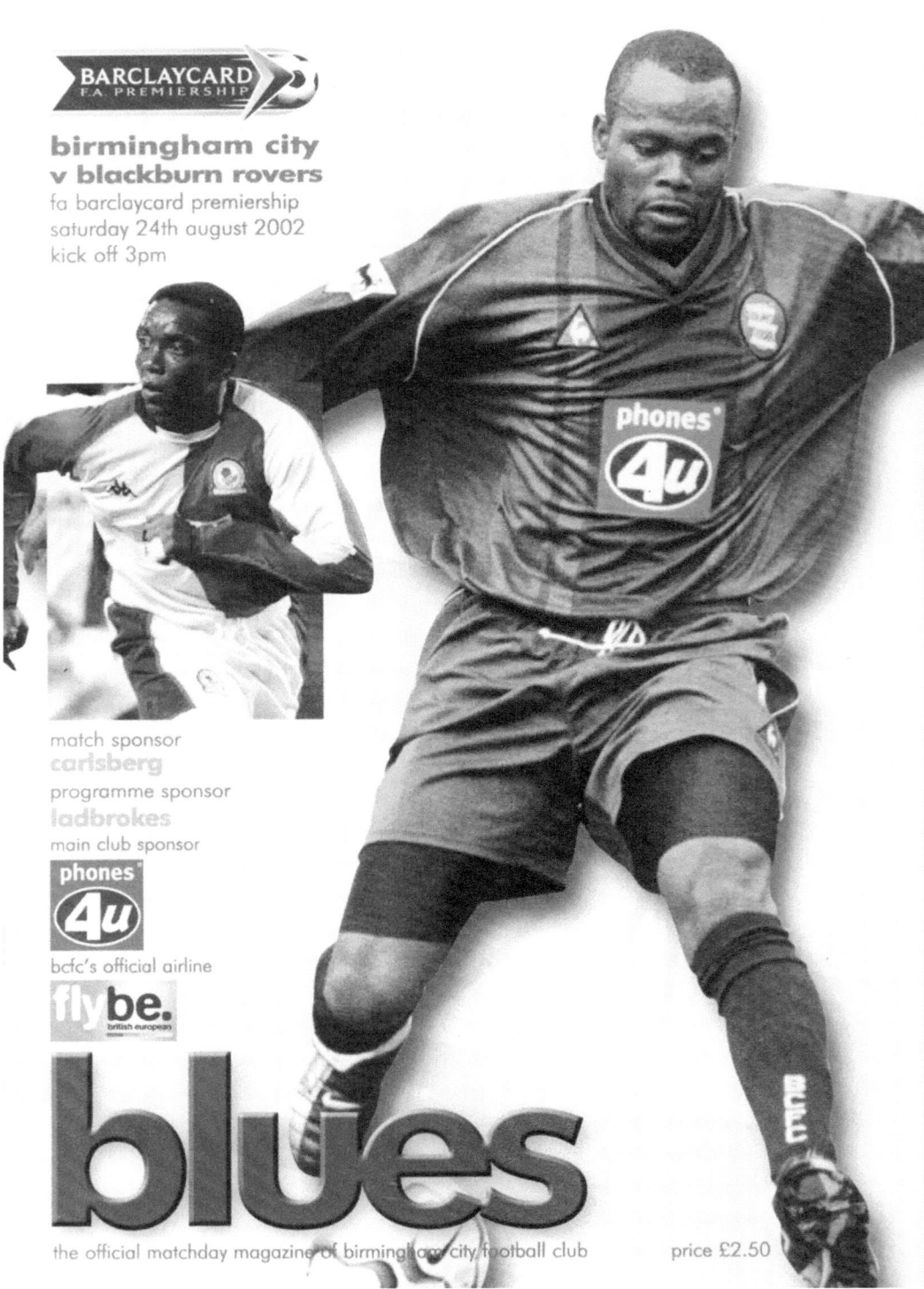

## Playing Career

| Club | From | To | Fee | Total Appearances incl (subs) | Goals |
|---|---|---|---|---|---|
| Ipswich Town | 2009 | 2010 | Loan | 9 | 1 |
| Crystal Palace | 2009 | 2010 | Free | 16 | 2 |
| Bristol City | 2008 | 2009 | Loan | 26 | 2 |
| Southampton | 2007 | 2009 | | 52 | 20 |
| Sunderland | 2007 | 2007 | | 16 | 5 |
| Derby County | 2005 | 2005 | Loan | 7 | |
| Coventry City | 2004 | 2007 | £200,000 | 88 | 29 |
| Birmingham City | 2002 | 2004 | £150,000 | 85 | 21 |
| Nottingham Forest | 1999 | 2002 | £1,500,000 | 78 | 20 |
| Columbus Crew | 1998 | 1999 | | | |

## Career in words

Stern moved to the US to attend Mercer County Community College in 1995. He joined Columbus Crew of Major League from New Orleans Riverboat Gamblers of the A-League for the 1998 season. After the 1999 season he was sold to Nottingham Forest for a fee of £1.5 million. Financial difficulties forced his sale to Blues for £150,000. He left Blues for Coventry City on 14 September 2004, finishing his first season with Coventry City as the team's second highest goalscorer scoring 12 goals. He was loaned to Derby County on 16 September 2005 for three months. On 29 January 2007 he joined Sunderland but his career in the North-East was short-lived as on 29 August 2007 he moved to Southampton as part of the deal which took Kenwyne-Jones in the opposite direction. He finished the 2007–08 season as the fourth -top scorer in the Championship with 19 goals. He went on loan to Bristol City in October 2008 until the end of the season. On 29 July 2009 he signed for Crystal Palace on a year-long contract making his debut on the opening day of the season v Plymouth Argyle. He went to Ipswich Town for a month long loan at the end of November. At the end of 2009–10 season he was released by Crystal Palace and was operating as a free agent. He made his Trinidad & Tobago international debut on 15 February 1995 against Finland in a friendly at the Queen's Park Oval scoring a goal. Stern is currently their all-time leading scorer with 69 goals in 109 caps (**Author's note:** As at 2 August 2009). He helped Trinidad & Tobago get to the 2006 FIFA World Cup playing in all three group games in Germany 2006. He was named as Trinidad & Tobago's Football Federation Player of the Year in 2002. Currently he is their second most capped international behind Angus Eve.

# Andrew Johnson

### Heroic claim to fame
Missed deciding penalty in 2001 League Cup Final.

### Vital statistics
*Date of birth:* 10 February 1981
*Place of birth:* Bedford
*Blues career:* 103 – 13 goals
*First appearance for Blues:* As a substitute 31 August 1998 (a) lost 1–2 v Bradford City. Crowd: 13,910
*Blues full debut:* 14 August 1999 (a) won 1–0 v Norwich City. Crowd: 15,261
*Team:* Poole, Rowett, Grainger, Hughes, Holdsworth, Johnson (M), McCarthy, Johnson (A), Furlong, O'Connor, Lazaridis
*Club honours:* Blues – First Division Play-off winner 2002, Worthington Cup runner-up 2001; Crystal Palace – Premier League Player of the Month October 2004 and September 2006, First Division Top Scorer 2003–04, Palace Player of the Year 2004 and 2005, Voted into Palace 'Centenary XI' 2005.
*Representative honours:* England: Youth – Under-20 2 caps, full 5 caps 2005–07

# BIRMINGHAM CITY

MODERN DAY HEROES

### Playing Career

| Club | From | To | Fee | Total Appearances incl (subs) | Goals |
|---|---|---|---|---|---|
| Fulham | 2008 | | £10,500,000 | 49 | 13 |
| Everton | 2006 | 2009 | £8,600,000 | 74 | 22 |
| Crystal Palace | 2002 | 2006 | £750,000 | 160 | 85 |
| Birmingham City | 1997 | 2002 | Trainee | 103 | 13 |

### Career in words

Andrew started his career at the Academy at Luton Town before moving to the Blues Academy when he was sixteen. He enjoyed the status of being one of the very few Blues Academy scholars who created a career at the highest level. Although renowned for his pace his scoring record of one goal every 10 games was not particularly impressive. He was sold to Crystal Palace in 2002 as a makeweight in the transfer deal which brought Clinton Morrison to St Andrew's with AJ being valued as £750,000. He made himself popular with the Palace fans by scoring back to back hat-tricks in October 2002 against Brighton & Hove Albion and Walsall in successive matches. Away from St Andrew's he found his shooting boots and finished the 2003–04 season as top scorer in the First Division with 32 goals. He joined Everton for £8.6 million on 30 May signing a five-year contract which was believed to have made him Everton's highest paid player on £40,000 per week. His move set two club transfer records both as Everton's most expensive purchase and Palace's most expensive sale. He scored his first goal for Everton on his debut on 19 August 2006 in a 2–1 win over Watford. He was their top scorer in the 2006–07 campaign with 11 goals. On 7 August 2008 he joined Fulham on a four-year contract for a fee in the region of £10.5 million making his debut in a 2–1 win over Bolton Wanderers on 13 September. He scored his first goal for The Cottagers against Wigan Athletic on 29 October 2008. He was first capped for England at Under-20 level being selected for the 1999 FIFA World Youth Championship. In 2004–05 he finished as the top English goalscorer in the Premier League. He made his full international debut as a substitute against Holland on 9 February 2005 after considering playing for Poland due to the birthplace of his grandfather. He made his full debut in a 2–1 friendly win over the United States of America

### About the man
#### How did you join Blues?

I was at Luton Town from the age of 12 and had been there for two years when Blues asked me for a trial after Lil Fucillo spotted me playing against Birmingham in a county game. I came with my friend Barrington Belgrade who ended up going to Norwich City and Plymouth Argyle. At the time I was about to sign YTS when Nottingham Forest who had showed an interest in me, Blues offered me professional terms which I was pleased to accept because I had already been at Blues for three years and I loved the club.

#### Who was the biggest influence on you?

My Dad was the biggest influence on my career in the early days particularly. Without him I would not have made it anywhere. He used to take me all over the country for football. He'd bring me to Birmingham twice a week, all over the country for district and county games.

#### Who was your schoolboy hero?

I used to support Arsenal so my boyhood footballing hero was Ian Wright.

#### How did you feel after scoring your first professional goal against West Bromwich Albion?

It was the best thing ever! It had been my dream to score for Blues and to do it in such a big game – a local derby with a full house at home was an unbelievable feeling.

#### Who was your craziest teammate at the Blues?

It has to be Martin Grainger because he is just off his head! He's crazy all the time.

# THE HEROES

**Who was the player with the worst dress sense at St Andrew's?**
No one in particular, but I do know Graham Hyde gets a lot of stick off the other lads. Although I wouldn't say too much because I room with him at away matches.

BIRMINGHAM CITY                                                    MODERN DAY HEROES

# Damien Michael Johnson

### Heroic claim to fame
Scored in Blues' first win in the Premiership 31 August 2002 – v Leeds United a 2–1 home win.

### Vital statistics
*Date of birth:* 18 November 1978
*Place of birth:* Lisburn, Ireland
*Blues career:* 214 – 4 goals
*Blues debut:* 12 March 2002 (a) won 3–1 v Bradford City. Crowd: 13,105
*Team:* Vaesen, Kenna, Grainger, Hughes, Purse, Johnson (M), Johnson (D), Mooney, John, Carter, Devlin
*First Blues goal:* 31 August 2002 (h) won 2–1 v Leeds United
*Club honours:* Blues – Championship runners-up 2006–07, Championship Play-off winners 2001–02
*Representative honours:* Northern Ireland – 56 appearances

### Playing Career

| Club | From | To | Fee | Total Appearances incl (subs) | Goals |
| --- | --- | --- | --- | --- | --- |
| Huddersfield Town | 2010 | | Loan | 3 | |
| Plymouth Argyle | 2010 | | Free | 20 | 2 |
| Birmingham City | 2002 | 2010 | £50,000 | 214 | 4 |
| Nottingham Forest | 1998 | | Loan | 6 | |
| Blackburn Rovers | 1997 | 2002 | Trainee | 81 | 4 |

### Career in words
His first English team was Blackburn Rovers for whom he signed as a trainee from Portadown FC in 1997. He made his debut in the League Cup on 30 September 1997 losing 1–0 to Preston North End. Loaned to Nottingham Forest on 28 January 1998 he only played six games before returning to Ewood Park for another four years. On 8 March 2002 Damien joined Blues for £50,000 and in September 2004 he signed a new three-year contract and was named Birmingham City captain for the 2006–07 season. Johnson earned his first call for the Northern Ireland squad on 29 May 1999 when he came on as a substitute in the 1–0 away win against the Republic of Ireland. Further substitute appearances followed against Finland, Luxembourg, Malta and Hungary before making his first full appearance against Yugoslavia at Windsor Park, Belfast in August 2000. He made his 49th appearance for NI in the 3–0 World Cup Qualifying victory in San Marino on 11 February 2009 when he was the BBC's Man of the Match. He left Blues for Plymouth Argyle on the deadline day of the January transfer window in January 2010. He was sent off 5 times in his Blues career which is a record for the club.

### About the man
**What do you recall of your Blues' debut?**
It was a damp, murky Valley Parade. I remember I had a nightmare I'd not been playing much for Rovers and it took me a while to settle in.

**Describe your ideal start to the day?**
Breakfast with Kelly Brook over a bowl of Frosties.

**Favourite music?**
Guitar rock music – something like The Strokes.

**Do you have investments?**
If I had money to invest I would ask for advice from Stan Lazaridis. He's into property development in Australia and seems to know what to do with money.

THE HEROES

**Who annoys you?**
The most annoying women on television recently must be Trinny Woodall and Susannah Constantine (**Author's note:** Their show was called *What not to Wear*.)

### Who is the funniest footballer?
David Dunn. We used to room together on away trips and he never stopped; telling jokes, taking the mickey out of himself, doing impressions. Nicky Eaden had a very dry sense of humour.

### What animal would you be?
A lion or a leopard, something strong and quick!

### Favourite holiday destination?
Rome, I love the history and the climate's good for me. I hate places that are too hot. I'm not a great sun lover.

### What sporting event would you like to attend?
An All Ireland Gaelic Football Final.

### What stadium would you like to play a game?
The Nou Camp.

### Best player you have played against?
Raul.

### Favourite sports programme?
*Match of the Day*

### First live match?
At the age of 12 it was Manchester United versus Coventry City.

### Most memorable match for Blues?
The first Aston Villa derby in the Premiership which we won 3–0.

### First sending off?
For Northern Ireland Under-21s in a tournament.

### Favourite TV programme?
*The Sopranos.*

### Favourite stadium?
Celtic Park.

### Favourite sports commentator?
Ian Crocker.

### Favourite newspaper?
*Belfast Telegraph.*

### Favourite food?
Steak.

### Favourite restaurant?
Teppen Yaki Shogun

### Favourite drink?
Lilt.

**Favourite film?**
*Usual Suspects.*

**Favourite pizza topping?**
Pepperoni.

**Favourite sport after football?**
Gaelic football.

**First pair of football boots?**
Arrow. When I was eight they had yellow luminous markings.

**First football team supported?**
Glasgow Celtic.

**First football team?**
Under-10s of Lisburn Youth a teammate was David Healy.

**First football hero?**
Paul McStay.

**First famous person met?**
Kenny Dalglish when I went over to Blackburn Rovers for a trial when I was 14.

**Favourite movie star?**
Robert De Niro.

**Favourite band?**
Stone Roses.

**First car?**
Peugeot 306.

**First wage?**
At Blackburn Rovers I was earning £40 per week as an apprentice. We used to get a bonus of £1 a draw and £2 a win.

# Stephen Michael Kelly

**Heroic claim to fame**
Played every minute of every Premiership game in 2007–08 season.

**Vital statistics**
*Date of birth:* 6 September 1983
*Place of birth:* Finglas, Dublin
*Blues career:* 88
*Blues debut:* 5 August 2006 (h) won 2–1 v Colchester United. Crowd: 24,238
*Team:* Taylor (Maik), Kelly, Sadler, Danns, N'Gotty, Tebily, Johnson (D), Dunn, Forssell, Campbell DJ, Clemence
*Club honours:* Blues – Championship runners-up 2006–07
*Representative honours:* 2003–05 Republic of Ireland Under-21 – 17 appearances, 2006 ROI full caps 14

# BIRMINGHAM CITY

# MODERN DAY HEROES

**Playing Career**

| Club | From | To | Fee | Total Appearances incl (subs) | Goals |
|---|---|---|---|---|---|
| Fulham | 2009 | | Free | 25 | |
| Stoke City | 2009 | 2009 | Loan | 6 | |
| Birmingham City | 2006 | 2009 | £750,000 | 88 | |
| Watford | 2003 | 2003 | Loan | 13 | |
| Queen's Park Rangers | 2003 | 2003 | Loan | 7 | |
| Southend United | 2003 | 2003 | Loan | 10 | |
| Tottenham Hotspur | 2000 | 2006 | Trainee | 44 | 2 |

**Career in words**

He joined Tottenham Hotspur in their youth scheme acting as an understudy to Stephen Carr, who ultimately took over Kelly's number-two shirt at St Andrew's. He made his first-team debut for Spurs in 2003 and made nearly 40 appearances in the Premiership scoring two League goals, one of which was ironically against Blues. Stephen joined Blues on 28 June 2006 for £750,000 with clauses which based on his success could result in a final payment of £1.25 million. He was the only outfield player in the 2007–08 Premier League season to have played every minute of every game for his club. On 4 February 2009 he joined Stoke City on loan, making his Stoke debut in a 2–0 defeat to Sunderland. On 16 June 2009 he signed for Fulham on a three-year deal. Kelly has represented the Republic of Ireland at junior level and made his full debut against Chile. He represented their Under-20 team in the 2003 FIFA World Youth Championship. He played as youth for Belvedere FC.

**About the man**
**Tell me about your early playing days?**
I played on the wing in my younger days because of my pace but when I went to Spurs I was only ever considered to be a full-back although I am 6ft 1in so I can play central defence as well if required.

**What made you decide to join Blues?**
Before I signed I spoke with Stephen Clemence who was with me at Spurs and he told me about the club and the people here, the place where he lived which amazed me. He told me Birmingham is a fabulous city with plenty to do.

**Which sporting event would you most like to attend?**
The World Cup Final.

**Which football stadium would you most like to play in?**
Croke Park Stadium Dublin.

**Sporting hero?**
Paul McGrath.

**Best player played against?**
Thierry Henry.

**Rule change you would like to see?**
Video evidence, as long as it does not slow the game down too much.

**First pair of football boots?**
Puma Kings – just black and white there was nothing fancy in those days.

**First team played for?**
Tolka Rovers I played for them from about six years of age until 11 or 12. Then Home Farm and Belvedere.

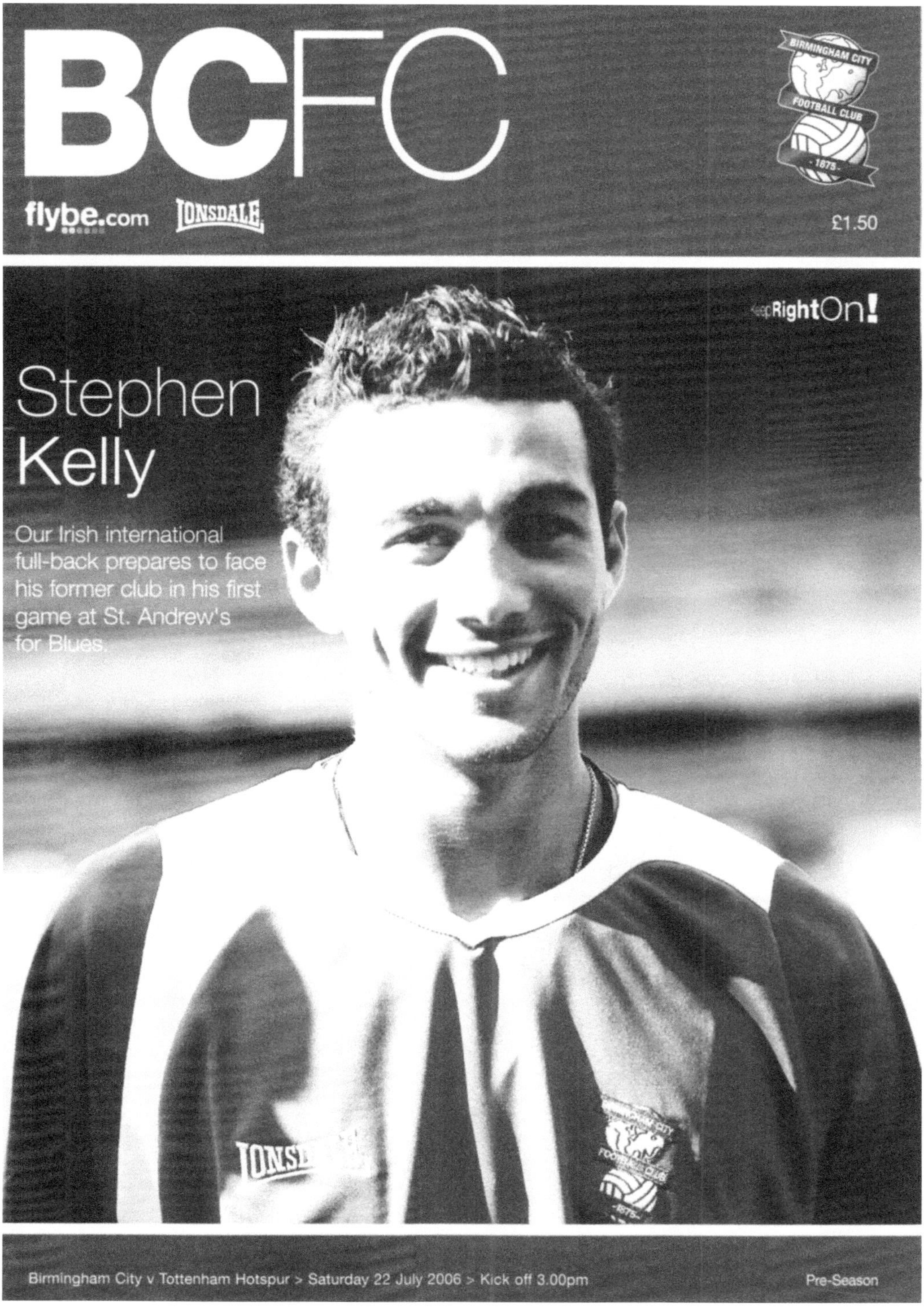

THE HEROES

# BCFC

flybe.com  LONSDALE

£1.50

KeepRightOn!

## Stephen Kelly

Our Irish international full-back prepares to face his former club in his first game at St. Andrew's for Blues.

Birmingham City v Tottenham Hotspur > Saturday 22 July 2006 > Kick off 3.00pm     Pre-Season

**Favourite TV programme?**
*Scrubs.*

**Favourite sports commentator?**
John Motson.

**Favourite newspaper?**
*Irish Times.*

**Favourite drink?**
Water.

**Favourite film?**
*Shawshank Redemption, The Godfather, Goodfellas.*

**Favourite pizza topping?**
Ham, chicken & pineapple.

**Favourite sport after football?**
Tennis.

**How would you describe the start to your career?**
I always wanted to be a footballer. Coming from a family of one boy and four sisters, it seemed like a great escape route! I started off back home in Dublin playing for my local team Tolka Rovers from the age of six or seven. They are a big team over there, and I played for them until I was 12, then I went to another big club called Home Farm. A lot of people in the game over here know them as they are seen as something of a nursery side for English clubs. I played for them for a couple of seasons and then for another team called Belvedere just before I came away. Then I went on trial at a number of clubs including Glasgow Celtic, West Ham United, Everton and Chelsea and, although lots of teams were interested in me, it was Tottenham Hotspur that made the first move. A Spurs scout saw me playing for Ireland Under-15s or 16s, I was offered a trial at White Hart Lane, came over, was impressed, was offered a contract and signed.

**Tell me about your record?**
I hold a unique appearance record for the year 2003. When I was still trying to claim a first-team place at White Hart Lane I went out on loan to three clubs. My first club was Southend United in January 2003, my second was Queen's Park Rangers in March until the end of the season and my third loan club was Watford from the beginning of the next season before I returned to White Hart Lane. I made my debut for Spurs on 28 December 2003 against Charlton Athletic so I had played in every Division of English professional football in the space of one calendar year.

# Jeffrey Jude Kenna

**Heroic claim to fame**
Won the Premier League with Blackburn Rovers.

**Vital statistics**
*Date of birth:* 27 August 1970
*Place of birth:* Dublin
*Blues career:* 84 – 3 goals
*Blues debut:* 26 December 2001 (a) won 1–0 v Sheffield Wednesday. Crowd: 24,335
*Team:* Bennett, Kenna, Grainger, Woodhouse, Purse, Vickers, McCarthy, Mooney, Horsfield, O'Connor, Lazaridis

THE HEROES

*First Blues goal:* 30 November 2001 (h) drew 1–1 v Tottenham Hotspur
*Club honours:* Blackburn Rovers – Premier League champions 1989; Blues – Division One Play-off winners 2001–02
*Representative honours:* 1988–92 Republic of Ireland Under-21 – 8 appearances, 1994 ROI B – 1 appearance, 1995–99 27 full caps.

# BIRMINGHAM CITY                                              MODERN DAY HEROES

## Playing Career

| Club | From | To | Fee | Total Appearances incl (subs) | Goals |
|---|---|---|---|---|---|
| Galway | 2008 | | | 6 | |
| Kidderminster Harriers | 2006 | | Free | 64 | 1 |
| Derby County | 2004 | 2006 | Free | 71 | |
| Birmingham City | 2002 | 2004 | Free | 78 | 3 |
| Birmingham City | 2001 | 2002 | Loan | 6 | |
| Wigan Athletic | 2001 | 2001 | Loan | 7 | 1 |
| Tranmere Rovers | 2001 | 2001 | Loan | 11 | |
| Blackburn Rovers | 1995 | 2002 | £1,500,000 | 196 | 1 |
| Southampton | 1989 | 1995 | Trainee | 136 | 4 |

## Career in words

He began his English career with Southampton in 1989, moving to Blackburn Rovers in March 1995 for £1.5 million and playing his part in their Premier League triumph. In 2001 he went out on loan to Tranmere Rovers, Wigan Athletic and Blues before moving to St Andrew's in February 2002. He joined Derby County on a free in March 2004 and was appointed club captain in 2005 before being released at the end of 2005–06 season. In August 2006 he joined Kidderminster Harriers, playing for them in the FA Trophy Final 2007 losing to Stevenage. He set a record with Steve Guppy, being the first players to play at both Wembley stadiums. He became manager of Galway United in April 2008, becoming player-manager on 15 July 2008. He took the post of manager at St Patrick's Athletic on 14 January 2009. On 25 November 2009 Kenna joined the Blues coaching staff after quitting as boss of St Patrick's Athletic in September 2009. He will work alongside Kevan Broadhurst Jerry Gill and Graham Hyde as a community development officer. Jeff's father Liam was an Irish snooker international and his brother Colin is a professional boxer.

## About the man
### Which famous person gets on your nerves?
Gareth Gates.

### What would be your specialist subject on *Mastermind*?
Guinness and hangovers.

### What do you do when you are not playing football?
I've got two young children that keep me busy and a wife. I listen to a bit of music I enjoy reading and the odd game of golf which I don't play regularly and haven't had lessons. But every now and then the lads will go out and if the sun's shining and there's not a cloud in the sky I will join them.

### What sort of books do you read?
I like thrillers. Fiction or non-fiction, I don't mind. I like John Grisham.

### What music do you listen to in the car?
I particularly like U2 and the Red Hot Chilli Peppers. I am not adverse to a bit of classical, but I have to be in the mood. I also like a bit of Frank Sinatra.

### What about when you hang your boots up?
I will spend more time abroad. I have a place out in Majorca so I will travel and chill out for as long as I feel it necessary.

### What bits of being a professional footballer do you not enjoy?
The travelling. I'm fortunate enough to have been an international and played in Europe, and certainly the travelling is the thing where you are away for long period of time. But other than that it's a fantastic life, and I would recommended it to anyone.

**Who are the biggest characters you've played alongside?**
For a laugh and joke I'd say people like Neil Ruddock and Terry Hurlock. I got on pretty well with everyone I've ever played with. Alan Shearer liked a laugh with the lads. Terry was a fierce competitor – even in five-a-sides on a Friday. He did not hold back and age did not come into it. Ruddock was a fantastic centre-half.

**Are then any conditions you hate playing in?**
Gale-force winds ruin games for me. I'm not too fussed about the cold.

# Martin Kuhl

### Heroic claim to fame
Never lost to Aston Villa.

### Vital statistics
*Date of birth:* 10 January 1965
*Place of birth:* Frimley, Surrey
*Blues career:* 132 – 6 goals
*Blues debut:* 19 August 1983 (a) lost 0–2 v West Bromwich Albion. Crowd: 20,682
*Team:* Coton, Hagan, Kuhl, Stevenson, Blake, Van Den Hauwe, Gayle (H), Halsall, Harford, Curbishley, Dillon
*Blues first goal:* 28 January 1984 (a) won 2–1 v Sunderland
*Club honours:* Blues – Division Two Promotion 1985

### Playing Career

| Club | From | To | Fee | Total Appearances incl (subs) | Goals |
|---|---|---|---|---|---|
| Aldershot | 2001 | 2002 | | | |
| Carshalton | 2000 | 2001 | | | |
| Farnborough | 1999 | 2000 | Free | | |
| Happy Valley (Hong Kong) | 1998 | 1999 | | | |
| Bristol City | 1994 | 1997 | £300,000 | 104 | 8 |
| Notts County | 1994 | | Loan | 2 | |
| Derby County | 1992 | 1994 | £650,000 | 84 | 2 |
| Portsmouth | 1988 | 1992 | £125,000 | 184 | 28 |
| Watford | 1988 | 1988 | | 4 | |
| Sheffield United | 1987 | 1988 | | 43 | 4 |
| Birmingham City | 1983 | 1987 | Apprentice | 132 | 6 |

### Career in words
Martin was an apprentice with Blues from 1981 before signing professional terms in 1987. He represented the Hong Kong League in matches against Mexico and Bulgaria. With Portsmouth he got to the 1992 FA Cup semi-final and was one of three players to miss their kick in the penalty shoot out against Liverpool. A qualified coach he is currently on the staff at Wycombe Wanderers after leaving Aldershot Town on 13 October 2009 where he was caretaker manager from 2007.

### About the man
#### How did you get into coaching?
I had come back from Hong Kong having played for a couple of years out there. I then played for a few clubs in non-League. As you drop down the Leagues your enjoyment is still there however it is a different sort of football because people don't trust each other as much. I really wanted to get back into coaching

# BIRMINGHAM CITY                                                 MODERN DAY HEROES

so I got involved running the Under-15s at Reading and was there for eight years and the same amount of time at Aldershot as assistant manager and coach.

**Born in Surrey, how did you end up at Blues?**
The Blues scout Don Dorman had a connection at Chelsea and there were about eight of us that came up to Birmingham. It was a fantastic start to my career. I really enjoyed my time at Blues. I still keep in touch with Hoppy and some of the boys. It was a fantastic club. Jim Smith was there and everything was okay then there were a few financial problems and other things happened but I loved it. The fans were fantastic. We had great support wherever we went, home and away. We had some good players like Tony Coton, Mick Harford, Frank Worthington and Archie Gemmill, they were fantastic people to be around and they taught you things.

**How many positions did you play for Blues?**
I started at left-back, then here or there, centre-half or centre-mid. I even played centre-forward. I think I was a bit too brainy to play in goal.

**What kind of player would you describe yourself?**
The words that were used to describe me were 'destroy and create'. People used to say that I put my foot in, but I thought I could play as well. I loved passing the ball. I was more of a passer than a runner with the ball. I was just an honest player who wanted to win and sometimes went over the top because I wanted to win too much, but I enjoyed the finer skills of the game as well.

THE HEROES

#### What were the highlights of your time at Blues?
Promotion was good in 1985, but then we got relegated the following year, so that was a bad time. We got to the quarter-finals of both the Cups in the season we went down in 1984, but going back up provided my best memories. It was always good to be in the top flight. The local games against the Villa were fantastic because of the atmosphere. They were my first derbies and I loved them. You just wanted to win so much, and I was lucky as we won two and drew one in the derbies that I played so I never lost to the Villa.

#### You had a few managers in your time?
Yes Jim Smith was good. I still come across him. He was good to me, and we had a great time at Portsmouth together. Ron Saunders had a good understanding, and John Bond was different in his ways. I was lucky to come across a lot of managers that were good and taught me things, and you take bits and pieces off all of them.

# David Francis Langan

#### Heroic claim to fame
Sustained the injury that spelt the end of his career in Ireland's famous 3–1 win over France.

#### Vital statistics
*Date of birth:* 15 February 1957
*Place of birth:* Dublin, Ireland
*Blues career:* 102 – 3 goals
*Blues debut:* 16 August 1980 (h) won 3–1 v Coventry City. Crowd: 21,877
*Team:* Wealands, Langan, Dennis, Curbishley, Gallagher, Givens, Ainscow, Bertschin, Worthington, Gemmill, Dillon
*Blues First goal:* 3 October 1981 (h) drew 2–2 v West Ham United
*Club honours:* Derby County – Division Two champions 1984–85, League Cup winners 1985–86
*Representative honours:* Republic of Ireland 1978–97 – 26 full caps

#### Playing Career

| Club | From | To | Fee | Total Appearances incl (subs) | Goals |
| --- | --- | --- | --- | --- | --- |
| Peterborough United | 1988 | 1989 | | 19 | |
| Bournemouth | 1987 | 1988 | | 23 | 5 |
| Bournemouth | | | Loan | 21 | 7 |
| Leicester City | | | Loan | 5 | 2 |
| Oxford United | 1984 | 1987 | Free | 136 | 2 |
| Birmingham City | 1980 | 1984 | £35,000 | 102 | 3 |
| Derby County | 1975 | 1980 | | 143 | 1 |

#### Career in words
Dave won his first cap for the Republic Of Ireland v Turkey in April 1978 and was a regular until sustaining a knee injury in Ireland's famous 3–2 win over France. He played youth football for Cherry Orchard before going to England in 1974 to join Derby County, making his debut as a 19-year-old in 1977, going on to make over 140 senior appearances. Jim Smith paid £350,000 to take him to St Andrew's for whom he played over 100 games, but his career was disrupted when he missed 18 months through injury, resulting in Ron Saunders letting him go. Jim Smith, then managing Oxford United, signed him, and he regained his fitness and his international place. He played over 100 games for Oxford, helping them to win the Division Two Championship in 1984–85 and the League Cup in 1985–86. He later played for Bournemouth and Peterborough United, but knee and back injuries put an end to his career, rendering him as a registered disabled person. On 14 June 1999 he had a benefit match in Ballyfermot.

113

BIRMINGHAM CITY                                                    MODERN DAY HEROES

### About the man
Dave ended up homeless and without a penny to his name. He fell on desperate times after crippling knee and back injuries robbed him of his career. Slowly he got back on track, he re-married and is living in Peterborough, yet he continues to struggle with the injuries that have registered him as disabled. There was a huge campaign to get him a testimonial match from the Football Association of Ireland because he had played 26 times for his country which at one stage would have been one over the requirement of 25 caps for a testimonial, but over time the FAI had increased the requirement to over 50 international appearances. Finally, a tribute dinner was arranged in recognition for his contribution to Irish football in London at the Burlington Hotel in 2008.

Dave said: 'I can't believe its going to happen because it s been such a long time. The support of people has been great. I got very emotional because I did not realise that people still thought of me because it has been such a long time.' He made his Irish international debut under Johnny Giles in 1978 against Turkey and suffered a knee injury in Ireland's 3–2 win over France and things were never the same after that match. He cracked a vertebrae during a gym session at Blues and missed 18 months of football. 'I am struggling with my legs, there is a lot of fluid and the doctors think it might be rheumatoid arthritis. It feels like my shins are on fire. It's horrible. Sitting is really uncomfortable, standing is better. There are times in the morning when my wife has to put my shoes and socks on.' He works at Peterborough Town Hall serving refreshments to guests and sweeping the floor. He started out as car park attendant. Three per cent of the Town Hall's staff have to be disabled, and that is how he got the job. 'It's a doddle of a job really. It keeps me off the street. The worst time was when I was sleeping in the store room of the Town Hall and suffering from severe depression. The lads were helping me out by bringing me food and taking my clothes away to be washed.' Council officials found out he was sleeping there and were forced to put a stop to it, but they helped him by arranging some legal advice. 'The Trust Fund people found our about it and they gave me a few bob. Terry Conroy came down to see me and helped me out.'

# Stanley Lazaridis

**Heroic claim to fame**
Blues' most-capped player at full international level.

**Vital statistics**
*Date of birth:* 16 August 1972
*Place of birth:* Perth, Australia
*Blues career:* 222 – 8 goals
*Blues debut:* 7 August 1999 (h) drew 2–2 v Fulham and he scored. Crowd: 24,042
*Team:* Poole, Rowett, Grainger, Hughes, Purse, Johnson (M), McCarthy, Adebola, Furlong, O'Connor, Lazaridis
*Club honours:* Blues – Division One Play-off winners 2002, Worthington Cup runners-up 2001. (**Author's note:** He scored in the penalty shoot-outs in both the 2001 Worthington Cup Final and the 2002 Division One Play-off Final.)
*Representative honours:* Australia – 1997 runners-up FIFA Confederations Cup, OFC Nations Cup 2000, 1989 Australia Under-17, 1993–2006 71 full caps.

**Playing Career**

| Club | From | To | Fee | Total Appearances incl (subs) | Goals |
|---|---|---|---|---|---|
| Perth Glory | 2006 | 2008 | | 13 | |
| Birmingham City | 1999 | 2006 | £1,500,000 | 222 | 8 |
| West Ham United | 1995 | 1999 | £300,000 | 87 | 3 |
| West Adelaide | 1992 | 1995 | | 73 | 5 |

**Career in words**
He began as a junior with Olympic Kingsway in Australia before making his senior debut for West Adelaide Hellas in the Australian National Soccer League in 1992. His dribbling ability and pace caught the attention of Harry Redknapp who eventually paid £300,000 to sign him for West Ham United. He stayed for four seasons at Upton Park, making 87 appearances before signing for Blues in the summer of 1999 for £1.5 million. He was part of the promotion team to the Premiership in 2002–03 and he played in the Worthington Cup Final in 2001. After seven seasons at St Andrew's he was released at the end of 2005–06 after making over 200 appearances. He returned to Australia to play for Perth Glory in the A-League. He had only 11 outings in 2006–07 for Perth and returned a positive drug test for anti-androgen Finasteride, a prescription alopecia medication which is banned due its potential as a masking agent for other performance enhancing substances. He was found guilty by the Australian Sports Anti-Doping Authority and received a 12-month suspension from football, which prompted him to retire.

**About the man**
*Pure Gold* by David Gold published in 2006 by Highdown.
'There are loyal players in football, such as our Australian Stan Lazaridis. They [*sic* players] are not all mercenaries after the extra pound, as Stan has proved over and over again…Stan stands out as the same

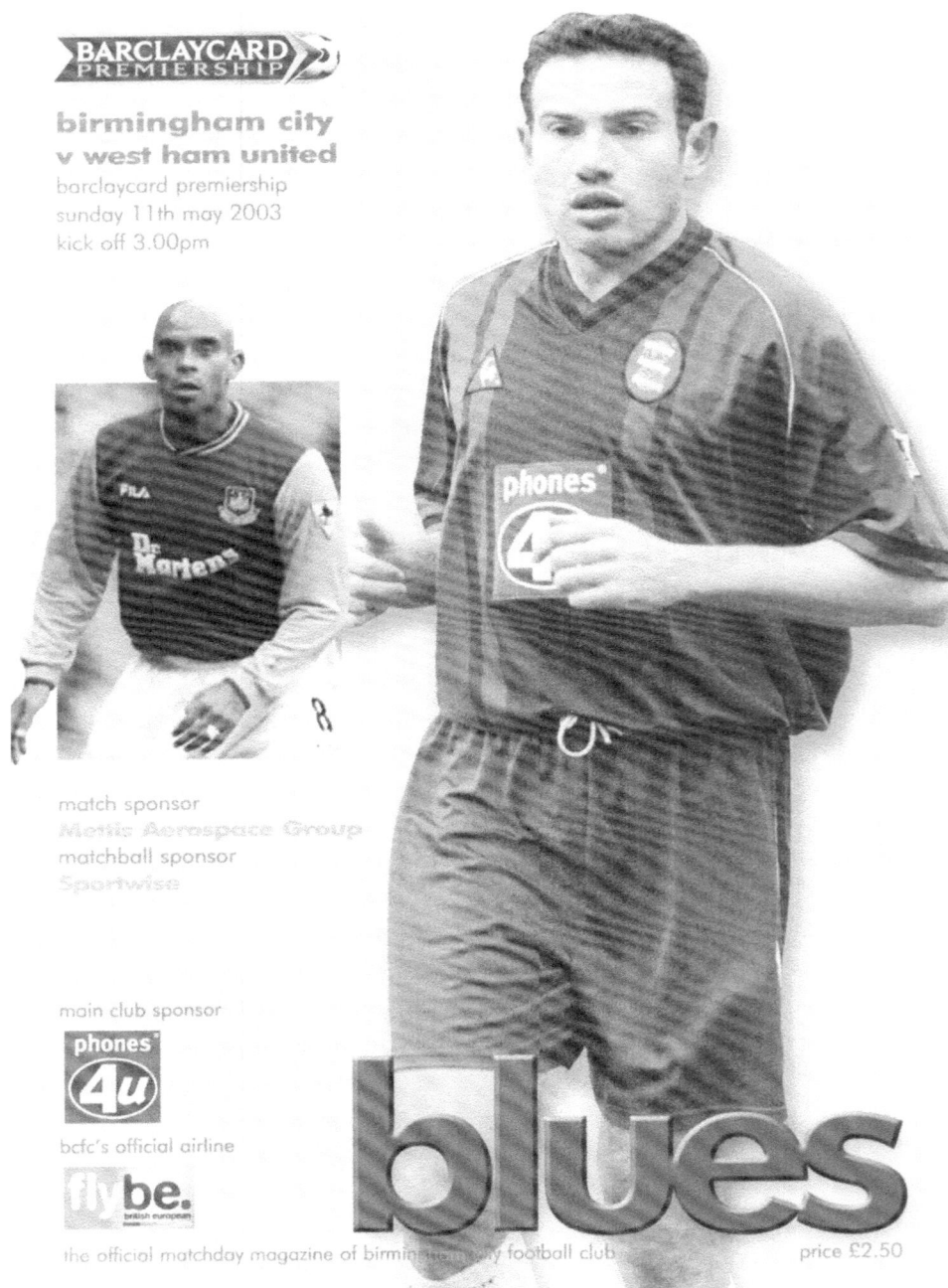

sort of person (*sic* Steve Bull of Wolverhampton Wanderers), as does our skipper Kenny Cunningham, who will play through the pain barrier for his manager and club.'

**Which famous person gets on your nerves?**
Lily Savage.

**Favourite actor?**
Arnold Schwarznegger.

**What would be your specialist subject on *Mastermind*?**
Finance.

# Christopher Marsden

### Heroic claim to fame
He captained Southampton in the 2003 FA Cup Final which they lost 0–1 to Arsenal.

### Vital statistics
*Date of birth:* 3 January 1969
*Place of birth:* Sheffield
*Blues career:* 59 – 6 goals
*Blues debut:* 12 October 1997 (h) won 1–0 v Wolverhampton Wanderers and he scored. Crowd: 17,822
*Team:* Bennett, Bass, Grainger, Bruce, Ablett, Marsden, Devlin, McCarthy, Furlong, Hughes, O'Connor
*Club honours:* Southampton – FA Cup runners-up 2003

### Playing Career

| Club | From | To | Fee | Total Appearances incl (subs) | Goals |
|---|---|---|---|---|---|
| Sheffield Wednesday | 2004 | 2005 | Free | 18 | |
| Buscon Icons (South Korea) | 2004 | 2004 | Free | 2 | 1 |
| Southampton | 1999 | 2004 | £800,000 | 152 | 8 |
| Birmingham City | 1997 | 1999 | £500,000 | 59 | 6 |
| Stockport County | 1996 | 1997 | Free | 73 | 3 |
| Stockport County | 1996 | | Loan | 14 | 1 |
| Notts County | 1994 | 1996 | £250,000 | 12 | 1 |
| Wolverhampton Wanderers | 1994 | 1994 | £250,000 | 11 | |
| Coventry City | 1993 | | Loan | 7 | |
| Huddersfield Town | 1988 | 1994 | | 155 | 9 |
| Sheffield United | 1987 | 1988 | Apprentice | 18 | 1 |

### Career in words
He started his career with Sheffield United going on to play for Huddersfield Town, Coventry City, Wolverhampton Wanderers, Notts County, Stockport County, Blues, Southampton, Buscon Icons and Sheffield Wednesday enabling him to make over 400 appearances in the Football League. As a lifelong fan of Sheffield Wednesday he was pleased to end his playing career at Hillsborough. Chris did not reach the heights of the Premiership until he was 30. After his spell in South Korea he signed for the Owls on a free transfer and captained them for 18 games, a hamstring injury cut short his spell at Hillsborough and he retired. His nickname at Southampton was 'Chrissy Marsden Football Genius' often reduced to CMFG. He was also known as 'the bald Beckenbauer' and 'the Midfield General'.

There were a few eyebrows raised in February 1999 when the then Saints manager Dave Jones signed one of his former charges at Stockport; Chris Marsden from First Division Birmingham City. Thirty-year-old Marsden had never played in the top flight and was seen as a journeyman footballer who had already played for seven clubs. With Southampton rooted to the bottom of the Premier League Jones felt that he needed some steel in midfield and so paid a fee of £800,000. In the final five games Marsden scored twice and the Saints were unbeaten gaining 11 points and avoided the drop – money

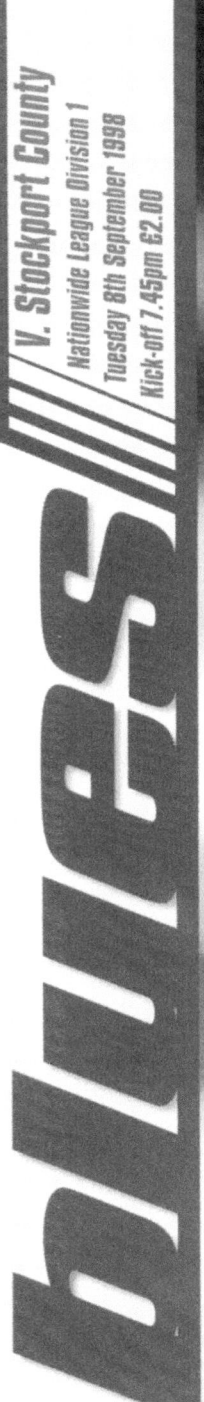

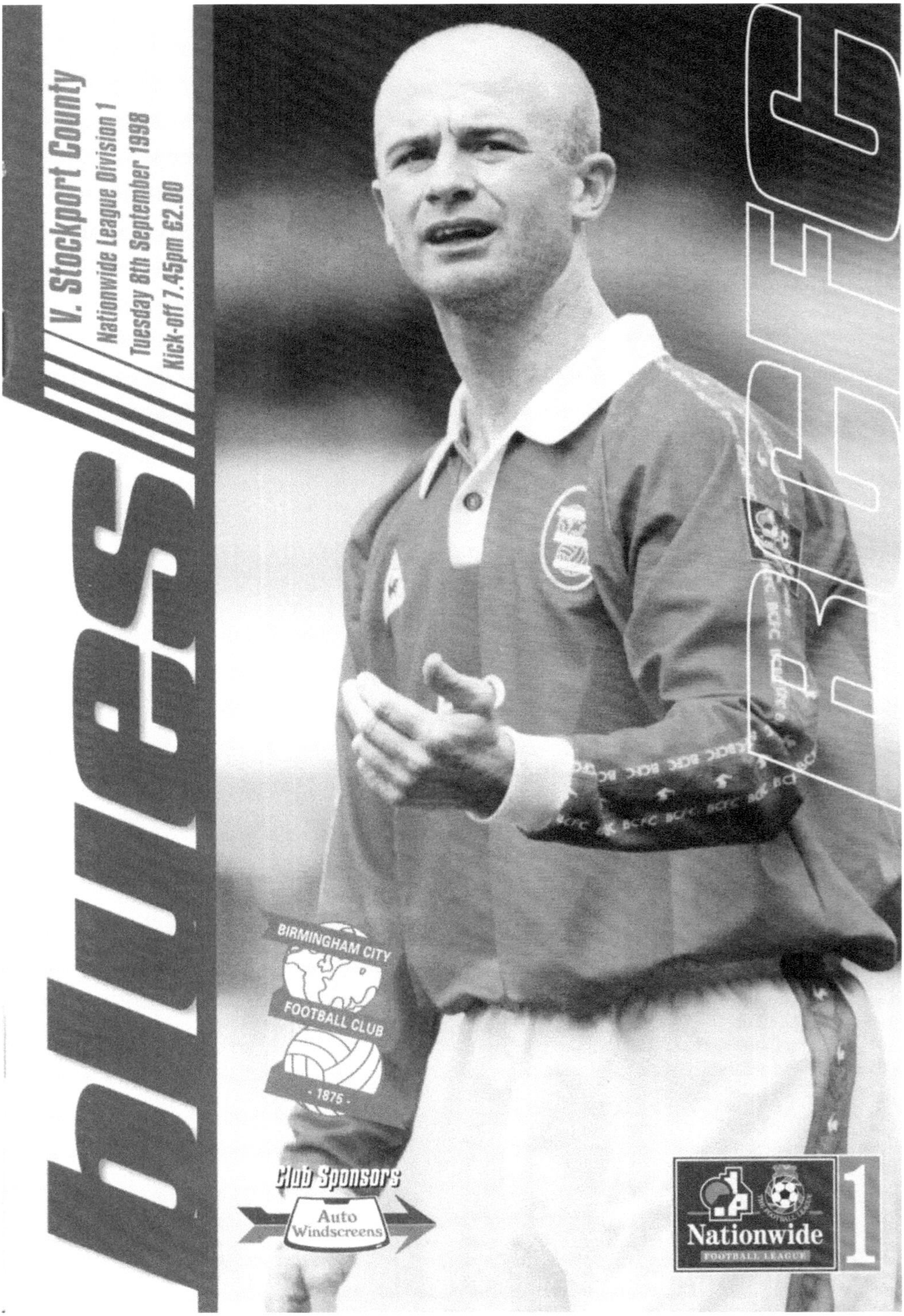
blues
V. Stockport County
Nationwide League Division 1
Tuesday 8th September 1998
Kick-off 7.45pm £2.00
BCFC
BIRMINGHAM CITY
FOOTBALL CLUB
1875
Club Sponsors
Auto Windscreens
Nationwide
FOOTBALL LEAGUE
1

well spent. After Jones, Marsden played for Glenn Hoddle and Stuart Gray but it was under the management of Gordon Strachan that elevated Chris to cult hero status. Strachan switched him to the left where he linked with left-back Wayne Bridge to form an extremely effective left-side partnership. He took over the captaincy from the injured Jason Dodd and lead the Saints out at Cardiff in the 2003 FA Cup Final which they lost 1–0 to Arsenal. He was voted Saints Player of the Season for 2001–02. He left in January 2004 to join Korean side Buscon Icons. It did not work out and he returned to his home town of Sheffield where he played a handful of games for Wednesday before persistent injury forced his retirement just before his 36th birthday. He severed all contact with football and now resides in Cyprus.

# Trevor Matthewson

### Heroic claim to fame
Sent off in the 12th minute v West Bromwich Albion on 8 February 1992 – Blues earliest dismissal.

### Vital statistics
*Date of birth:* 12 February 1963
*Place of birth:* Sheffield
*Blues career:* 203 – 13 goals
*Blues debut:* 19 August 1989 (h) won 3–0 v Crewe Alexandra. Crowd: 10,447
*Team:* Thomas, Clarkson, Frain, Atkins, Sproson, Matthewson, Peer, Bailey, Yates, Langley, Sturridge
*First Blues goal:* 16 April 1990 (h) drew 2–2 v Bristol Rovers
*Club honours:* Blues – Division Three runners-up 1991–92, Leyland Daf winners 1991

### Playing Career

| Club | From | To | Fee | Total Appearances incl (subs) | Goals |
|---|---|---|---|---|---|
| Hereford United | 1996 | 1998 | Free | 23 | |
| Bury | 1994 | 1996 | £10,000 | 49 | |
| Preston North End | 1993 | 1994 | | 14 | |
| Birmingham City | 1989 | 1993 | £45,000 | 203 | 13 |
| Lincoln City | 1987 | 1989 | £13,000 | 51 | 2 |
| Stockport County | 1985 | 1987 | Free | 88 | |
| Newport County | 1983 | 1985 | Free | 90 | |
| Sheffield Wednesday | 1981 | 1983 | Apprentice | 5 | |

### Career in words
Trevor comes from a footballing family: Tommy, his grandfather played for Sheffield Wednesday and Uncle Reg turned out for South Shields. He started his career as an apprentice with Wednesday in 1981 but failed to make the grade. So after two seasons as a professional he joined Newport County and two years later he joined Stockport County. After a further two years he dropped out of the Football League to join Lincoln City in the Conference, where as captain they won the Conference title and promotion to the Football League in 1988. In 1989 he joined Blues for a tribunal fee of £45,000. In his first season 1989–90 he became the first Blues player to appear in every match of a 46-game League season a feat he repeated the following year. He played in the Leyland Daf Cup Final in 1991 and helped them to promotion to the newly-designated First Division the following season. After leaving Blues he had spells at Preston North End, Bury, Hereford United, Ilkeston Town and Gresley Rovers. After his retirement through cartilage trouble he returned to Sheffield where he is a fish and meat trader. Another claim to fame was as a substitute for Martin Thomas he saved a penalty in the Cup game against Reading on 15 November 1992.

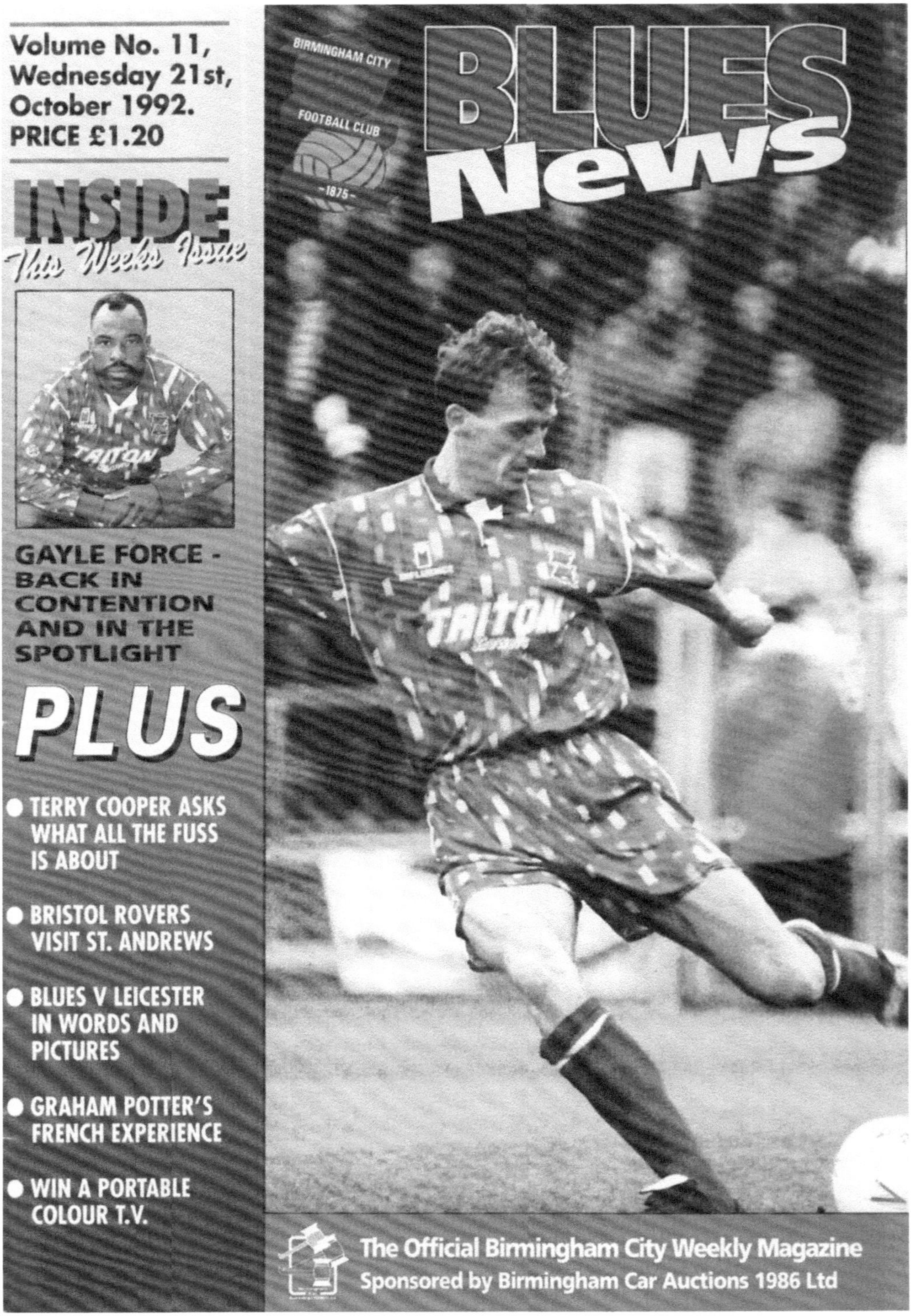
Volume No. 11,
Wednesday 21st,
October 1992.
PRICE £1.20
INSIDE
This Weeks Issue
GAYLE FORCE - BACK IN CONTENTION AND IN THE SPOTLIGHT
PLUS
TERRY COOPER ASKS WHAT ALL THE FUSS IS ABOUT
BRISTOL ROVERS VISIT ST. ANDREWS
BLUES V LEICESTER IN WORDS AND PICTURES
GRAHAM POTTER'S FRENCH EXPERIENCE
WIN A PORTABLE COLOUR T.V.
BIRMINGHAM CITY FOOTBALL CLUB 1875
BLUES News
The Official Birmingham City Weekly Magazine
Sponsored by Birmingham Car Auctions 1986 Ltd

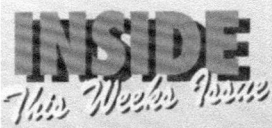

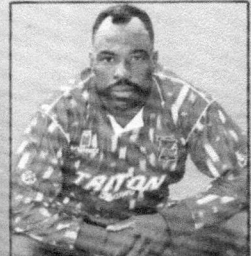

## About the man
### How did your move to Blues come about?
I got a phone call from the Lincoln City manager, Colin Murphy saying that Birmingham City (under the management of Dave Mackay) had come in for me, and obviously you don't think twice about it. You want to play at the highest level you possibly can, and Birmingham City were and still are a big club.

### What memories do you have of the Leyland Daf?
I still think about it even now. To play at Wembley in front of 80,000 people, just to go to Wembley, the ride on the bus, it was amazing – I've even get goose pimples thinking of it now.

We were cruising at 2–0 and Mark Yates, I think, had a great chance to put us three up before half-time. Then they brought on two substitutes, and it was like the Alamo. When they got it back to 2–1 I thought we were going to be hanging on – then John Gayle pulled that one out of the bag and what a fantastic feeling. You're going back a few years now, but people still talk about it. You cherish these moments as they don't come around every year unless you're one of the top players in the Premier League. For where we were, struggling near the bottom, and for all our supporters it was absolutely amazing.

### How did your departure from Blues happen?
Terry Cooper bought one or two players in, and I don't think I was wanted at that time. These things happen in football, though, and although I didn't want to move it was a chance to move back to Sheffield and sign for Preston North End for a couple of years.

### You only managed 12 appearances at Deepdale, Why?
We had a manager in John Beck up there who was stuck in his ways. He had a reputation from when he was at Cambridge United. He didn't treat you as adults, he treated you as kids, and I just didn't like it.

### How would you describe your time at St Andrew's?
I really enjoyed my time there. Out of my football career it is the four years that I will cherish for the rest of my life. I've still got all the cuttings from the *Argus*, all my shirts and shorts.

# Jonathan David McCarthy

### Heroic claim to fame
Broke his leg twice in 1990.

### Vital statistics
*Date of birth:* 18 August 1970
*Place of birth:*
*Blues career:* 142 – 8 goals
*Blues debut:* 14 September 1997 (h) lost 0–1 v Sunderland. Crowd: 17,478
*Team:* Bennett, Wassall, Grainger, Bruce, Ablett, O'Connor, Devlin, McCarthy, Furlong, Hughes, Ndlovu
*First Blues goal:* 26 December 1997 (a) v Ipswich Town won 1–0
*Club honours:* York City – Football League Third Division Play-off winners 1993; Blues – Worthington Cup runners-up 2001, Division One Play-off winners 2001–02
*Representative honours:* Northern Ireland – 19 full caps

### Playing Career
| Club | From | To | Fee | Total Appearances incl (subs) | Goals |
|---|---|---|---|---|---|
| Carlisle United | 2002 | 2003 | Free | 27 | 2 |
| York City | 2002 | 2002 | Free | 1 | |

# BIRMINGHAM CITY                                    MODERN DAY HEROES

| | | | | | |
|---|---|---|---|---|---|
| Doncaster Rovers | 2002 | 2002 | Free | 1 | |
| Port Vale | 2002 | 2002 | Free | 9 | |
| Sheffield Wednesday | 2002 | 2002 | Loan | 4 | |
| Birmingham City | 1997 | 2002 | £1,500,000 | 142 | 8 |
| Port Vale | 1995 | 1997 | £450,000 | 119 | 17 |
| York City | 1990 | 1995 | | 233 | 38 |
| Shepshed Carterhouse | 1989 | 1990 | Free | | |
| Hartlepool United | 1987 | 1989 | Junior | 1 | |

## Career in words

'Macca' began his career with Hartlepool United in 1987. After a short spell outside of the professional game with Shepshed Carterhouse in the 1989–90 season he joined York City where he stayed for five years. He joined Port Vale in August 1995 for £450,000 joining Blues in September 1997 for £1.5 million. Despite breaking his leg three times in five years at the Blues he made nearly 150 appearances. He had a one month loan period with Sheffield Wednesday in April 2002 before he was released on a free in August 2002 which resulted in a return to Port Vale. Two months later Jon left Port Vale due to a lack of cash and moved to Doncaster Rovers, the following month he signed for York City for a second time. His fourth club in three months was Carlisle United who he joined at the end of September 2002 and stayed to the end of the season but after failing to agree terms he was released in May 2003. In 2003–04 he signed for Hucknall Town and helped them win the Northern Premier League title. He then went to Northwich Victoria at the start of 2004–05 while working as a full-time teacher and stayed there until the end of 2006–07 when he retired. He represented Northern Ireland 19 times, earning his debut while at Port Vale against Sweden.

## About the man

### Who was your craziest teammate?

Goalkeepers usually are. I roomed with Pooley (Kevin Poole) and he was actually quite sane. Benno (Ian Bennett) was as daft as anything even though he didn't not show it on the pitch. Some of his choice of underwear is amazing – you should see it! He was the daft one in the dressing room.

### Any funny moments from your career?

Probably Michael Johnson trying to get back from corners.

### What is your current job?

Sport Science Lecturer at Mid-Cheshire College, Northwich.

### Who was your favourite player as a boy? And why?

Terry Cochrane. Right winger for Middlesbrough and Northern Ireland. Remember him playing without shin pads, with his socks rolled down. Always looking to go past defenders.

### Which game in your career stands out in your memory?

The best performance I ever had was in a 4–0 defeat to Germany in a European Championship qualifier in Dortmund. Just felt like for one night only I was able to compete with some of the world's top players. None of my family friends will have ever seen the performance. I need to get a copy of the DVD to see if I played as well as I thought I did or was I kidding myself!

**What's your best football experience?**
The chance to play International football against some of the world's greatest players was incredible. I was fortunate enough to play against the likes of France, Italy, Spain and Germany. To share a pitch and compete with those players was memorable.

**Who was the best player you played with and why?**
Steve Bruce was an outstanding player. I played with him at the end of his career, but the quality of his touch and passing was top class, but what I really learned from him was how important positioning was as a defender. He read the game so well and organised things around him that he always appeared to be in the right place.

**If you could go back to your days at Blues what one thing would you do differently?**
Loved my time at Blues. Working my way through the lower Leagues, I knew what a privilege it was to be signed by such a big club with its tradition and fan base. I regret getting injured just as I was producing my best form for Blues and developing a relationship with the fans. Differently…avoided that leg breaking challenge against Tranmere!

**What was your best moment while at St Andrew's?**
Worthington Cup Final was an amazing experience. Blues fans created an unbelievable atmosphere. Mixed feelings ultimately. So glad that we performed and gave the fans a memorable day and yet so disappointed that we lost on penalties and didn't bring home the silverware that our fans deserved.

**If you hadn't chosen football as a career what would you be?**
Sport Science Lecturer, which is my current profession. I was a late developer in football. I had been to university to study for a Sport Science degree before I received an opportunity in the professional game. I really appreciated my career coming from the non-League game. Natural progression into my current career.

**What is your opinion of football today?**
It has its good and its bad points like it always has. I could find negatives and positives concerning the relationship between football and the media money. However, the game still excites me and I still want to talk football, still want to go to football matches, take my children to matches. I would pay money to play in one more professional game – I had the best job in the world, but if I hadn't got the opportunity I would still have played on a Saturday/Sunday and still gone to watch football. Ultimately, everybody who plays the game at whatever level is a fan. The relationship between the fans and the players at their football club is vital. I hope the divide/connection doesn't become too wide.

**If you could be one of today's Premier League stars who would you want to be and why?**
So much respect for Ryan Giggs and how he has adapted his game as he has matured. The level of consistency and longevity at the top level of the game is unparalleled.

# James McFadden

**Heroic claim to fame**
Scored in Blues first-ever match with Rochdale in August 2010.

**Vital statistics**
*Date of birth:* 14 April 1983
*Place of birth:* Springburn, Glasgow

# BIRMINGHAM CITY

MODERN DAY HEROES

*Blues career:* 104 – 14 goals (At the end of 2010)
*Blues debut:* 19 January 2008 (h) lost 0–1 v Chelsea. Crowd: 26,567
*Team:* Taylor (Maik), Kelly, Queudrue, Muamba, Ridgewell, Scmitz, Larsson, Johnson (D), Jerome, McFadden, Kapo
*First Blues goal:* 9 February 2008 (a) drew 1–1 v West Ham United
*Club honours:* Blues: Championship runners-up 2008–09
*Representative honours:* Scotland Under-21 –9 caps, full 59 caps 15 goals

## Playing Career

| Club | From | To | Fee | Total Appearances incl (subs) | Goals |
|---|---|---|---|---|---|
| Birmingham City | 2008 | | £4,750,000 | 104 | 14 |
| Everton | 2003 | 2008 | £1,250,000 | 139 | 18 |
| Motherwell | 1999 | 2003 | Youth | 70 | 32 |

## Career in words

It is July 2002 and it is a pre-season friendly as part of Blues' preparation for their first season in the Premier League. We are playing Terry Butcher's Motherwell in Scotland. In the seventh minute a young 19-year-old player danced past four Blues players before squaring the ball to his colleague to open the scoring, the second goal was his with a cheeky chip over the head of Ian Bennett. Only stout defending prevented the youngster from scoring a hat-trick – that youth was James McFadden!

'Fadds' went into Scottish folklore with his brilliant 30-yarder against France in September 2007. His long distance strike earned Scotland a shock win in Paris. His goal for Scotland in the Euro 2008 qualifier on 12 September 2007 against France in the Parc des Princes is regarded as one of Scotland's most famous goals, alongside the two other historic goals he scored: the winner to beat The Netherlands and against Macedonia.

James joined the Motherwell youth system and made his first-team debut at the age of 17. In 2002–03 season he was awarded the title Scottish Young Player of The Year in recognition of him scoring 19 goals in 34 starts in a season when Motherwell finished bottom of the Scottish Premier League. (**Author's note:** Motherwell escaped relegation as the First Division champions Falkirk could not be promoted as their ground did not meet the SPL criteria.) In that season James had been given 15 yellow cards and a red! His final game for Motherwell saw him score a hat-trick in a 6–2 victory over Livingston at Fir Park.

In 2003 he signed for Everton for a fee of £1.25 million and he scored his first goal in their 5–2 defeat at Spurs on 1 January 2005 more than a year after joining the club. On 18 January 2008 he signed a three-and-a-half-year contract with an option for a further two years for the Blues for an initial fee of £5 million, rising to £6 million depending on appearances. He scored in his fourth game, a penalty kick against West Ham at Upton Park after he had been fouled by Lucas Neill. In his second season he suffered a serious knee injury which reduced his appearances. He scored Blues' first goal in the 2009–10 Premier League season a 92nd-minute penalty to secure a 1–0 win against Portsmouth at St Andrew's.

He gained his first cap aged 19 on a Far East tour against South Africa at the end of which a night out drinking caused him to miss his flight home. Despite his domestic performances he became a regular in Berti Vogts' Scotland set-up, scoring his first goal against the Faroe Islands during a 3–1 win in a Euro 2004 qualifier at Hampden Park on 6 September 2003.

His goals for Scotland:

| Goal | Date | Venue | Opposition | Result |
|---|---|---|---|---|
| 1. | 6 September 2003 | Glasgow | Faroe Islands | 3–1 |
| 2. | 15 November 2003 | Glasgow | Netherlands | 1–0 |
| 3. | 31 March 2004 | Glasgow | Romania | 1–2 |
| 4. | 27 May 2004 | Estonia | Estonia | 1–0 |
| 5. | 3 September 04 | Valencia Spain | Spain | 1–1 |
| 6. | 17 November 2004 | Edinburgh | Sweden | 1–4 |
| 7. | 4 June 2005 | Glasgow | Moldova | 2–0 |
| 8. | 12 October 2005 | Slovenia | Slovenia | 3–0 |
| 9. | 11 May 2006 | Kobe Japan | Bulgaria | 5–1 |
| 10. | 2 September 2006 | Glasgow | Faroe Islands | 6–0 |
| 11. | 8 September 2007 | Glasgow | Lithuania | 3–1 |
| 12. | 12 September 2007 | Paris | France | 1–0 |
| 13. | 13 October 2007 | Glasgow | Ukraine | 3–1. |
| 14. | 10 September 2008 | Reykjavik | Iceland | 2–1 |
| 15. | 5 September 2009 | Glasgow | Macedonia | 2–0 |

# Thomas John Mooney

### Heroic claim to fame
Won two Division One Play-off Finals.

### Vital statistics
*Date of birth:* 11 August 1971
*Place of birth:* Middlesbrough
*Blues career:* 39 – 15 goals
*Blues debut:* 11 August 2001 (a) lost 1–3 v Wimbledon. Crowd: 9,142
*Team:* Vaesen, Gill, Grainger, Sonner, Purse, Johnson (M), Eaden, Mooney, Horsfield, O'Connor, Lazaridis
*First Blues goal:* 25 August 2001 (a) won 2–1 v Walsall
*Club honours:* Watford – Second Division champions 1997–98, Division One Play-off winners 1998–99; Blues – Division One Play-off winners 2001–02

### Playing Career

| Club | From | To | Fee | Total Appearances incl (subs) | Goals |
|---|---|---|---|---|---|
| UD Marbella | 2008 | 2009 | | 4 | |
| Walsall | 2007 | 2008 | | 36 | 11 |
| Wycombe Wanderers | 2005 | 2007 | | 87 | 29 |
| Oxford United | 2004 | 2005 | | 42 | 15 |
| Swindon Town | 2003 | 2004 | | 45 | 19 |
| Derby County | 2003 | | Loan | 8 | |
| Sheffield United | 2003 | | Loan | 3 | |
| Stoke City | 2002 | | Loan | 12 | 3 |
| Birmingham City | 2001 | 2003 | | 39 | 15 |
| Watford | 1994 | 2001 | £95,000 | 241 | 58 |
| Watford | 1994 | | Loan | 10 | 2 |
| Southend United | 1993 | 1994 | £100,000 | 14 | 5 |
| Scarborough | 1990 | 1993 | | 129 | 40 |
| Aston Villa | 1989 | 1990 | | 0 | |

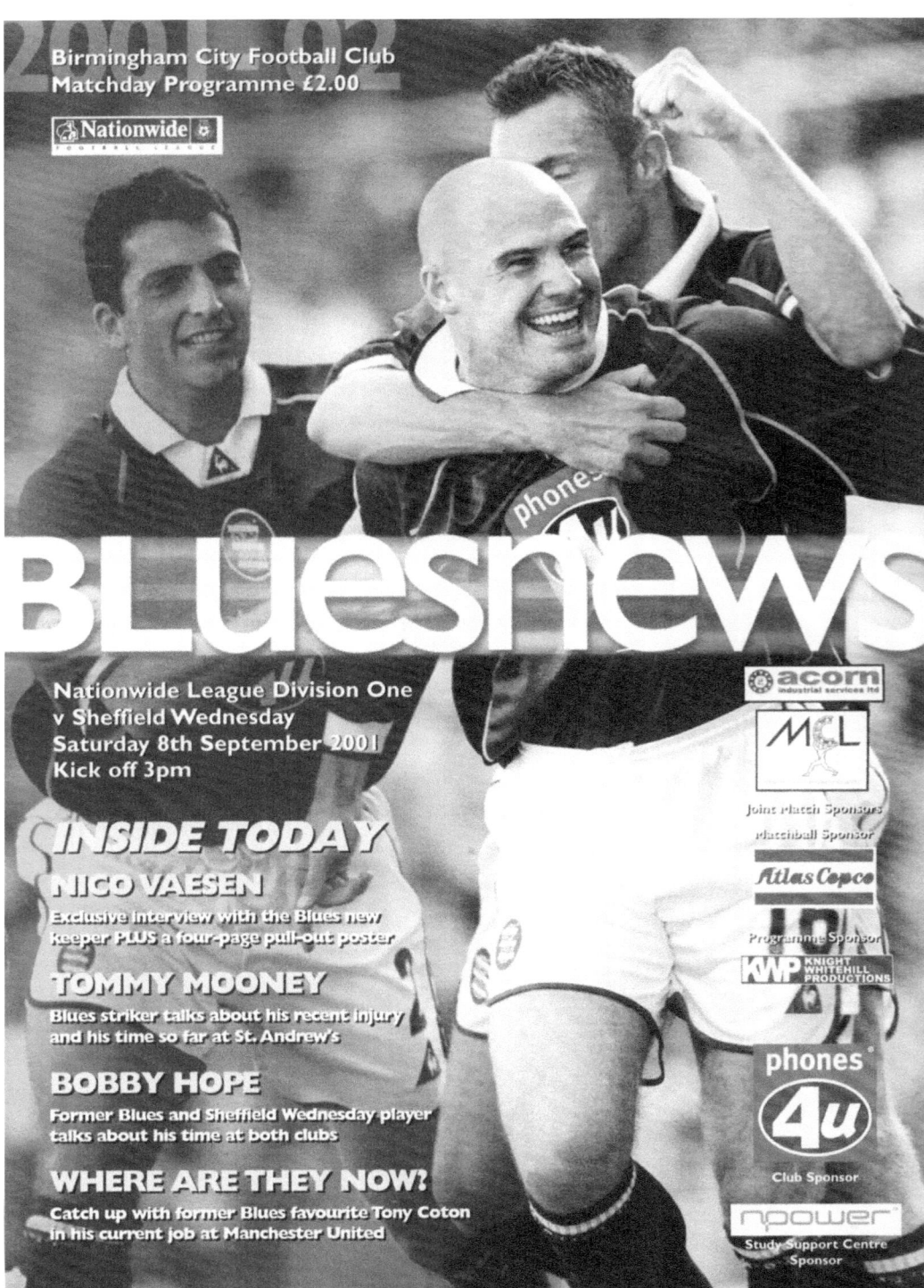

### Career in words
He began his professional career at Aston Villa but was released in 1990, having never played for the first team. He joined Scarborough, where he spent three years, helping himself to 40 goals in 129 outings, before moving to Southend United for £100,000. After one season on the south coast he went to Watford, initially on loan before signing a permanent deal in July 1994 for £95,000 as part of deal which sent Keith Dublin in the opposite direction. He had a difficult time at Vicarage Road under Glenn Roeder eventually ending up as part of the defence when the Hornets won the Second Division Championship in 1997–98. He was restored to the firing line when Graham Taylor became manager and was instrumental in helping them to the Premiership Play-offs in which they were successful to the detriment of Bolton Wanderers and Blues! Watford only had the one season in the top flight and on their return to the First Division in 2000 saw Tommy scored 20 League goals for the club – the first time in a decade! In May 2006 he became the fourth inductee into the Watford Hall of Fame following Luther Blissett, John McClelland and former Blues' goalkeeper, Tony Coton.

Out of contract at Watford, he signed for Blues in June 2001, helping them to promotion to the Premier League via the Play-offs in 2001–02. He only played one game in the Premier League before being loaned to Stoke City. Two other loan periods were completed in the season with Sheffield United and Derby County. He made a permanent move to Swindon Town at the start of the 2003–04 season, and his 20 goals helped them reach the Play-offs. In the summer of 2004 he made the short move to Oxford United and was their top scorer in 2004–05. He signed a two-year contract with Wycombe Wanderers prior to the 2005–06 season and again he contributed to them getting to the Play-offs. He captained the side when they played Chelsea in the League Cup semi-final which they lost 4–1 on aggregate having held them to a 1–1 draw in the first leg at Adams Park. He rejected a new contract with Wycombe in July 2007 and moved back to the Midlands with Walsall, after one season he moved to sunnier climes with UD Marbella. He is currently working with Dean Holtham in the Blues Community Programme.

# Mehdi Nafti

### Heroic claim to fame
Bought to replace Robbie Savage.

### Vital statistics
*Date of birth:* 28 November 1978
*Place of birth:* Toulouse, France
*Blues career:* 74 – 1 goal
*Blues debut:* 5 February 2005 (a) lost 0–2 v Manchester United. Crowd: 67,838
*Team:* Taylor (Maik), Melchiot, Clapham, Johnson (D), Taylor (Martin), Cunningham, Pennant, Blake, Pandiani, Nafti, Gray
*First Blues goal:* 13 August 2008 (a) won 4–0 v Wycombe Wanderers League Cup
*Club honours:* Blues – Promotion to Premier League 2006–07 and 2008–09
*Representative honours:* Tunisia – 41 full caps 1 goal

### Playing Career
| Club | From | To | Fee | Total Appearances incl (subs) | Goals |
| --- | --- | --- | --- | --- | --- |
| Aris FC | 2009 | | | | |
| Birmingham City | 2005 | 2009 | | 74 | 1 |
| Racing de Santander | 2001 | 2005 | | 75 | 3 |
| Toulouse | 1998 | 2001 | Youth | | |

### Career in words
He left Blues in June 2009 after his contract was not renewed and signed a two-year deal with Aris FC. He joined Blues initially on loan in the January transfer window of 2005 from Racing de Santander,

# BIRMINGHAM CITY                                    MODERN DAY HEROES

eventually being signed permanently to replace Robbie Savage and provide 'bite' into the midfield. Early in the 2005–06 season he damaged his cruciate ligaments which kept him on the injury list until reappearing on the last day of the season against Bolton Wanderers. Although already relegated, he was a major part of the team which regained Premier League status in 2006–07. He was used to being part of a 'Yo-Yo' club as in 1998–99 he went down and came back up with Toulouse and in 2000–01 went down and came back up with Santander in Spain. His nickname of 'Nasty' began with Toulouse when in his second professional game at the age of 19 he came on as a substitute on 70 minutes v Nantes in 1998–99 and was red carded seven minutes later for a dangerous tackle. Every year while in Spain he got around 15 yellow cards.

### About the man
**Favourite newspaper?**
*France Football.*

**Favourite drink?**
Diet Coke – occasional beer.

**What was the highlight of your career?**
Winning the African Cup of Nations for the first time for my country was amazing. We were at home in Tunisia and we beat Morocco 2–1 in the Final. The stadium was full, the atmosphere was crazy. A great, great moment.

**Best player you have played against?**
Zinedine Zidane. No question. He's the best. A top, top, top player and was always quiet off the pitch. You never read about him in the newspaper unless it is to do with football. He did his talking on the pitch and that is my philosophy. I have played him one on one. It was very hard, but I did OK.

**Nickname?**
When I came to England, everyone called me 'Nasty'. My friends call me 'Med'.

**Favourite food?**
Italian – my favourite pizza topping is Jalapeno chilli peppers.

**Favourite holiday destination?**
Spain, I like to go to Santander. Majorca and Ibiza are good. I'd love to go to Brazil one day.

**What other sports do you like?**
Tennis.

# Peter Ndlovu

**Heroic claim to fame**
Sent off for diving against Huddersfield Town in October 1998.

### Vital statistics
*Date of birth:* 25 February 1973
*Place of birth:* Bulawayo, Zimbabwe

THE HEROES

*Blues career:* 134 – 28 goals
*Blues debut:* 9 August 1997 (h) won 2–0 v Stoke City and he scored. Crowd: 20,608
*Team:* Bennett, Wassall, Grainger, Bruce, Ablett, O'Connor, Devlin, Hey, Hughes, Robinson, Ndlovu.
*Representative honours:* Zimbabwe – 16 full caps

**BIRMINGHAM CITY**  MODERN DAY HEROES

### Playing Career

| Club | From | To | Fee | Total Appearances incl (subs) | Goals |
|---|---|---|---|---|---|
| Sheffield United | 2001 | 2004 | Free | 164 | 29 |
| Huddersfield Town | 2000 | 2001 | Loan | 6 | 4 |
| Birmingham City | 1997 | 2001 | £1,600,000 | 134 | 28 |
| Coventry City | 1991 | 1997 | £10,000 | 196 | 43 |
| Highlanders FC (Zimbabwe) | 1989 | 1991 | | | |

### Career in words
Peter started his football career in his native Zimbabwe, but his performances attracted the attention of the UK scouting system and Coventry City paid £10,000 for his services in August 1991. He spent six years at Highfield Road, scoring over 40 goals in nearly 200 first-team outings. He signed for Blues in July 1997 for £1.6 million. He played out wide for the Blues and caused problems for defenders with his pace, ball skills and commitment. He suffered from injuries in the latter part of his time at St Andrew's, and after going to Huddersfield Town on loan he moved to Sheffield United on a free transfer. He had three good years at Bramall Lane and returned to his goalscoring ways.

### About the man
Early on 25 February 1973 in a crime-ravaged and poverty-ridden suburb of Makaboba in Bulawayo a middle-aged woman Abigail Mary Nyoni went into labour to deliver her seventh child. She delivered a baby boy and named him Peter, after the biblical Simon Peter – a football genius who was to dominate the world of soccer had emerged. Peter is the seventh of 11 brothers and sisters. From the tender age of 16 he catapulted himself from the ashes of ghetto life to the affluent surroundings afforded by playing in the English Premiership. In England they called him the Bulawayo Bullet or the Flying Elephant. In Zimbabwe, he was a footballing god. He completed his primary education at Lotshe Primary School and then went to Mzilikazi High School, where he first played football. In 1989 he inspired his High School to win the nationwide Coca-Cola Cup. He was the longest-serving African player in the UK.

# Ricky Junior Otto

### Heroic claim to fame
From prison to the probation service.

### Vital statistics
*Date of birth:* 9 November 1967
*Place of birth:* Hackney, London
*Blues career:* 62 – 8 goals
*Blues debut:* 26 December 1994 (h) drew 1–1 v Cambridge United and he scored. Crowd: 20,743
*Team:* Bennett, Poole, Whyte, Ward, Barnett, Howell, Donowa, Claridge, McGavin, Otto, Cooper
*Club honours:* Blues – Division Two runners-up 1994–95, Auto Windscreens Shield winners 1995

### Playing Career

| Club | From | To | Fee | Total Appearances incl (subs) | Goals |
|---|---|---|---|---|---|
| Rhyl | 2001 | | | | |
| Notts County | 1997 | 1997 | Loan | 6 | |
| Peterborough United | 1997 | 1997 | Loan | 20 | |
| Charlton Athletic | 1996 | 1996 | Loan | 9 | |

THE HEROES

| | | | | | |
|---|---|---|---|---|---|
| Birmingham City | 1994 | 1998 | £800,000 | 62 | 8 |
| Southend United | 1993 | 1994 | £100,000 | 76 | 19 |
| Leyton Orient | 1990 | 1993 | Free | 68 | 15 |
| Haringey Borough | 1989 | 1990 | | | |

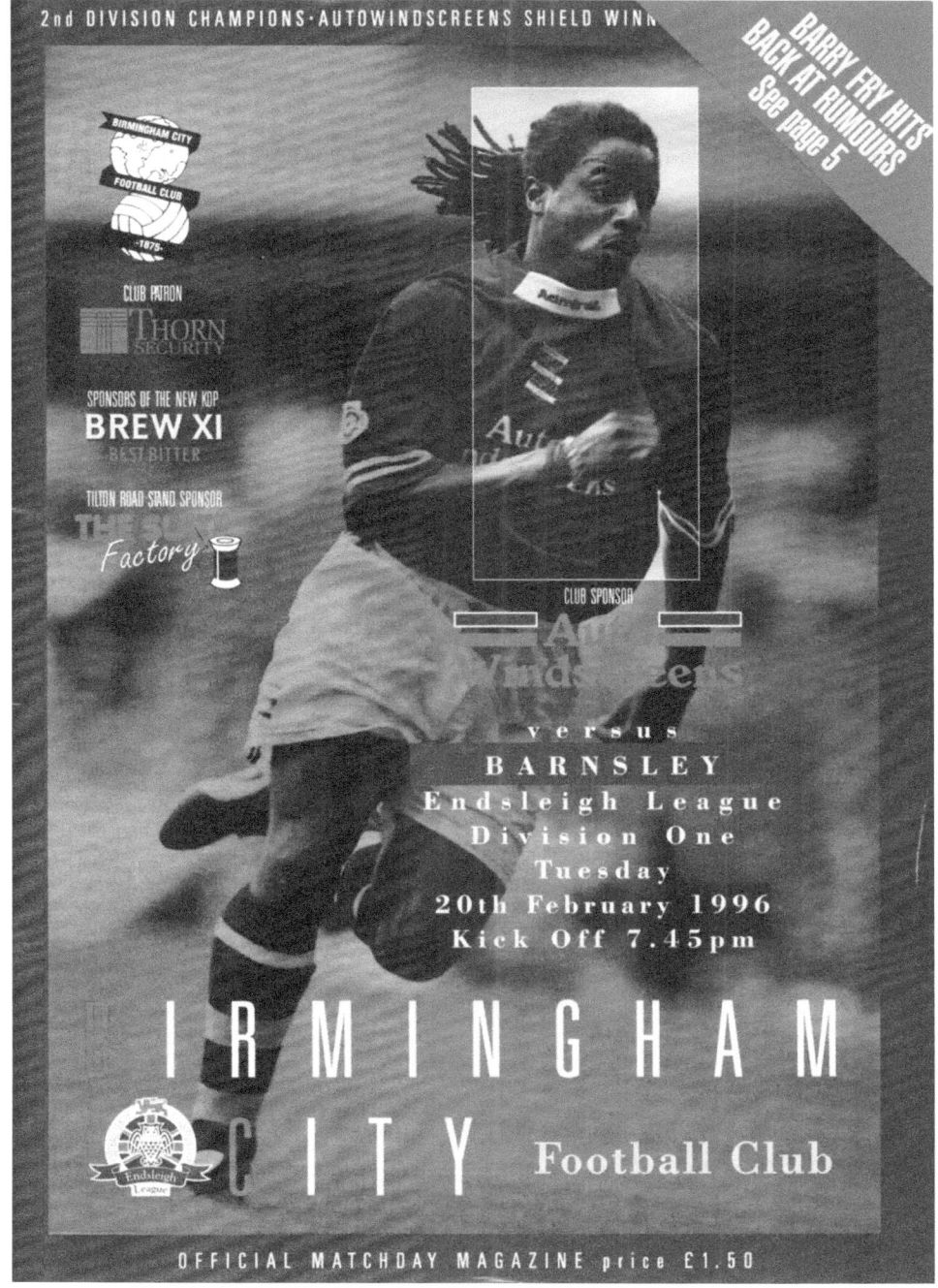

### Career in words
He began his career with the amateur side Haringey Borough before signing for Leyton Orient in 1990. Barry Fry signed him for Southend United for £100,000 in 1993. He moved to Blues for £800,000 in 1994 and he never justified the fee resulting in loan spells at Charlton Athletic, Peterborough United and Notts County. He has the unenviable record of scoring both goals in a 1–1 draw on his debut against Cambridge United. Released in 1998 he had a spell in non-League football with Halesowen, Bloxwich United and Romulus before signing for Rhyl in 2001.

Edwin Stein was an integral part of the Barry Fry regime that won the Division Two Championship in 1994–95 season. He had this to say about Ricky Otto's contribution to the triumph: 'Ricky didn't have the best of starts when we got him in from Southend United in December, and he knew that. People wondered if he had the ability, we never doubted and stuck by him. In my opinion for a winger he got in a great amount of crosses and shots in for us. People tend to forget that. He scored vital goals. He had a lot of pressure on him after becoming the club record signing. I don't think you could say it affected him, it was more that he took time to settle.'

### About the man
In 2001 after retiring from football Ricky became a probation officer, which in a way he is perfect for as he once spent four years detained at Her Majesty's pleasure for armed robbery. In 2007 he was studying for a degree in Theology. 'After my criminal past I always knew I wanted to work with offenders. When I started the job it felt as though I was delivering the programme to myself – so heavily entrenched in that behaviour. It was weird working with prisoners on the wing and in the cells. The memories all came flooding back and it made me realise how far I'd come as I still have friends doing life sentences. When I was involved in crime, hanging out on the street or playing football I was caught up in a materialistic society. Pride was a big part of that. I was young and hot-headed. I felt I had to live up to my reputation, it was weight on my back. I believed the life I was living was the greatest life, but I paid a great price for it. To be honest I'm just glad to be alive. Three years ago I gave my life to God and was baptised – that's when I decided to study the Bible. Some people must think I must have freaked out, but I always say that God can take out the baddest man and humble him. Playing football was a privilege, and I do miss the banter. I go to St Andrew's now and again, but usually I'm studying at weekends. After my start in life it's amazing that I had a football career. It was only when I finished playing that I realised the magnitude of what I'd done. Without football I would probably be dead now.'

(**Author's note:** I remember Ricky playing in a pre-season friendly at Atherstone United when there was an announcement over the tannoy system: 'Will the owner of a black BMW R80TT0 please return to their vehicle as it is causing an obstruction.' Needless to say, Ricky was on the pitch and the obstruction remained.)

# Dean Peer

### Heroic claim to fame
Moor Green Clubman of the Year 2003.

### Vital statistics
*Date of birth:* 8 August 1969
*Place of birth:* Wordsley, Stourbridge
*Blues career:* 150 – 12 goals
*Blues debut:* 20 September 1986 (a) lost 2–3 v Hull City. Crowd: 6,851
*Team:* Hansbury, Roberts, Dicks, Hagan, Overson, Kuhl, Peer, Clarke, Rees, Mortimer, Cooke (RE)
*First Blues goal:* 18 April 1989 (h) lost 1–2 v Swindon Town
*Club honours:* Blues – Leyland Daf Trophy 1991, Third Division runners-up 1992; Northampton Town – Third Division Promotion 1997

## THE HEROES

**Playing Career**

| Club | From | To | Fee | Total Appearances incl (subs) | Goals |
|---|---|---|---|---|---|
| Ipswich Town | 2009 | 2010 | Loan | 9 | 1 |
| Shrewsbury Town | 2000 | 2001 | Free | 60 | |
| Northampton Town | 1995 | 2000 | Free | 155 | 7 |
| Walsall | 1993 | 1995 | Free | 56 | 8 |
| Mansfield Town | 1992 | | Loan | 11 | |
| Birmingham City | 1987 | 1993 | Trainee | 150 | 12 |

**Career in words**

His junior career involved spells with Stourbridge Falcons and Lye Town before joining Blues on the Youth Training Scheme in July 1985. Two years later he signed professional terms. After making 150 appearances for the Blues and a loan period at Mansfield Town he moved to Walsall on a free transfer. He had two years with the Saddlers before moving to the Cobblers in 1995, where once again he made over 150 appearances. An ever present in the Cobblers squad in his first season, he helped them in their transition season of 1995–96 to a top-half finish before the two seasons that culminated in Wembley appearances. Peer came on as 79th-minute substitute in 1997 and was probably brought on to add some energy as extra-time loomed! But luckily for Northampton they did not need an extra half hour, and the job was done in breathtaking fashion by John Frain's left foot.

A year later Peer returned to Wembley with the Cobblers and missed a glaring opportunity late on. With Grimsby Town 1–0 up and the game coming to an end, Peer blazed over from just a few yards out.

His League career ended at Gay Meadow, where in two years he made 60 outings for Shrewsbury Town. He then spent some time on the non-League circuit with Moor Green, Solihull Borough and Evesham United.

# Jermaine Lloyd Pennant

**Heroic claim to fame**
Sold for a record £6.7 million to Liverpool in July 2006.

**Vital statistics**
*Date of birth:* 15 January 1983
*Place of birth:* Nottingham
*Blues career:* 60 – 3 goals
*Blues debut:* 2 February 2005 (h) won 2–1 v Southampton. Crowd: 28,797
*Team:* Taylor (Maik), Melchiot, Clapham, Johnson (D), Upson, Cunningham, Pennant, Blake, Pandiani, Gray
*First Blues goal:* 26 October 2005 (h) won 2–1 v Norwich City League Cup round three

# BIRMINGHAM CITY

*Club honours:* Arsenal – FA Community Shield 2004, FA Youth Cup 2001; Liverpool – FA Community Shield 2006, UEFA champions League runners-up 2006–07
*Representative honours:* England Under-21 – 24 caps

## Playing Career

| Club | From | To | Fee | Total Appearances incl (subs) | Goals |
|---|---|---|---|---|---|
| Stoke City | 2010 | | Loan | | |
| Real Zaragoza | 2009 | | Free | 2 | |
| Portsmouth | 2009 | 2009 | Loan | 14 | |
| Liverpool | 2006 | 2009 | £6,700,000 | 81 | 3 |
| Birmingham City | 2005 | 2006 | | 48 | 3 |
| Birmingham City | 2005 | 2005 | Loan | 12 | |
| Leeds United | 2003 | 2004 | Loan | 36 | 2 |
| Watford | 2002 | 2003 | Loan | 14 | 1 |
| Watford | 2002 | 2002 | Loan | 9 | 2 |
| Arsenal | 1999 | 2005 | £2,000,000 | 26 | 3 |
| Notts County | 1998 | 1999 | Trainee | 2 | |

## Career in words

Jermaine is of Jamaican descent, his mother died when he was three, his father Gay was a semi-professional footballer. He had three younger siblings (two sisters and a brother). He grew up in a crime and drug-infested neighbourhood, and he credits football for saving him from a life of crime. He joined Notts County as a trainee before joining Arsenal at the age of 15 for £2 million a record fee at the time for a trainee but he failed to impress twinned with a troublesome disciplinary record. He made his debut for the Gunners on 30 November 1999 in a League Cup fixture against Middlesbrough with three months to go to his 17th birthday (16 years and 319 days to be exact) which made him the youngest-ever first-team player at that time subsequently surpassed by Cesc Fabregas. While he continued to play in League Cup fixtures, it was a further two and a half years before his League debut against West Ham United on 24 August 2001 as a substitute. His first full League debut was in May 2003 against Southampton on which he scored a hat-trick. Between 2002 and 2004 he had loan spells at Watford and Leeds United. He joined Blues on loan for the 2004–05 season a spell which resulted in him being arrested and convicted for drink-driving while disqualified and uninsured. Blues showed great loyalty to him and gave him a permanent contract in April 2005. Blues were relegated from the top division and it was no surprise when Pennant signed for Liverpool on 26 July 2006 for a record incoming fee of £6.7 million for the Blues, with add-ons which if triggered would bring in a further £1.3 million to the St Andrew's coffers. His Liverpool debut was in the Champions League third round qualifying match against Maccabi Haifa at Anfield. He scored his first Liverpool goal in their 2–0 defeat of Chelsea on 20 January 2007. He was chosen to be part of the England squad for the games against Israel and Andorra in March 2007. In January 2009 he joined Portsmouth on loan for the second half of 2008–09 making 13 League appearances. Upon his return to Anfield he was not offered a new contract, and as a free agent he signed a three-year deal with Real Zaragoza on 9 July 2009, making his La Liga debut against CD Tenerife. He represented England at Under-21 level but even then his troubles followed him when he was sent home after breaking a curfew, and he was sent off for punching an opponent in a fixture against Croatia. Nevertheless, he made 24 appearances, making him one of the five most-capped Englishmen at that level.

In February 2004 given a 16-month ban from driving after being seen driving in the wrong lane in Paddington, West London. He was arrested on 23 January 2005 for drink driving after crashing into a lamp post in Aylesbury. At the time he was serving the previously imposed ban. He was sentenced to 90 days imprisonment on 1 March. He was released early from his custodial sentence at Woodhill Jail in Milton Keynes on 31 March 2005. He served a third of his three-month sentence for motoring offences. As a condition of his early release for good behaviour he was required to wear an electronic tag for the next two weeks and observe a night time curfew. His father was arrested for drug dealing in early 2009.

THE HEROES

### About the man
*Pure Gold* by David Gold published in 2006 by Highdown:
'On the face of it, we swapped one problem [Robbie Savage] for another when we took on the young winger Jermaine Pennant after he had suffered problems at Arsenal and was in danger of missing out on what

promised to be a glittering career in the game. Here is a young man with amazing potential but also with the baggage of personal problems. I can empathise with the man as the problems he has brought upon himself come from his impoverished background. It is a classic case of too much, too soon. It took me 20 years to claw my way out of poverty, but he was pulled out almost overnight and was given money beyond his wildest dreams. He has subsequently struggled to adjust, but I am convinced he will. The football club (Birmingham City) has done its best for him, but he is not going to take too kindly to being nannied 24 hours a day, seven days a week. All we can do is make sure he knows we are available to help him whenever he needs us. He has the skill to play for England, and better judges of footballers than me believe that to be the case. I sincerely hope he does, because he is such a charming young man. He has the opportunity because he will improve under Steve Bruce. When you are an attacking winger you have to have loads of self-belief, and he has this quality in abundance. Jermaine knows I am always available to him. I have, in the past, flown up so see him, and other players when they have needed it. I will sit and have lunch and an informal chat with them, and listen to their problems. After the latest episode there was only so much I dared do; I cannot become his father. I have to pace things and judge what part I am going to play. I am there for every match, in the dressing room before and after the game; I am there to pat him on the back after a game, and at the training ground. But, I repeat, I am not his father. After this latest issue the club made itself available to help him, though of course much of what we did must remain private. He wrote to Karren Brady saying how sorry he was for having a drink too many and suffering because of it. Nothing too unusual for a 21-year-old, except when you are under the spotlight, as he is and always will be as long as he is in football. He was suitably sorry and embarrassed, and that is what makes him durable and endurable. I could not cope with arrogance. If he had said, "So what?" there would have been little we could have done. At least he gave himself a chance, and it has to be said he bounced back brilliantly during our fight to stave off relegation.'

### Which sporting event would you most like to attend?
World Cup Final either watching or playing.

### Football stadium you would love to play in?
Wembley.

### Favourite sports programme?
*Soccer AM.*

### Best player played against?
Ashley Cole.

### First pair of football boots?
Quasar with yellow tongue sponsored by Gary Lineker.

### First team played for?
Clifton All-Whites.

### Favourite stadium?
Anfield.

### Favourite sports commentator?
Andy Gray.

### Favourite newspaper?
*The Sun.*

### Favourite food?
Nandos.

THE HEROES

**Favourite drink?**
Fanta.

**Favourite film?**
*Scarface*.

**Favourite holiday destination?**
Jamaica.

**Favourite pizza topping?**
Hawaiian.

**Favourite sport after football?**
Basketball.

# Kevin Mark Phillips

### Heroic claim to fame
Over 250 goals in over 500 matches and still scoring.

### Vital statistics
*Date of birth:* 25 March 1973
*Place of birth:* Hitchin, Hertfordshire
*Blues career:* 110 – 19 goals (at the end of 2010)
*Blues first appearance:* As a substitute 7 August 2008 (h) won 1–0 v Sheffield United and he scored. Crowd: 24,019
*Blues full debut:* 23 August 2008 (h) won 2–0 v Barnsley and he scored. Crowd 17,413
*Team:* Taylor (Maik), Parnaby, Murphy, Carsley, Ridgewell, Taylor (Martin), Larsson, Owusu-Abeye, O'Connor (G), Phillips, McSheffery
*Club honours:* Sunderland – Division One champions 1998–99; West Bromwich Albion – Championship winners 2007–08; Blues – Championship runner-up 2008–09, Carling Cup winner 2011
*Representative honours:* England B –1 cap, 8 full caps

### Playing Career

| Club | From | To | Fee | Total Appearances incl (subs) | Goals |
| --- | --- | --- | --- | --- | --- |
| Birmingham City | 2008 | | Free | 62 | 18 |
| West Bromwich Albion | 2006 | 2008 | £700,000 | 81 | 46 |
| Aston Villa | 2005 | 2006 | £1,000,000 | 27 | 5 |
| Southampton | 2003 | 2005 | £3,250,000 | 73 | 27 |
| Sunderland | 1997 | 2003 | £325,000 | 236 | 132 |
| Watford | 1994 | 1997 | £10,000 | 65 | 25 |
| Baldock Town | 1994 | 1994 | | | |

### Career in words
He started his career at non-League Baldock Town as a right-back after being rejected as a striker by Southampton. In 1999–2000 he was the Premier League top scorer, with 30 goals for Sunderland, going on to win the 'Golden Boot' for Europe which says something for The Saints' scouting system. Baldock switched him back to being a striker, and his exploits resulted in a move to Watford on 19 December 1994 for £10,000. At the end of the 1995–96 season he was signed by Sunderland for a fee of £350,000, which grew to £600,000 based on appearances and the achievements of the club. Sunderland had just been

relegated from the Premiership, and Kevin scored in seven consecutive games, equalling the club record. He also became the first Sunderland player to scored 30 goals in a season since Brian Clough. In all competitions he hit 35 goals which was the most by any Sunderland player since World War Two. In 1998–99 he scored 23 goals in 26 League games and 25 goals in all competitions in a season impacted negatively by a toe injury which kept him out for nearly four months. This form earned him an England call-up making his debut against Hungary. He joined Southampton after the Black Cats relegation from the Premier League in a £3.25 million deal. When Southampton suffered a similar fate to Sunderland Kevin joined Aston Villa for £1 million on 29 June 2005. He failed to establish a regular first-team place at Villa Park and therefore moved across Birmingham to join West Bromwich Albion for £700,000, scoring his 200th career goal in a FA Cup fifth round tie v Middlesbrough. In March 2008 he was named Championship Player of The Year. He scored his 200th League goal in a 1–1 draw v Palace on 13 March 2008. In 2007–08 'Super Kev' helped the Baggies win promotion to the Premiership as champions, earning him the Player of the Year award from both the supporters and the club after scoring 24 goals from 30 starts. He was also named in the PFA Championship Team of the Year. His contract ended at the end of the 2007–08 season, and he was offered a one-year contract with a further year if he made 19 or more League appearances. He rejected the offer and joined Blues, signing a two-year deal on 9 July 2008. At the end of the season he was top scorer with 13 goals. Although he gained eight caps for England, he never played a full 90 minutes, and his final appearance was against Holland in February 2002.

**About the man**
Phillips is married to Julie and they have four children: Millie, twins Toby and Tua and Alfie.

# Gary John Poole

**Heroic claim to fame**
Captained the Blues to the League Cup semi-finals in February 1996.

**Vital statistics**
*Date of birth:* 11 September 1967
*Place of birth:* Stratford, London
*Blues career:* 103 – 4 goals
*Blues debut:* 18 August 1994 (h) won 4–0 v Peterborough United. Crowd: 10,600
*Team:* Bennett, Poole, Small, Ward, Whyte, Dryden, Hunt, Claridge, Bull, Tait, Wallace
*First Blues goal:* 6 January 1996 (h) drew 1–1 v Wolverhampton Wanderers
*Club honours:* Barnet – Conference champions 1991; Blues – Division Two champions 1995 Auto Windscreens Shield winners 1995.

## Playing Career

| Club | From | To | Fee | Total Appearances incl (subs) | Goals |
|---|---|---|---|---|---|
| Charlton Athletic | 1996 | 1999 | £250,000 | 16 | 1 |
| Birmingham City | 1994 | 1996 | £500,000 | 103 | 4 |
| Southend United | 1993 | 1994 | £350,000 | 52 | 2 |
| Plymouth Argyle | 1992 | 1993 | Free | 48 | 7 |
| Barnet | 1989 | 1992 | £3,000 | 55 | 3 |
| Cambridge United | 1987 | 1989 | Free | 50 | |
| Tottenham Hotspur | 1985 | 1987 | Junior | | |

## Career in words

He came through the juniors at Spurs and was given a professional contract but never played for the first team, resulting in his release after two years. He signed for Cambridge United in the Fourth Division and after 18 months was sold for £3,000 to Conference side Barnet who were managed by Barry Fry. In Gary's first full season Barnet were promoted as champions to Division Four. He joined Plymouth Argyle on a free, where he captained the side. After one season Fry signed him again, this time for Southend United in Division One for a club-record fee of £350,000. One year later he joined up with Fry again at Blues who were newly relegated to Division Three for a fee of £500,000. When Liam Daish went to Coventry Gary became Blues captain taking them to the League Cup semi-finals where they lost to Leeds United. He was banned for four matches in 1996 when he pushed referee Richard Poulain with such force that he needed treatment for whiplash after the game. A month later new manager Trevor Francis sold him to Charlton Athletic for a fee of £250,000. He played 16 games for Charlton before a knee injury ended his first-team career, retiring in August 1999.

DEEP IN CONCENTRATION, GARY POOLE DELIVERS ANOTHER PIN-POINT BALL

PHOTO CREDIT: ASSOCIATED SPORTS PHOTOGRAPHY

## About the man

Liam Daish recalls 'Baz [Barry Fry] was a larger-than-life character, and you couldn't help but like him. I remember him once having a row with Gary Poole. Baz has gone "Gaz, what the f**k are you doing?" "What do you mean?" said Gary, "what do you want me to do?" Baz turned round and said: "Well if you don't f**king know, I don't either!"

Edwin Stein had this to say about Gary Poole: 'He was a great signing since moving from Southend United in September 1994. I think he at last found a club to match his ambition. He's very solid defensively and a fierce competitor. A real asset. When Scott Hiley got injured he came in and held the right-back place down so much that he became a member of the PFA Division team of the year. Pooley or Brucie because of his chin was also good off the pitch. He got team spirit going and got the lads feathers ruffled a few times which is need at some stages in a long season.'

BIRMINGHAM CITY                                                            MODERN DAY HEROES

# Kevin Poole

### Heroic claim to fame
In June 2009 he was the oldest player in the Football League, aged 46.

### Vital statistics
*Date of birth:* 21 July 1963
*Place of birth:* Bromsgrove
*Blues career:* 67
*Blues debut:* 3 May 1998 (h) drew 0–0 v Charlton Athletic. Crowd: 25,877
*Team:* Poole Gill, Charlton, Bruce, Johnson (M), McCarthy, O'Connor, Adebola, Ndlovu, Furlong
*Club honours:* Leicester – Division One Play-off winner 1995–96, League Cup winner 1997; Burton Albion – Conference champions 2008–09

### Playing Career

| Club | From | To | Fee | Total Appearances incl (subs) | Goals |
|---|---|---|---|---|---|
| Burton Albion | 2006 | | Free | 132 | |
| Derby County | 2005 | 2006 | Free | 7 | |
| Bolton Wanderers | 2001 | 2005 | Free | 16 | |
| Birmingham City | 1997 | 2001 | Free | 67 | |
| Leicester City | 1991 | 1997 | £400,000 | 194 | |
| Hartlepool United | 1991 | | Loan | 12 | |
| Middlesbrough | 1987 | 1991 | Free | 42 | |
| Northampton Town | 1984 | | Loan | 3 | |
| Aston Villa | 1981 | 1987 | Apprentice | 32 | |

### Career in words
His first club was Aston Villa, joining initially as an apprentice before turning professional in 1981. He was third choice behind Jimmy Rimmer and Nigel Spink when the Villa won the European Cup in 1982. He made his League debut while on loan at Northampton Town in late 1984 and played the first of his 32 games for the Villa later in the 1984–85 season. He moved to Middlesbrough in 1987 who had been promoted to Division Two. In 1987 he played 42 first-team games in four seasons spending the latter part of 1990–91 on loan at Hartlepool United where he started their last 12 games of the season keeping five clean sheets and never being on the losing side to clinch promotion from Division Four. He signed for Leicester City and went on to make 194 appearances in all competitions, between 1991 and 1997 being part of the side that won promotion to the Premier League in 1996 but eventually lost his place to Kasey Keller. He moved to Blues in August 1997 achieving a regular place when Ian Bennett was injured in September 1998. He was released in May 2001. He returned on a short-term contract again when 'Benno' was injured in September 2001 and played in one League Cup game before joining Bolton Wanderers in the October. He spent 4 years with the Trotters as back up to Jussi Jaaskelainen. During 2003–04 he was part of the squad that reached the League Cup Finals and was an unused sub v Middlesbrough. He joined Derby County as goalkeeping coach in July 2005 although he was still registered as a player for emergency purposes, only due to injuries to Lee Clamp and Lee Grant he was brought into the first team playing seven times as a 42-year-old before returning to his coaching duties. He was released in May 2006, after a trial with Walsall he signed for Burton Albion on a match-to-match basis in August 2006 keeping a clean sheet on his debut a day later at Morecambe and continued to play until the end of 2006–07 season when he was named Player of the Season. He then helped them reach the Conference Play-off semi-finals before playing a key role in the 2008–09 title-winning side. He signed a new contract in June 2009, making him the oldest player in the Football League aged 46, and he is also their goalkeeping coach. He made two League appearances coming as a substitute for the red-carded Artur Krysiak at Port Vale in January 2010 and then played in place of the suspended Krysiak in the next League game, a 3–2 win v Torquay.

# THE HEROES

**About the man**
**What is your current job?**
I am currently goalkeeping coach-player at Burton Albion Football Club.

**Who was your favourite player as a boy? And why?**
Peter Shilton was my hero as a young lad, as he was a fantastic goalkeeper and I wanted to model myself on him and become a footballing legend like he is.

**Which game in your career stands out in your memory?**
Playing for Leicester City v Crystal Palace at Wembley in the Championship Play-off Final and winning 2–1 after extra-time to gain promotion to the Premier League.

**What's your best football experience?**
Making my football debut in the old First Division at Tottenham Hotspur against the likes of Ray Clemence and Glenn Hoddle and keeping a clean sheet in a 2–0 victory.

**Who was the best player you played with and why?**
While at Bolton I played with Jay Jay Okocha. He could tie defenders up in knots with his unbelievable quick feet and fantastic skills and tricks.

**If you could go back to your days at Blues what one thing would you do differently?**
Nothing really, as I enjoyed every minute of my time there, just would have like to have played more games than I actually did.

**What was your best moment while at St Andrew's?**
The Worthington Cup Final v Liverpool at Cardiff, although I was only substitute and we lost too, but still a great day out. Also scoring my one and only goal in the penalty shoot-out v Watford at St Andrew's in the Play-off semi-final, although we lost that one too.

**If you hadn't chosen football as a career what would you be?**
Probably a professional cricketer, as at 16 I had to choose between a football apprenticeship with Aston Villa or playing cricket for Worcestershire Cricket Club. Football won hands down.

**What is your opinion of football today?**
It's still a great game but a lot quicker and more physical these days, but they should limit the amount of foreign players at each club in order for youngsters to get a better chance of coming through and making the grade.

**If you could be one of today's Premier League stars who would you want to be and why?**
At the moment I would like to be in Joe Hart's shoes as he is a fantastic young goalkeeper with a great future ahead of him.

BIRMINGHAM CITY                                              MODERN DAY HEROES

# Franck Queudrue

### Heroic claim to fame
Captained the reserves to triumph in the Birmingham Senior Cup in 2008.

### Vital statistics
*Date of birth:* 27 August 1978
*Place of birth:* Paris, France
*Blues career:* 56 – 3 goals
*Blues debut:* 12 August 2007 (a) lost 2–3 v Chelsea. Crowd: 41,590
*Team:* Doyle, Kelly, Queudrue, Nafti, Ridgewell, Djourou-Gbadjere, Larsson, Muamba, Forssell, Kapo, McSheffrey
*First Blues goal:* 15 November 2008 (h) won 3–2 v Charlton Athletic
*Club honours:* Blues – Championship runners-up 2008–09; Middlesbrough – League Cup winners 2004, UEFA Cup runners-up 2006
*Representative honours:* France B cap

### Playing Career

| Club | From | To | Fee | Total Appearances incl (subs) | Goals |
| --- | --- | --- | --- | --- | --- |
| Colchester United | 2010 | 2010 | Loan | 3 | |
| Birmingham City | 2007 | 2010 | £2,000,000 | 56 | 3 |
| Fulham | 2006 | 2007 | | 32 | 1 |
| Middlesbrough | 2002 | 2006 | £2,500,000 | 165 | 10 |
| Middlesbrough | 2001 | 2002 | Loan | 34 | 2 |
| Lens | 1999 | 2002 | | 2 | |

### Career in words
Franck joined Middlesbrough on loan from Lens in October 2001 and stayed until the summer of 2006 after earning a permanent move in May 2002 for £2.5 million. He has a poor disciplinary record and earned five yellow and three red cards in 2002–03 season contributing to Middlesbrough missing out on a place in the UEFA Cup through the Fair Play League. He was part of the Boro team that won the League Cup in 2004, beating Bolton Wanderers as well as starting in the 2006 UEFA Cup Final. In 2006 he became a UK citizen and in the same year joined Fulham. On 3 August 2007 he signed a three-year deal with Blues for an estimated £2.5 million. In 2009 he was voted the fan's Player of the Year and the *Birmingham Mail's* Player of the Season for 2008–09 after David Sullivan had branded him a 'rubbish signing' in the summer of 2008. Blues reserves won the Birmingham Senior Cup in 2008, beating Burton Albion 5–0. Franck captained the side which was: Colin Doyle; Stuart Parnaby, David Joyce, Franck Q. (Jack Rutter), Rafael Scmitz, Jordan Mutch, Daniel De Ridder (Jamie Sheldon), Garry O'Connor (Jake Jervis), Cameron Jerome, Ashley Sammons, Semith Aydilek. Scorers: O'Connor (3), Parnaby, Jerome.

On 14 December 2009 it was reported that Franck had won a cook-off with James McFadden to have the official Blues curry named after him. At the NEC Golf Show he topped the leaderboard for the simulated longest drive, beating five of his fellow pros; Lee Bowyer, Roger Johnson, Maik Taylor, Gary McSheffery and Stephen Carr. Franck plays off a handicap of 16 and registered a drive of 290 yards, beating Johnson into second place.

The *Sunday Mercury* reported on 21 March 2010 that he was appealing against a £1,000 speeding fine and a 14-day ban, even though he earned allegedly £20,000 per week at Blues. He was caught driving at 76mph on a 50mph restricted zone near junction 15 on the M40 in Warwickshire. He pleaded guilty and as well as the fine and ban ordered to pay a £15 victim charge and court costs of £85.

THE HEROES

**About the man**
**Early days?**
I grew up in Cessom a small town near Paris. I was OK at school, a good lad never in trouble. My best subjects were history and sport, of course. We did lots of sport – football, rugby and gymnastics.

**Pets?**
Two French bulldogs.

**Spare time pursuits?**
I play golf, I have been playing for six years and have got a 16 handicap.

**Previous jobs?**
My family had a pizza restaurant. I used to help in there washing up and stuff.

**Favourite sport after football?**
Rugby.

**World's greatest ever sportsman?**
Roger Federer.

**Best place for a holiday?**
Corsica.

**Six-a-side dream team?**
Buffon, Sagnol, Nesta, Queudrue, Ronaldo, Van Nistelrooy.

# Liam Matthew Ridgewell

**Heroic claim to fame**
Developed a knack for scoring vital goals at the back post.

**Vital statistics**
*Date of birth:* 21 July 1984
*Place of birth:* Bexleyheath, London
*Blues career:* 137 – 10 goals (As at the end of 2010)
*Blues debut:* 12 August 2007 (a) lost 2–3 v Chelsea. Crowd: 41,590
*Team:* Doyle, Kelly, Queudrue, Nafti, Ridgewell, Djourou-Gbadjere, Larsson, Muamba, Forssell, Kapo, McSheffrey
*First Blues goal:* 27 October 2007 (h) won 3–2 v Wigan Athletic
*Club honours:* Aston Villa – FA Youth Cup 2002; Blues – Championship runners-up 2008–09, Carling Cup winner 2011
*Representative honours:* 2002 England Under-19 – 1 cap 1 goal, Under-21 – 7 caps

**Playing Career**

| Club | From | To | Fee | Total Appearances incl (subs) | Goals |
|---|---|---|---|---|---|
| Birmingham City | 2007 | | £2,000,000 | 116 | 7 |
| Bournemouth | 2002 | 2002 | Loan | 5 | |
| Aston Villa | 2001 | 2007 | Trainee | 93 | 7 |

**Career in words**
He began his career with West Ham United but moved to Aston Villa in February 2001 being part of the team that won the FA Youth Cup in May 2002 v Everton. In October 2002 he went on loan to Bournemouth playing five games between 13 October to 13 November. His debut for Villa's first team came on 4 January 2003 in a 4–1 defeat to Blackburn Rovers in the FA Cup, coming on as a substitute after 69 minutes. He joined Blues for a fee of £2 million on 3 August 2007, becoming the captain in the absence of Damien Johnson and the first player to move directly from Villa to Blues since Des Bremner

# THE HEROES

in 1984. On 13 April 2009 Liam broke a leg, returning to the first team on 24 October 2009.

## About the man
**Who did you support as a boy?**
I supported Queen's Park Rangers. My father, Bob, is a Crystal Palace fan, as is one of my brothers, while the other follows Arsenal.

**How did you become a footballer?**
I was spotted playing for junior side Long Lane. I had been to Manchester United a couple of times for trials, as well as Aston Villa; their south-east scout Alfie Apps recommended me. I had been at West Ham since I was eight, so moving away from home at the age of 15 made me grow up quickly. I was a member of the FA Youth Cup-winning side which beat Everton in the 2002 Final. The Toffees featured a young lad called Rooney!

**Favourite TV programme?**
*Prison Break* or *Lost*.

**Famous person you would like to meet?**
Ricky Hatton.

**Favourite shop?**
Dolce & Gabanna.

**Favourite comedian?**
Lee Evans.

**Best friend in football?**
Steve David.

**Favourite sport after football?**
Formula One.

**World's greatest sportsman?**
For football Pele or Maradonna. Outside football Tiger Woods.

**Favourite holiday destination?**
Dubai.

**Best six-a-side team?**
Given, Terry, Ridgewell, Messi, Henry, Rooney.

BIRMINGHAM CITY                                                MODERN DAY HEROES

# Steve Robinson

**Heroic claim to fame**
Middle name is Eli and his nickname is Turbo.

**Vital statistics**
*Date of birth:* 17 January 1975
*Place of birth:* Nottingham
*Blues career:* 95 – 2 goals
*Blues first appearance:* As a substitute 4 March 1995 (a) drew 0–0 v Hull City. Crowd: 9,894
*Blues full debut:* 11 March 1995 (h) lost 0–1 v Swansea. Crowd: 16,191
*Team:* Bennett, Poole, Whyte, Ward, Barnett, Daish, Robinson, Claridge, McGavin, Otto, Tait
*First Blues goal:* 17 September 1997 (h) won 4–1 v Stockport County League Cup round two
*Club honours:* Blues – Leyland Daf winners 1991, Division Two champions 1994–95

**Playing Career**

| Club | From | To | Fee | Total Appearances incl (subs) | Goals |
|---|---|---|---|---|---|
| Grantham | 2008 | 2009 | Loan | 4 | |
| Worksop | 2005 | 2009 | | | |
| Lincoln City | 2005 | 2006 | | 12 | |
| Swindon Town | 2001 | 2005 | £50,000 | 161 | 5 |
| Peterborough United | 1996 | | Loan | 5 | |
| Kidderminster Harriers | 1995 | | Loan | | |
| Birmingham City | 1991 | 2001 | | 95 | 2 |

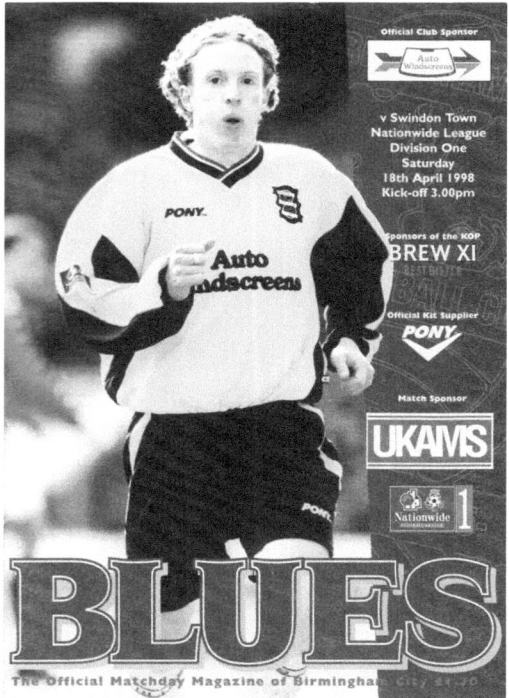

**Career in words**
He began his career as a trainee with Blues in 1991 turning professional in June 1993. He had loan spells with Kidderminster Harriers in 1995 and Peterborough United in 1996. After appearing in only four games in the 2000–01 season he joined Swindon Town for a fee in the region of £50,000 in February 2001. He was released when the 2004–05 season ended and he joined Lincoln City on a one-year deal in July 2005 before joining Worksop Town on loan in November 2005. He returned to The Imps before being released in May 2006 and rejoining Worksop Town. In November 2008 he joined Grantham Town on a three-month loan deal after he was released by them at the end of 2008–09. While at Swindon he endured a broken leg, and then when he moved to Lincoln he broke his foot in two places on a pre-season tour of Ireland.

**About the man**
Edwin Stein was an integral part of the Barry Fry regime that won the Division Two Championship in 1994–95 season. He had this to say about Steve Robinson's contribution to

the triumph: 'We threw little Robbo in for his seasonal debut at Hull in March, and then he started his first ever Blues game against Swansea days later. He lifted us with his enthusiasm, attitude and tigerish play. It was great to see.'

# Ian Rodgerson

## Heroic claim to fame
From pitch to touchline as qualified physiotherapist.

## Vital statistics
*Date of birth:* 9 April 1966
*Place of birth:* Hereford
*Blues career:* 116 – 16 goals
*Blues debut:* 15 December 1990 (h) won 2–1 v Rotherham United. Crowd: 4,734
*Team:* Thomas, Clarkson, Downs, Frain, Overson, Matthewson, Rodgerson, Gayle (J), Aylott, Gleghorn, Tait
*First Blues goal:* 2 March 1991 (h) won 2–0 v Swansea
*Club honours:* Blues – Division Three runners-up 1991–92

## Playing Career

| Club | From | To | Fee | Total Appearances incl (subs) | Goals |
|---|---|---|---|---|---|
| Hereford United | 1997 | 2002 | Free | 92 | 8 |
| Cardiff City | 1995 | 1997 | Free | 65 | 2 |
| Sunderland | 1993 | 1995 | £140,000 | 10 | |
| Birmingham City | 1990 | 1993 | £50,000 | 116 | 16 |
| Cardiff City | 1988 | 1990 | £35,000 | 124 | 4 |
| Hereford United | 1985 | 1988 | Junior | 119 | 6 |

## Career in words
His youth career began with Pegasus Juniors and Hereford United. He signed professional for Hereford in 1985 and made over 100 appearances. In 1988 he joined Cardiff City for £35,000. He had a loan spell at Blues during 1990–91 before making it a permanent move in 1991. He cost Blues £50,000, but they made a significant profit when Ian was sold to Sunderland for £140,000. After lengthy and successful spells with Cardiff City and a return to Hereford United, he quit the League game to qualify as a chartered physiotherapist. He is currently working for Blues Academy and Forest Green Rovers.

## About the man
**What is your current job?**
Chartered physiotherapist.

**Who was your favourite player as a boy? And why?**
Kevin Keegan – one of the biggest stars of the 1970s and '80s.

**Which game in your career stands out in your memory?**
Shrewsbury Town at St Andrew's. We gained promotion to the old Division Two.

**What's your best football experience?**
Playing the Blues.

# BIRMINGHAM CITY
## MODERN DAY HEROES

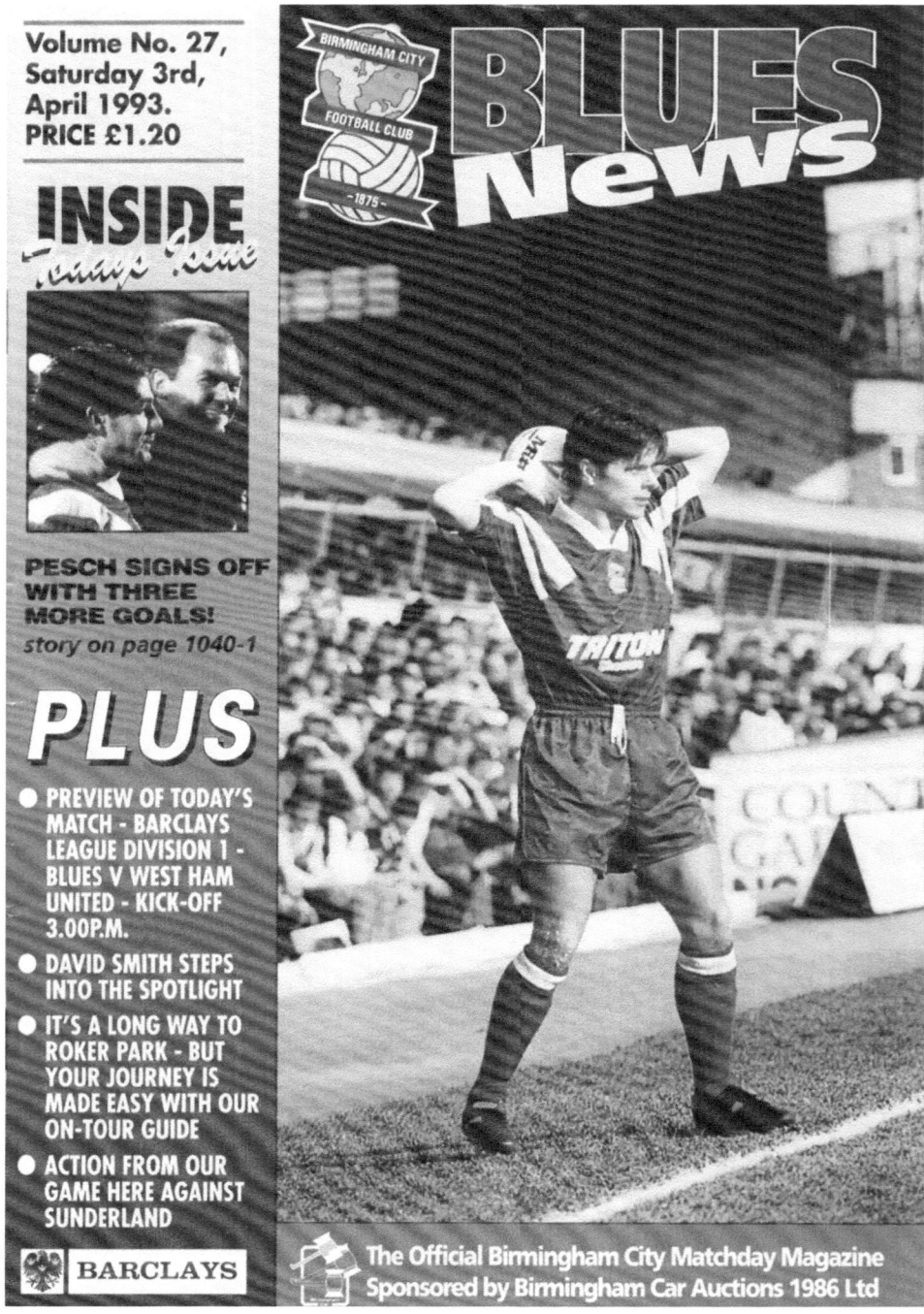

**Who was the best player you played with and why?**
Ian Clarkson – great defender and when he won the ball he passed it to me.

**If you could go back to your days at Blues what one thing would you do differently?**
Work harder.

**What was your best moment while at St Andrew's?**
Every time I scored a goal for the Blues.

**If you hadn't chosen football as a career what would you be?**
I did a plumbing apprenticeship before turning pro at 19 years of age. So probably a plumber.

**What is your opinion of football today?**
Big improvement.

**If you could be one of today's Premier League stars who would you want to be and why?**
Gareth Bale – likes to get forward and score goals.

# Mathew Sadler

### Heroic claim to fame
A Bluenose through and through.

### Vital statistics
*Date of birth:* 26 February 1985
*Place of birth:* Marston Green, Birmingham
*Blues career:* 61
*Blues debut:* 2 October 2002 (a) won 3–2 v Leyton Orient. Crowd: 3,615
*Team:* Bennett, Kenna, Lazaridis, Woodhouse, Purse, Vickers, Powell, John, Horsfield, Sadler, Kirovski
*Club honours:* Blues – Championship runners-up 2006–07
*Representative honours:* England Youth Cap

### Playing Career

| Club | From | To | Fee | Total Appearances incl (subs) | Goals |
|---|---|---|---|---|---|
| Shrewsbury Town | 2010 | | Loan | 8 | |
| Stockport County | 2010 | | Loan | 20 | |
| Watford | 2008 | | £750,000 | 43 | |
| Northampton Town | 2003 | 2004 | Loan | 8 | |
| Birmingham City | 2002 | 2008 | Trainee | 61 | |

### Career in words
He began his career as a junior with Blues before making his first appearance in the Premiership in a 3–2 win over Bolton Wanderers at St Andrew's 2 November 2002. After making a further top-flight appearance against Manchester United, he was sidelined for the nearly three and a half years with two bad ankle injuries. In November 2003 he spent two months on loan at Northampton Town, playing eight games which did little to help his injuries, and he was forced into a lengthy period of rehabilitation which thankfully did not stop Blues offering him a new contract, which he signed in May 2004. Sadler joined Watford on 24 January 2008 for an initial fee of £750,000, rising to £900,000 depending on appearances, signing a three-and-a-half year contract.

### About the man
### As a Bluenose which ex-player impressed you?
When I watched Blues from the terraces, I used to admire Martin Grainger who was such a tough-tackling player.

BIRMINGHAM CITY                                   MODERN DAY HEROES

**When you were in the Blues Academy, did any senior players help the young lads?**
Mario Melchiot was always available to help all the young Academy lads. He would often come and chat for a good 20 minutes or so, offering words of wisdom. He's a good person to have about.

**What are your earliest memories as a Blues fan?**
It was when I was about four or five years old. My Dad took me to see Blues v Leyton Orient, which we won 1–0. Before the goal I kept asking him if we could go because as far as I could see there was nothing happening, but then we scored and I was bitten. I realise now that it was the emotion of everyone around when the goal went in that did it. After that I wanted to go to every game just to hear the moment when you do score and the crowd's reaction.

**Which sporting event would you most like to attend?**
World Cup Final as a player – to watch? Masters golf or men's singles final at Wimbledon.

**Football stadium you would love to play at?**
Wembley.

**Sporting hero?**
Bobby Moore.

**Best player played against?**
Arjen Robben, Damien Duff and Joe Cole.

**Rule change you'd like to see?**
Offside.

**First football boots?**
Nicks from Littlewoods.

**First team played for?**
Arden Forest.

**Favourite TV programme?**
*The Sopranos.*

**Favourite sports commentator?**
John Motson.

**Favourite newspaper?**
*The Sun.*

**Favourite magazine?**
*Kerrang.*

**Favourite food?**
Surf 'n turf.

**Favourite drink?**
Budweiser.

**Favourite film?**
*Life of Brian.*

**Favourite pizza topping?**
Cheese, tomato & pineapple.

**Favourite sport after football?**
Cricket.

**Favourite city after Birmingham?**
There is not one!

# Robert William Savage

**Heroic claim to fame**
He holds the record of the most yellow cards in the Premiership's history – almost 90.

**Vital statistics**
*Date of birth:* 18 October 1974
*Place of birth:* Wrexham
*Blues career:* 88 – 12 goals
*Blues debut:* 28 August 2002 (a) drew 1–1 v Everton. Crowd: 37,197
*Team:* Vaesen, Tebily, Grainger, Savage, Purse, Cunningham, Johnson (D), John, Horsfield, Cisse, Hughes
*First Blues goal:* 2 November 2002 (h) won 3–1 v Bolton Wanderers
*Club honours:* Manchester United – Youth Cup winners 1992; Crewe Alexandra – Division Two Play-off winners 1997; Leicester City – League Cup runners-up 1999, League Cup winners 2000
*Representative honours:* Wales – 39 full caps

**Playing Career**

| Club | From | To | Fee | Total Appearances incl (subs) | Goals |
|---|---|---|---|---|---|
| Brighton & Hove Albion | 2008 | | Loan | 7 | |
| Derby County | 2008 | | £1,500,000 | 102 | 3 |
| Blackburn Rovers | 2005 | 2008 | £3,000,000 | 100 | 3 |
| Birmingham City | 2002 | 2005 | £1,250,000 | 88 | 12 |
| Leicester City | 1997 | 2002 | £400,000 | 204 | 9 |
| Crewe Alexandra | 1994 | 1997 | Free | 95 | 11 |
| Manchester United | 1993 | 1994 | Trainee | | |

**Career in words**
He attended Ysgol Bryn Alyn, Gwersyllt, until he completed his GCSE studies in July 1991. On leaving school he joined Manchester United as an apprentice striker, playing in the FA Youth Cup-winning team of 1992. He was given a professional contract but never played for the first team and signed for Crewe Alexandra in 1994, switching to midfield, helping them reach the Division Two Play-offs in his first two seasons at the club. In 1997 Crewe made it third time lucky by sealing promotion via the Play-offs. He joined Premier League side Leicester City in July 1997 for £400,000, spending five years at Leicester. In 1999 he reached the League Cup Final v Spurs, and a year later they reached the League Cup Final again, this time beating Tranmere 2–1. With Leicester City relegated at the end of 2001–02 season he moved to newly promoted Blues for a fee of £1.25 million on a three-year contract. On 19 January 2005 he moved to Blackburn Rovers for a fee of £3 million to be nearer his ailing father in Wrexham. On 9 January 2008 he joined Derby County for a fee of £1.5 million on a two-and-a-half year contract, being appointed skipper after the departure of Matt Oakley to Leicester City. He was sent out on loan to Brighton & Hove Albion in October 2008 for a month to keep match fit. At the start of 2009–10 season he signed a new two-year deal. He retired from international football in September 2005, having earned 39 caps. Sav has

BIRMINGHAM CITY MODERN DAY HEROES

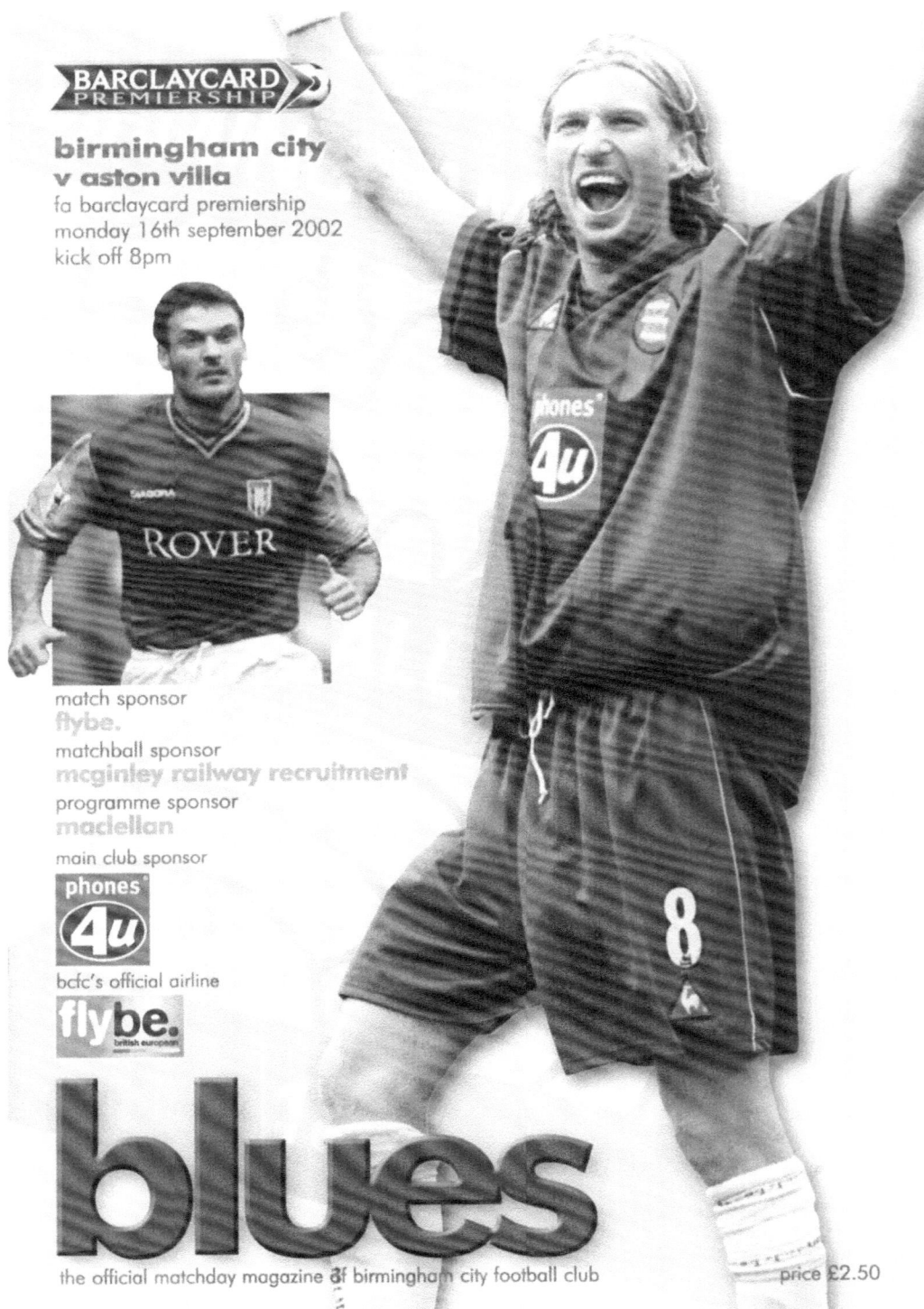

**BARCLAYCARD PREMIERSHIP**

**birmingham city v aston villa**
fa barclaycard premiership
monday 16th september 2002
kick off 8pm

match sponsor
flybe.

matchball sponsor
mcginley railway recruitment

programme sponsor
maclellan

main club sponsor
phones 4u

bcfc's official airline
flybe. british european

**blues**
the official matchday magazine of birmingham city football club

price £2.50

only been sent off twice in his career – in an international game v Northern Ireland in September 2004 and in a Premier League game for Blackburn Rovers on 18 February 2006 v Middlesbrough. He used the referee's toilet before a game, resulting in a FA fine of £10,000 while Leicester City fined him two weeks wages.

## About the man
*Pure Gold* by David Gold, published in 2006 by Highdown:
'It hurts me to say it, but we have to admit that we missed Robbie Savage, and we did not replace him. I supported him and did everything to hold on to him and persuade him to stay at St Andrew's. His move to Blackburn Rovers left a sour taste in the mouths of all of us at The Blues. There were so many reasons and so many excuses and all the sob stories about him wanting to be nearer his home because he was worried about his family, but they all failed to stand up. What he was really doing was reneging on a four-year contract offered and signed, we thought, in good faith. He signed that contract when he was due to go into hospital for surgery at the end of the 2003–04 season, with his future as a professional footballer in doubt. He had realised the back/neck operation was not as simple as he thought and he rushed in to sign the contract out of fear for his playing career. He was outstanding when he came back, but as we moved towards the transfer window through Christmas 2004 he organised and worked out his own move. He made himself intolerable to work with and orchestrated his own demise. He had made up his mind he was going to Blackburn, and nothing was going to change his mind. He told the press it was closer to his parents' house and it was important to him to be near them. Needless to say, the press do not believe everything they are told. They measured the distances involved and found that his parents' home was closer to Birmingham than Blackburn. The truth was he wanted a new challenge, and he just abandoned Birmingham City. He had an excellent contract with us but he moved because of the money and because he wanted to be with his former Welsh coaching team of Mark Bowen and Mark Hughes, both of whom had moved to Blackburn. Had he had the courage to come out and say as much we would have accepted it much more readily. But he was childlike in his approach. It was a good as saying, "I want that – giss it!" I loved Robbie Savage. I thought he was a fantastic character, and he was great for Birmingham City…'

## The funniest footballer?
John Hartson. He's mad. I've got a lot of stories about him because we roomed together when we played for Wales. One of the things he always keeps reminding me about is that he's had £24 million worth of moves. Another is Ian Bennett. If anyone has seen Galeon off *Planet of the Apes*, it's Benno.

## The worst programme ever on the TV?
*Footballer's Wives*.

## First football boots?
Panther 'four stripes' I think they cost less than £10 from Woolworths.

## First football team you supported?
Wrexham.

## First football team you played in?
Llay United who I joined as Under-12 – I was centre-forward and scored 73 goals in one season.

## First footballing hero?
Mark Hughes.

## First famous person you met?
Terry Griffiths the snooker player.

## Favourite actor?
Robert de Niro.

**Favourite singer?**
George Michael.

**First car?**
Ford Fiesta D reg with a 1.1 engine.

**First pet?**
Tortoise called Dixie.

**First wage?**
As an apprentice it was £29.50. My first professional contract was worth £140 per week with Manchester United.

**Which sporting event would you most like to attend?**
The Ryder Cup in the USA.

**Football stadium you would love to play in?**
The Bernabeau.

**Favourite sports programme?**
*Question of Sport*.

**Best player played against?**
Steven Gerrard.

# David Andrew Seaman

### Heroic claim to fame
Another England 'keeper to add the greats from the past Gil Merrick et al and the current crop Joe Hart and Ben Foster.

### Vital statistics
*Date of birth:* 19 September 1963
*Place of birth:* Rotherham
*Blues career:* 84
*Blues debut:* 6 October 1984 (a) lost 0–2 v Brighton & Hove Albion. Crowd: 13,695
*Team:* Seaman, Jones (MAW), Roberts, Wright, Armstrong, Daly, Hagan, Clarke, Harford, Bremner, Rees
*Club honours:* Blues – Division Two runners-up 1984–85; Arsenal – three League Championships (1991, 1998, 2002), four FA Cups (1993, 1998, 2002, 2003), League Cup winners 1993, European Cup-Winners' Cup in 1994, Winner Tournoi de France 1997.
*Representative honours:* England B – 6 caps, Under-21 – 10 caps, 75 full caps playing in two World Cups (1998, 2002), two Euro Championships in 1996 and 2000.

### Playing Career

| Club | From | To | Fee | Total Appearances incl (subs) | Goals |
| --- | --- | --- | --- | --- | --- |
| Manchester City | 2003 | 2004 | Free | 26 | |
| Arsenal | 1990 | 2003 | £1,300,000 | 566 | |
| Queen's Park Rangers | 1986 | 1990 | £225,000 | 175 | |
| Birmingham City | 1984 | 1986 | £100,000 | 84 | |
| Peterborough United | 1982 | 1984 | £4,000 | 106 | |
| Leeds United | 1981 | 1982 | Apprentice | | |

### Career in words
He retired on 13 January 2004 and was awarded the MBE in 1997 for services to football. He is England's second-most capped goalkeeper with 75 caps after Peter Shilton. He is left-handed but threw with his right arm and kicked with his right foot. He was brought up in Rotherham, where he attended Kimberworth Comprehensive School. He began his career at Leeds, whom he supported as a boy; however, he was released by the then manager Eddie Gray who had been David's favourite player. In August 1982 he went to Division Four side Peterborough United for a fee of £4,000. Just two years later in October 1984 Second Division Blues paid £100,000 for his services ending up winning promotion at the end of that season but were relegated the following season so in August 1986 he moved to Queen's Park Rangers for £250,000. He won his first cap in a friendly v Saudi Arabia in November 1988. In 1990 he moved to Arsenal for £1.3 million, at the time a British record for a goalkeeper. Before making his Arsenal debut he was selected as third goalkeeper for England's 1990 World Cup squad behind Peter Shilton and Chris Woods but after arriving in Italy he was injured and replaced by Dave Beasant. In 1990–91 he only conceded 18 goals when playing in every match of the 38-game season in which Arsenal won the title. In June 2008 he was voted seventh in the list of 50 Gunners' Greatest Players. In the summer of 2003 he was released by Arsenal and joined Kevin Keegan's Manchester City, but by January 2004 he had sustained an injury and announced his retirement at the age of 40 due to a recurring shoulder injury.

International debut v Saudi Arabia (away in Riyadh) 16 November 1988 drew 1–1. Final appearance v Macedonia at Southampton on 16 October 2002 drew 2–2.
Voted into UEFA Euro 1996 Team of the Tournament, PFA Team of the Year 1997, Premier League 10 seasons Awards (1992–93 to 2001–02), Domestic Team of the Decade, Goalkeeper with most clean sheets (130).

### About the man
Since retiring he has carved out a successful media career including a cameo role in *My Summer with Des* starring Rachel Weisz and Neil Morrissey, appointed as the Brand Ambassador for Yorkshire Tea during the early 1990s and a team captain in the TV quiz *They Think Its All Over*. In December 2004 he took part in *Strictly Ice Dancing* and then in January 2006 *Dancing On Ice*. He also hosts a 'Safe Hands' annual charity golf event and has released two DVDs: *Seaman's Goalkeeping Nightmares* in 2003 and *Jeepers Keepers* the following year.

# Peter A. Shearer

### Heroic claim to fame
Capped for the England semi-professional team.

### Vital statistics
*Date of birth:* 4 February 1967
*Place of birth:* Birmingham
*Blues career:* 38 – 13 goals

# BIRMINGHAM CITY

*Blues first appearance:* As a substitute on 3 November 1984 (h) drew 0–0 v Shrewsbury Town. Crowd: 9,807
*Blues full debut:* 10 October 1984 (a) lost 0–1 v Manchester City. Crowd: 25,369
*Team:* Seaman, Gorman, Hagan, Wright, Armstrong, Shearer, Kuhl, Clarke, Harford, Bremner, Hopkins
*First Blues goal:* 7 November 1984 (a) lost 1–3 v West Bromwich Albion
*Club honours:* Blues – Division Two runners-up 1984–85, Second Division champions 1994–95, Auto Windscreen Shield winners 1995

## Playing Career

| Club | From | To | Fee | Total Appearances incl (subs) | Goals |
|---|---|---|---|---|---|
| Peterborough United | 1997 | 1998 | | | |
| Birmingham City | 1994 | 1996 | | 35 | 12 |
| Bournemouth | 1989 | 1994 | £18,000 | 85 | 10 |
| Cheltenham Town | 1988 | 1989 | | | |
| Nuneaton | 1986 | 1988 | | | |
| Rochdale | 1986 | | Loan | 1 | |
| Birmingham City | 1983 | 1986 | | 3 | 1 |

## Career in words

He began his football career as a schoolboy with Coventry City. He left school in 1983 and joined Blues as an apprentice, signing professional two years later. He made his first-team debut as a 17-year-old, he played four more games that season which saw Blues promoted to the top flight. In April 1986 he was released and moved to Rochdale where he played only 1 game for the Third Division side before dropping into non-League football six months later with Nuneaton Borough. A year with Nuneaton and successful spell with Cheltenham Town during which he was capped for the England's semi-professional representative side brought him an £18,000 move to Bournemouth in the Second Division. His form at Bournemouth resulted in a proposed £500,000 move to First Division Wimbledon but a knee injury spoilt his plans. He returned to fitness and after trials with Coventry City and Dundee he re-joined Blues in January 1994 for £50,000. An achilles tendon operation prevented him playing in the final games of the title season, and he never played for the first team again. He had a trial with Notts County in 1997 before joining Peterborough United as player-coach, playing for the reserves, but his only first-team outings were three as an unused sub.

## About the man

Edwin Stein was an integral part of the Barry Fry regime that won the Division Two Championship in 1994–95 season, and he had this to say about Peter Shearer's contribution to the triumph: 'Big Daddy was the find of the season. Shears had injury problems after he first arrived and never got into his stride. On the opening day at Leyton Orient we had to use him as an emergency centre-half and that's not really his best position. He didn't get back in until we were short for a Coca-Cola Cup game. He did well then and after he scored two goals in a preliminary round of the Auto Windscreens Trophy he came into his own. His late runs into the box and aerial prowess brought him 12 goals from 27 games. Many of which were vital strikes. We desperately missed him when he was out. He was a fierce competitor and provided our midfield with a great balance.'

In the *Birmingham Evening Mail* Wembley special of 3 April 1995 Colin Tattum wrote an article entitled 'Peter Stung Into Action':

Peter Shearer wondered whether his Blues career was over in October after the tongue lashing he received from manager Barry Fry after a reserve game. Fry threatened to pay him up and Shearer, struggling to get into the first team, wondered what lay ahead. The answer was Blackburn Rovers days later in the Coca-Cola Cup as injuries forced Fry to turn to his combative midfielder. Shearer did well and held his place in the side with goalscoring performances that have turned him into one of the first names Fry pencils in on his team sheet. 'I'd never played for Barry before and it was very difficult to get used to the way he'd slaughter you.' Said the 28-year-old. 'After that reserve game he laid into me and said I wasn't doing it. I thought I was a better player than I actually was etc. etc. The next thing I knew I got in because of injuries and began to play to my potential. To be now considered as one of his first choices for the Wembley team is a dream come true. I had wondered what the hell was going on earlier in the season, I was at a low. I can't wait for the final to come and it's still hard to believe. He still calls me all sorts, especially at half-time but I think I've got used to him a bit more now.' He suffered a career-threatening injury at Bournemouth which came 24 hours before he was due to sign for Wimbledon for £500,000. 'Not knowing whether I'd play again was the worst point in my life,' he said 'I realise just what I have got at the moment and I appreciate it so much. That's why I'm determined to keep up the standards I've set myself. What has helped me this season is that I have been given licence to get forward. Before I've always been the anchor man. It just seems natural to make blind side runs and arrive in the box late and I always said to Barry that once the first goal went in I'd carry on getting more' Shearer netted 10 times from 19 appearances after getting his extended run in the side. Not bad for a player who cost just £50,000 from the Cherries in December 1993. His double against Walsall in the preliminary round lifted the pressure of him and showed the fans what he could do. 'Those goals definitely were a turning point.' He said 'I had been getting in positions but missing badly before. My confidence picked up after that and I began to win the fans over. It's hard to establish yourself at any club but the goals helped me. I only played two games last season because of an Achilles injury and Barry was getting stick from people like Karren Brady for bringing someone in who wasn't doing anything. It was difficult for both of us at first but I remained positive and have always believed in myself.' It is such strength of character that Shearer believes Blues have to show to beat Carlisle United. 'It will be all about who wants to win it the most' he said 'It's down to the determination on the day. We will be so hyped up purely because we are playing at Wembley we'll give one of our best performances I'm sure'.

# Daniel James Sonner

### Heroic claim to fame
Never spent more than two seasons at any of his clubs.

### Vital statistics
*Date of birth:* 9 January 1972
*Place of birth:* Wigan
*Blues career:* 56 – 3 goals
*Blues debut:* 12 August 2000 (a) drew 0–0 v Queen's Park Rangers. Crowd: 13,926
*Team:* Bennett, Eaden, Johnson (M), Hughes, Holdsworth, Purse, Lazaridis, Grainger, Horsfield, Sonner, Ndlovu
*First Blues goal:* 18 August 2000 (h) lost 1–3 v Fulham

*Club honours:* Burnley: Fourth Division champions 1991–92 Blues: League Cup runners-up 2001 Division One Play-off winners 2001–02
*Representative honours:* Northern Ireland B –4 caps 1 goal, full – 13 caps

## Playing Career

| Club | From | To | Fee | Total Appearances incl (subs) | Goals |
| --- | --- | --- | --- | --- | --- |
| Wrexham | 2008 | 2008 | Free | 9 | 1 |
| Walsall | 2007 | 2008 | Free | 7 | |
| Port Vale | 2005 | 2007 | Free | 74 | 2 |
| Port Vale | 2005 | 2005 | Loan | 13 | |
| Peterborough United | 2004 | 2005 | Free | 17 | |
| Nottingham Forest | 2003 | 2004 | Free | 32 | |
| Walsall | 2002 | 2003 | Free | 28 | 4 |
| Birmingham City | 2000 | 2002 | Free | 56 | 3 |
| Sheffield Wednesday | 1998 | 2000 | £75,000 | 63 | 4 |
| Ipswich Town | 1996 | 1998 | Free | 69 | 4 |
| FC Erzgebirge | 1995 | 1996 | | 21 | 6 |
| Preussen | 1994 | 1995 | | N.K. | |
| Viktoria Koln | 1993 | 1994 | | 21 | 3 |
| Bury | 1992 | 1993 | Loan | 9 | 4 |
| Burnley | 1991 | 1993 | | 9 | 1 |
| Wigan Athletic | 1990 | 1991 | Trainee | | |

## Career in words

He spent 18 years as a professional footballer but never spent more than two seasons at any one club. He started his professional career with Third Division Wigan Athletic in 1990. Danny never made a first-team appearance so signed for Burnley in March 1991. He barely featured at Turf Moor during their table-topping season of 1991–92 and so was loaned out to Bury in November 1992 staying for the remainder of the season. He moved to Germany for the start of the 1993–94 season with Viktoria Koln in the Oberliga he spent the following season with BFC Preussen; both teams were in the depths of the German Football League. He spent the 1995–96 season with FC Erzgebirge Aue in the Regionalliga Nordost. It was while at Erzgebirge that he was plucked from obscurity by Ipswich Town manager George Burley. Sonner therefore spent the 1996–97 season in the First Division. In his two seasons at Portman Road he played 56 League games, half of which were substitute appearances. However, he and Burley soon fell out and Sonner was on the move to Sheffield Wednesday in October 1998 for an undisclosed fee believed to be around £75,000 thereby spending 1998–99 in the Premier League. When Wednesday were relegated at the end of 1999–2000 Sonner was released. Signing for Blues where he helped them to the 2001 League Cup Final scoring v Sheffield Wednesday in the quarter-final 2–0 win on 12 December 2000. In the Final he was replaced by Bryan Hughes after 71 minutes. In the Play-off semi-final defeat at Preston North End Sonner and Michael Johnson, together with manager Trevor Francis, were charged with misconduct by the FA, with Sonner and Johnson also charged for using abusive language. Sonner was fined £1,000. He left Blues at the end of 2001–02, playing his last game for the club on 7 November 2001 and was sent off on 77 minutes after a poor challenge at St Andrew's on Phil Gilchrist in the 1–0 defeat by WBA, resulting in him being suspended for the 2002 Play-off Final. After training with Wolverhampton Wanderers he spent 2002–03 with Walsall, followed by time at Nottingham Forest. In 2004–05 season he was with Peterborough United but spent the period from February to May on loan to Port Vale, making 13 appearances in which he impressed enough to be offered a permanent deal for the start of the 2005–06 season. He played more games at Vale Park than at any of his other clubs; however, at the age of 35 he rejected Vale's contract offer on the basis it was too low paying, so he moved back to Walsall but due to injury played just seven games in the 2007–08 season before leaving in the September. In January 2008 he joined Wrexham leaving in the May following their relegation to the Conference. His international debut came on 10 September 1997 in a 1–0 defeat to Albania in Zurich.

# Byron Stevenson

### Heroic claim to fame
He was given a four-and-a-half-year European ban which effectively ended his international career.

### Vital statistics
*Date of birth:* 7 September 1956
*Date of death:* 6 September 2007 of throat cancer
*Place of birth:* Llanelli, Wales
*Blues career:* 91 – 3 goals
*Blues debut:* 18 September 1982 (h) won 1–0 v Coventry City. Crowd: 11,681
*Team:* Blyth, Langan, Dennis, Stevenson, Blake, Phillips, Hagan, Evans, Whatmore, Curbishley, Handysides
*First Blues goal:* 2 April 1983 (h) drew 1–1 v Swansea
*Club honours:* Blues – Division Two runners-up 1984–85
*Representative honours:* Wales Youth, Under-21, full –15 caps

### Playing Career

| Club | From | To | Fee | Total Appearances incl (subs) | Goals |
|---|---|---|---|---|---|
| Bristol Rovers | 1985 | 1986 | | 31 | 3 |
| Birmingham City | 1981 | 1985 | | 91 | 3 |
| Leeds United | 1975 | 1981 | | 95 | 4 |
| Leeds United | 1972 | 1975 | Youth | | |

### Career in words
He started his career at Leeds United in 1972 making his debut in 1975 and went onto establish himself in the first team, making nearly 100 appearances for the Elland Road club. He joined Blues in 1981 to become Ron Saunders's first signing with Frank Worthington going in the opposite direction. Initially he played at the heart of the defence before being switched to midfield. Again he made nearly 100 appearances for his club before moving to Bristol Rovers, where he stayed for one season before retiring due to injury. He moved back to Leeds and spent some time managing the Garforth Miners Welfare Football Club. He left football in the early 1990s. He made his debut for Wales in May 1978 at Wrexham v Northern Ireland in a 1–0 win in the Home Championship. In 1979 v Turkey he was accused of fracturing the cheekbone of Buyak Mustafa. He was given a four and a half year European ban which effectively ended his international career.

## About the man
Byron was forced to retire at the age of 29 after struggling with injuries. He ran the New Inn public house on Elland Road, Churwell Leeds which had previously been managed by John Charles, another Leeds and Wales stalwart. In *Match Weekly* in the 1970s Byron answered the following questions:

**Club nickname?**
Johnnie Carson.

**Most difficult opponent?**
Kenny Dalglish.

**Other sports?**
Golf and snooker.

**Favourite actor?**
Clint Eastwood.

**Favourite actress?**
Barbara Streisand.

**Favourite film?**
*Jazz Singer.*

**Favourite player?**
Eddie Gray.

**Favourite away ground?**
Ipswich Town.

**Favourite stadium?**
Cologne.

**TV show you would switch off?**
*Emmerdale Farm.*

**Favourite pop star?**
Leo Sayer.

**Favourite food?**
Fillet steak and beef stroganoff.

**Favourite drink?**
Tetley's bitter.

**Best country visited?**
Yugoslavia.

**What don't you like about football?**
Hooliganism.

**Pre-match meal?**
Steak.

BIRMINGHAM CITY                                               MODERN DAY HEROES

# Simon Andrew Sturridge

**Heroic claim to fame**
Scored the opening goal in the Leyland Daf Final at Wembley.

**Vital statistics**
*Date of birth:* 9 December 1969
*Place of birth:* Birmingham
*Blues career:* 186 – 38 goals
*Blues first appearance:* As a substitute on 15 October 1988 (h) lost 1–4 v West Bromwich Albion. Crowd: 10,453
*Blues full debut:* 5 November 1988 (h) drew 0–0 v Portsmouth. Crowd: 5,866
*Team:* Thomas, Ranson, Roberts, Atkins, Bird, Langley, Bremner, Childs, Yates, Sturridge, Wigley
*First Blues goal:* 27 March 1989 (h) lost 1–2 v Shrewsbury Town
*Club honours:* Blues – Division Three runners-up 1991–92, Leyland Daf winners 1991

**Playing Career**

| Club | From | To | Fee | Total Appearances incl (subs) | Goals |
|---|---|---|---|---|---|
| Shrewsbury Town | 2000 | 2000 | Loan | 11 | 1 |
| Northampton Town | 1999 | 2000 |  | 19 | 1 |
| Blackpool | 1999 | 1999 | Loan | 5 | 1 |
| Stoke City | 1993 | 1999 | £50,000 | 93 | 15 |
| Birmingham City | 1988 | 1993 | Trainee | 186 | 38 |

**Career in words**
He attended Duddeston Manor and St George's schools in Birmingham and played for William Cowper before joining Blues as a YTS trainee in June 1985 and turned professional in July 1988. He was a prolific scorer in the Birmingham Boys League which brought him to the attention of the Blues' scouting system. 'Studger' followed his brother Michael to St Andrew's, although his brother never made the first team. He continued to score in the Youth set up, and therefore his call-up to the first team was inevitable. His pace, control of the ball and vision made him a fan's favourite, a position that was confirmed when he scored the goal against Brentford that secured Blues' return to Wembley for the Leyland Daf Cup. He scored the opening goal at Wembley on that memorable day. He joined Stoke City in 1993 for a fee of £50,000 and stayed in the Potteries for six years before going on loan to Blackpool in 1999. The year later he moved to Northampton Town but after one season moved to Shropshire with Shrewsbury Town on loan.

**About the man**
**The beginning of the end of your career had an ironic twist?**
Yes I was playing for Stoke City against the Blues, and I had come on as a substitute with 15 minutes to go. I'd made a few runs and done a few things and then the ball came to me and I tried to go between Steve (Bruce) and Michael (Johnson) and one of them caught me as I turned and my knee went. What was tragic about it was that was my first game back for months, having suffered a similar injury to my other knee the year before.

**So what happened?**
I more or less spent two seasons out of the game. It was very frustrating, and in all honesty I knew I was on the back foot then. It's bad enough spending two years out of any profession, but to spend two years out of football, one after the other, I was always going to be struggling from then on, and so it proved.

**Any regrets?**
I am certainly not bitter that my career ended at the age of 31; after all, I know plenty of players who suffered career-ending injuries in their teens so I am grateful to have had 12 good years in the game.

THE HEROES

#### Tell me about your early days at Blues?
I was lucky I saw many players come into Blues during my time who I thought looked good players, but so few of those players actually made it through. The drop out happened to my brother. He joined Blues as a YTS but it never worked out for him. When I joined Blues as a YTS I would have to do my normal training in the morning, but you'd have jobs to do in the afternoon and we'd also go to college. You would sweep the terraces and clean the boots. To be honest, part of the reason the game is better now is because you've got more young players spending more time on the training ground. In my day you would spend more time cleaning the ground and getting snow off the pitch in the winter than you would training. Mind you, I think it made us realise what a good job it was to be a professional footballer and to make the most of every opportunity.

#### Who were influencing your career in those days?
The youth coaches Kevin Reeves and Fred Davies gave me a great education both on and off the park. Your YTS and apprentice years are where you are moulded as a player and a person and they were both great teachers.

#### That crop of youth players resulted in a number breaking through?
I and a number of Blues youngsters benefitted from the club's demise and we got not only a chance to play in the first team during this period, but also went on to have good careers in the game. Initially coming through the youth team there were quite a few faces, besides me, who eventually broke into the first team, like Ian Clarkson, Mark Yates, Dean Peer, John Frain and Kevin Ashley. A good grounding in the youth team and the club being in financial difficulty gave us the opportunity to break through, but you've still got to be at the club and good enough compared to the lads that are there to take your chances when they come.

#### The club's financial situation resulted in you playing for a few managers?
In the eight years between signing YTS forms and my departure to Stoke in 1993 I played under no less than six bosses: Ron Saunders, John Bond, Garry Pendrey, Dave Mackay, Lou Macari and Terry Cooper.

#### Tell us about the Leyland Daf Cup Final?
The occasion was unbelievable and it was one hell of a party. Mind you it was only made great because we won. Winning the Leyland Daf was the beginning of a turnaround for the Blues. The following year we gained promotion under Terry Cooper and that's when David Sullivan and Karren Brady came in and revolutionised the club. I'm sure they will have realised the potential of Birmingham City as an investment from the time of the Wembley victory. The manager was given a bit of money to spend for the first time and brought in a load of new faces. Even though I'd played in every game in the promotion-winning season, it was clear that I wasn't going to get much of a chance after that.

# Maik Stefan Taylor

#### Heroic claim to fame
Blues' first million-pound goalkeeper.

#### Vital statistics
*Date of birth:* 4 September 1971
*Place of birth:* Hildesheim, Germany
*Blues career:* 242 (As at the end of 2010)
*Blues debut:* 16 August 2003 (h) won 1–0 v Tottenham Hotspur. Crowd: 29, 358
*Team:* Taylor (Maik), Kenna, Clapham, Savage, Purse, Cunningham, Johnson (D), Dugarry, Horsfield, Clemence, Dunn
*Club honours:* Fulham – Second Division champions 1999, First Division champions 2001; Blues – The Championship runners-up in 2007 and again in 2009.
*Representative honours:* Northern Ireland B – 1 cap, full – caps 90

## Playing Career

| Club | From | To | Fee | Total Appearances incl (subs) | Goals |
|---|---|---|---|---|---|
| Birmingham City | 2004 | | £1,500,000 | 247 | |
| Birmingham City | 2003 | 2004 | Loan | 32 | |
| Fulham | 1997 | 2004 | £700,000 | 235 | |
| Southampton | 1996 | 1997 | £500,000 | 18 | |
| Barnet | 1995 | 1996 | | 83 | |
| Farnborough | 1994 | 1995 | | | |

## Career in words

He began his career with ASC Nienburg before moving to Princes Marina College, Petersfield Town, Farnborough Town, Barnet and Southampton. He signed for Fulham in 1997 for £700,000, helping them to win the Second Division title in 1999. The Cottagers won the First Division Championship in 2001 gaining promotion to the Premier League. Because of his parentage; an English father and a German mother he qualified to represent Northern Ireland through his British passport. He signed for Blues in August 2003 on a year-long loan gaining a permanent contract in January 2004. He was replaced by Colin Doyle as first choice goalkeeper in February 2007 but regained his first-team place after the first three matches of the 2007–08 Premier League season. Taylor has over 80 caps for NI including playing in their famous victory over England in September 2005. His debut was against Germany in 1999 where Northern Ireland lost 3–0. While at Farnborough Town he won the Southern League Premier Division Championship in 1993–94.

## About the man
### First team supported?
Southampton. One of my first footballing memories was watching the 1976 FA Cup Final on television. I wasn't a great follower of the English game as I was living out in Germany at the time, but that match against Manchester United stuck with me, and I supported them every since.

### First team?
My first team was called SV Fallinghostel, near Hamburg, Northern Germany, when I was 11 or 12. They were the local team near to the Army base where my father was stationed. I wasn't treated any differently, I mixed in the normal way and I could speak German. When I played for Northern Ireland in a World Cup qualifier in Dortmund, 12 members of my old team turned up at the hotel we were staying at, I was gobsmacked. They never thought I would be a goalkeeper as I used to play outfield, as a defender.

### Football hero?
My first was Kevin Keegan who was with SV Hamburg when I was out there. I loved his enthusiasm and the way he wore his heart on his sleeve. I think the fans and his teammates appreciated him for that.

### First car?
Chrysler Hillman Avenger. Parents bought it for £300.

### First football boots?
They were a pair of Adidas with moulded soles. I must have been about 11 years old, and I remember they were four sizes too big.

### Favourite actor?
Bruce Willis.

### First record?
*Prince Charming* by Adam and The Ants.

### Favourite singer?
R. Kelly.

**First house?**
A mid-terrace three-bedroomed place in Barnet. It cost £68,000.

**First pet?**
A black Border Collie called Sukie.

**First pay packet?**
As a boy soldier in the Army I was on a salary of £7,000 per annum.

**What's the best stadium who have played at?**
Old Trafford is fantastic but the Millenium Stadium.

**Anything quirky about your kit?**
I wear cycling shorts which are padded on the sides.

**Who would you least like to face from the penalty spot?**
Andrew Johnson because he just smashes them and gives you no time to react. But the all-time best penalty-taker was Matt Le Tissier of Southampton. I spent a year with him, and he is out of this world.

**Which sporting event would you most like to attend?**
Ryder Cup.

**Football stadium you would love to play in?**
Maracana in Rio de Janerio, Brazil.

**Sporting hero?**
Steve Redgrave.

**Favourite sports programme?**
*They Think It's All Over.*

**Best player played against?**
Alan Shearer.

**Favourite sports commentator?**
Andy Gray.

**Favourite newspaper?**
*The Sun.*

**Favourite food?**
Pasta.

**Favourite restaurant?**
Teppen Yaki Shogun.

**Favourite drink?**
Orange juice.

**Favourite holiday destination?**
Dubai.

**Favourite pizza topping?**
Ham and mushroom.

**Favourite sport after football?**
Tennis.

**BIRMINGHAM CITY** — MODERN DAY HEROES

**Favourite other goalkeeper?**
Peter Schmeichel.

**Favourite foreign team?**
Barcelona.

**Best away fans?**
Liverpool.

# Martin Taylor

**Heroic claim to fame**
While at Stockport County he scored an own-goal with a header from 20 yards.

**Vital statistics**
*Date of birth:* 9 November 1979
*Place of birth:* Ashington, Northumberland
*Blues career:* 117 – 3 goals
*Blues first appearance:* As a substitute on 11 February 2004 (h) won 3–0 v Everton. Crowd: 29,004
*Blues full debut:* 3 March 2004 (h) won 3–1 v Middlesbrough and he scored. Crowd: 29,369
*Team:* Taylor (Maik), Tebily, Upson, Savage, Taylor (M), Cunningham, Johnson (D), Forssell, Clemence, Hughes
*Club honours:* Blackburn Rovers – League Cup winners 2002; Blues – Championship runners-up 2006–07 and 2008–09
*Representative honours:* England Under-21 – 1 cap

**Playing Career**

| Club | From | To | Fee | Total Appearances incl (subs) | Goals |
| --- | --- | --- | --- | --- | --- |
| Watford | | | | | |
| Norwich City | 2007 | | Loan | 8 | 1 |
| Birmingham City | 2000 | | | 117 | 3 |
| Stockport County | 2000 | | Loan | 7 | |
| Darlington | 2000 | | Loan | 4 | |
| Blackburn Rovers | 1997 | 2004 | | 88 | 5 |

**Career in words**
'Tiny' was born in Ashington, Northumberland, the same place as Bobby and Jack Charlton. He played for Cramlington Juniors, who were one of Alan Shearer's junior sides, before joining Newcastle United as a junior. The nickname 'Tiny' was given to him by Dave Hall, the youth manager at Blackburn Rovers, whom he joined as a schoolboy at the age of 17 signing his first full contract at the start of 1997–98 season. After loan spells at Darlington and Stockport he gained his one and only representative honour when he came on as a second half substitute for John Terry in a 3–0 friendly win for the England Under-21 against Mexico in May 2001. In 2002 he played in Rovers' League Cup win over Tottenham Hotspur by 2–1 in Cardiff. On 2 February 2004 he was sold to Blues for £1.25 million on a three-year contract. In April 2007 he signed a further three-year contract with an option for a further two years. On 1 November 2007 he joined Norwich City on a month's loan. On 23 February 2008 Martin achieved football notoriety when in the third minute of the home game v Arsenal he fouled Eduardo, who suffered a compound fracture of his left fibula and an open dislocation of his left ankle, a tackle which saw Martin sent off. He was a trainee with Blackburn along with David Dunn and Damien Johnson. Married to Nikki, he has two sons, Coel and Caleb. He moved to Watford on a free in the January 2010 transfer window in a two-and-a-half-year deal.

# BIRMINGHAM CITY                              MODERN DAY HEROES

**About the man**
**Toughest opponent?**
Herman Crespo.

**Best advice given?**
Don't make excuses.

**Which sporting event would you most like to attend?**
A World Cup Final.

**Football stadium you would love to play in?**
Nou Camp.

**Favourite Sports programme?**
*Match of the Day.*

**Any football rules you would like to change?**
The obstruction rule, when a defender shepherds the ball out of play for a goal kick it would be more interesting if the player had to deal with the ball.

**First pair of football boots?**
Adidas with moulded soles.

**Team supported as a boy?**
Newcastle United.

**How do you spend your spare time?**
With my kids.

**Favourite TV?**
The Soaps.

**Favourite stadium?**
Nou Camp.

**Favourite sports commentator?**
John Motson.

**Favourite foreign team?**
Juventus, I had one of their kits as a lad.

**Favourite newspaper?**
*Daily Mirror.*

**Favourite food?**
Fish.

**Favourite restaurant?**
Gastro Pub.

**Favourite drink?**
Pepsi Max.

**Favourite holiday destination?**
Center Parcs.

**Favourite pizza topping?**
Everything.

**Favourite sport after football?**
Swimming.

# Olivier Tebily

**Heroic claim to fame**
He won a 50/50 tackle in his stockinged feet against Millwall.

**Vital statistics**
*Date of birth:* 19 December 1975
*Place of birth:* Abidjan, Cote d'Ivoire
*Blues career:* 95
*Blues debut:* 24 March 2002 (a) drew 1–1 v Coventry City. Crowd: 17,945
*Team:* Vaesen, Kenna, Grainger, Hughes, Tebily, Johnson (D), Devlin, Mooney, John, Carter, Williams
*Club honours:* Glasgow Celtic – Scotland Premier League winners 2001–02; Blues – Championship runners-up 2006–07
*Representative honours:* Ivory Coast – 18 full caps

## Playing Career

| Club | From | To | Fee | Total Appearances incl (subs) | Goals |
| --- | --- | --- | --- | --- | --- |
| Toronto | 2008 | | | 4 | |
| Birmingham City | 2002 | 2007 | £700,000 | 95 | |
| Glasgow Celtic | 1999 | 2002 | £1,250,000 | 52 | 2 |
| Sheffield United | 1999 | 1999 | £200,000 | 8 | |
| Chateauroux | 1998 | 1999 | | 23 | 1 |
| Niort | 1993 | 1998 | | 91 | 5 |

**Career in words**
He was raised in France and became a naturalised Frenchman. He began his career as a junior at Ligue 2 Niort. In January 1998 he moved to Chateauroux, who were promoted to Ligue 1. In March 1999 he was signed by Steve Bruce for Sheffield United for £200,000 and three months later, in June 1999, he joined Glasgow Celtic for a fee of £1.25 million being signed by John Barnes. He scored an own-goal in a pre-season friendly against Leeds United, his first Celtic appearance which gave an early indication of his erratic nature which earned him the nickname 'Bombscare' from the Hoops fans. He was a member of the Cote d'Ivoire squad for the 2000 African Cup of Nations. In 2001–02 he earned a Scotland Premier League-winners' medal. On 22 March 2002 he joined Blues for £700,000, making his last appearance for the Blues first team in October 2006. His contract was paid up, thus becoming a free agent after nearly six years at St Andrew's. After a trial he signed for Toronto FC in the Major League of Canada on 24 April 2008, but an ankle injury cut short his time in North America and on 31 July 2008 he was released to return to his family in France. Steve Bruce affectionately labelled 'Tebs' as 'The Beast' because he is big, powerful and quick and, more importantly, fearless. There was a tackle in the Millwall Play-off semi-final game when a 50/50 ball had to be won against the opposition defender, Stuart Nethercot. Olivier won that ball to the delight of the Blues' fans, and he was missing a boot at the time!

# BIRMINGHAM CITY

# MODERN DAY HEROES

Brucie has always been a fan of this aggressive defender, bringing him to Bramall Lane from France when he was manager of The Blades. Brucie remembers: 'I took him to Sheffield United from France for 70 grand. Kenny Dalglish watched him against Ade Akinbiyi, and we sold him to Celtic for £1.3 million – that was after just six League games.' His cousin is Didier Drogba of Chelsea.

### About the man
Olivier was an enigma. The initial impression he gave was that of an athlete with an extremely muscular frame who would stand no nonsense from any opponent, and to an extent that was true. But he was blighted by either an inability to concentrate for any length of time or a continuing streak of bad luck. He seemed supremely confident as he strolled around the heart of a team's defence, but no sooner had he completed a timely interception or emerge victorious from a tackle than he would have a seemingly massive surge of aberrant brainwave activity and cause complete mayhem in the defence where a few seconds previously there had been relative peace and harmony. As a result of his eccentric approach to the art of defending he quickly acquired the nickname 'Bombscare', although Heart Attack and Hospital Pass were synonyms that could have been equally appropriate. As an indication of how his luck was; during his first season at Glasgow Celtic he went to the African Nations Cup with the Ivory Coast and promptly found himself being held at gunpoint by the country's military following a series of results that left the president somewhat underwhelmed.

# Martin Richard Thomas

### Heroic claim to fame
One of England's goalkeeping coaches.

### Vital statistics
*Date of birth:* 28 November 1959
*Place of birth:* Senghenydd, Glamorgan
*Blues career:* 176
*Blues debut:* 4 October 1988 (h) lost 0–1 v Plymouth Argyle. Crowd: 4,435
*Team:* Thomas, Ranson, Roberts, Atkins, Overson, Bird, Bremner, Langley, Whitton, Robinson (CR), Wigley

*Club honours:* Newcastle United – Division Two Promotion 1984; Blues – Division Two Promotion 1992, Leyland Daf winner 1991

*Representative honours:* Wales – Under-21 two caps, full 1 cap

## Playing Career

| Club | From | To | Fee | Total Appearances incl (subs) | Goals |
|---|---|---|---|---|---|
| Cheltenham Town | 1993 | 1994 | | 80 | |
| Crystal Palace | | | Loan | 0 | |
| Aston Villa | | | Loan | 0 | |
| Birmingham City | 1988 | 1993 | £75,000 | 176 | |
| Middlesbrough | 1984 | | Loan | 4 | |
| Newcastle United | 1983 | 1988 | £50,000 | 115 | |
| Newcastle United | 1983 | | Loan | 3 | |
| Southend United | 1983 | | Loan | 6 | |
| Tottenham Hotspur | | | Loan | 0 | |
| Cardiff City | | | Loan | 15 | |
| Bristol Rovers | 1977 | 1983 | | 162 | |
| Bristol Rovers | 1975 | 1977 | Youth | | |

## Career in words

He moved from his native Wales to England to join Bristol Rovers as a youth player. He made his first-team debut on 3 January 1977 as a substitute for Jim Eadie in an away game at Charlton Athletic. He turned professional in September 1977 and went on to become Rovers' first-choice goalkeeper. During 1982–83 he went on loan to Cardiff City, Tottenham Hotspur and Southend United before joining Newcastle United in 1983 for £50,000 winning promotion to the top flight in 1984. He stayed as first choice for 1985–86 and in the following season won his first cap for Wales in a European Championship qualifier v Finland. Currently he is a goalkeeping coach with England FA as 'Assistant National Goalkeeping Coach'. After a loan spell with Middlesbrough he joined Blues in Division Two for £75,000 in October 1988. He was a member of the promoted side in 1992. In 1993 after loan spells with Aston Villa and Crystal Palace he joined non-League Cheltenham Town, where he made 80 appearances before retiring as a player in 1995. While at Newcastle he gained a preliminary coaching certificate and gained further coaching badges while at Blues. He got the UEFA 'A' Coaching licence, joining the FA in the early 90s as a Regional Development Officer in the Midlands on a part-time basis. In 1996 he coached England's Under-16s before joining on a full-time basis in 1997. In 2007 Martin was part of the England Under-21 coaching staff which got to the semi-finals of Euro 2007.

## About the man
### How did it start for you?

I spent my schooldays playing Rugby Union until my final year at Cardinal Newman School when I was allowed for the first time to play with the round ball. Due to my handling skills as a scrum-half, I naturally favoured the goalkeeper's position and began to play competitive soccer as an Under-12 with Senghenydd Imps. Although my Dad and elder twin brothers were successful rugby players they encouraged me to answer an advertisement in the *South Wales Echo* for open trials with Bristol Rovers. That was in 1974. I obviously did well and was signed as an apprentice in July 1976, turning professional a year later. Having played just the one senior game in 1976–77, Don Megson, the manager, decided to trust me as a 17-year-old with the first-team jersey. I doubt whether it would happen in today's game, but it worked out really well, we avoided relegation to the old Division Three and I was voted Player of the Season by the supporters. My League debut was away at Charlton, who were also the opposition for my last-ever League outing, funny the little coincidences that litter footballer's careers.

### What is the story behind the number of loan deals you were involved in?

Everything was going fine at Rovers until I started having trouble with my ring finger on my right hand, it kept dislocating so I had to play with it strapped up. In a match against Luton I was involved in a one

on one with Brian Stein, and I further damaged my hand such that I was out the first team for six months. By the time I was back my contract was due for renewal, and I decided not to re-sign and was transfer listed. I wanted to improve. I went to Cardiff, the team I supported as a lad, for three months and then onto Spurs. There was serious talk about a permanent move to White Hart Lane, but it fell through and I went to Southend in Division Two and played five games for Dave Smith.

### What happened then?
Arthur Cox, manager of Newcastle United took me on loan just before the transfer deadline of 1983 and signed me permanently shortly after for a fee which ended up, after add-ons, around £60,000. I had played around 200 senior games for Rovers and it was a great move for me going to a big club like Newcastle United particularly after the Spurs disappointment. I had a loan period at Middlesbrough in October 1984 again for five games!

### How did your move to Blues come about?
Newcastle had paid about £1 million for Dave Beasant so my days as number one were going to be limited so I was interested when Garry Pendrey, who had been at Bristol Rovers when I was there offered to take me initially on loan (there it is again!) with a view to a permanent move.

### What were your initial thoughts of the Blues?
Terrible, they were so short of money that the light switches were taped over to prevent you switching them on! But somehow they managed to raise the money to sign me, £75,000 in October 1988, and I moved to Tamworth. I signed on the Monday and made my debut a few days later on the fourth at home to Plymouth Argyle, a match we lost 1–0 in front of 4,435 spectators. That team had some characters in it: Ray Ranson, Brian Roberts, Ian Atkins, Vince Overson, Des Bremner, Steve Whitton and Steve Wigley, who is now involved with me in the England international set up.

During my first season Blues had four goalkeepers who played for the first team: myself, Tony Godden, Roger Hansbury and, here's a teaser for Blues' fans…Tony Elliott who only played the one game, a League Cup tie against Villa which we lost 5–0. He was released shortly after.

### What was your proudest moment at Blues?
That has to be the Leyland Daf Final as it presented me with my only opportunity to play at Wembley.

### What do you remember of the game?
I had played at big clubs, Spurs and Newcastle, but as I came out of the tunnel and saw the massed Blues contingent I had a lump in my throat the size of a golf ball! Fantastic experience.

### What was your least most memorable game at Blues?
27 March 1989 at St Andrew's against Shrewsbury in front of nearly 5,000 fans. Tony Kelly took a wide free kick from the Railway End and it was an in swinger, the cross came in and I caught the ball to look up at the netting behind the cross bar, I had carried the ball over the line by about a yard. I was too close to my far post and would have been better pushing it over the bar for a corner. We lost 2–1. But everyone was fine about it, the players and the fans, but I have never forgotten that moment.

### What was your happiest moment?
That was my first and only full Welsh Cap away at Finland in the European Championship in 1987. Neville Southall had dominated the position for many years, leaving me on the bench, so when I got my chance it was a great thrill to get a full cap to go with my Youth and Under-21 caps. At Blues I was kept happy by Brian 'Harry' Roberts who is the funniest man I have met in football. He's hilarious, like a stand-up comedian.

### How did your career end at Blues?
My final League game was at home against Charlton that we won 1–0, thanks to a Paul Moulden goal in front of 22,234 fans. It meant we finished 19th in Division Two which had particular significance because the following season the Premier League was formed, and we became members of the new Division One (The Championship) I only played five League games in 1992–93 as I had suffered a cruciate ligament injury in the Littlewoods Cup game at Crystal Palace in November 1991 which effectively ended my career. I was 32 and had to have three operations on the knee.

### Tell me about your loan period at Aston Villa.
Ron Atkinson was at Villa Park and the 'keepers were Bosnich, Nigel Spink (once Blues' goalkeeping

coach) and young Michael Oakes, I was signed as cover for two games as both senior goalkeepers were carrying injuries. After that I had another loan deal this time Steve Coppell took me, along with Louie Donowa to Crystal Palace where I was sub to Nigel Martyn for three games.

**What did you do then?**
I had 18 months as a part-timer with Cheltenham Town for Lyndsey Parsons, their manager who I had known from Bristol Rovers. My knee was so troublesome that I could only play as the daily training aggravated the injury.

Throughout my playing career I had prepared myself for a career in coaching, I gained my Level 2 Coaching Badge while at Newcastle. When I was at Blues I completed a three-year course in Leisure Management at Henley College, Coventry. I got my Full Badge and Advanced UEFA Licence in 1991 and started working part-time at Lilleshall for the National School of Excellence. In 1995–96 I got involved with the England International set up, in 1997 I was with the Under-20s in their World Cup over in Malaysia, the squad involved Michael Owen, Kieron Dyer and Matthew Upson to name a few!

In 1998 I became a full-time goalkeeping coach along with Ray Clemence and together with Ray and later Tony Parks, we set up the Goalkeeping Coaching/Education programme.

It is a funny old game because when I was on loan at Spurs in 1982 the three goalkeepers were… you've guessed it, Ray Clemence, Tony Parks and me.

**What about your leisure time?**
Recently most of my spare time has gone into building the new house, which I share with Alison my wife of 23 years. We have two children at university, Sian who is studying Culinary Art Management in Birmingham and Gareth who is reading Sociology at Cardiff.

# Nico-Jos Theodoor Vaesen

**Heroic claim to fame**
Sent off on his English League debut with Huddersfield Town.

**Vital statistics**
*Date of birth:* 28 September 1969
*Place of birth:* Hasselt, Belgium
*Blues career:* 63
*Blues debut:* 11 August 2001 (a) lost 1–3 v Wimbledon. Crowd: 9,142
*Team:* Vaesen, Gill, Grainger, Sonner, Purse, Johnson (M), Eaden, Mooney, Horsfield, O'Connor, Lazaridis
*Club honours:* Blues – Championship Play-off winners 2002; Crystal Palace – Championship Play-off winners 2004

**Playing Career**

| Club | From | To | Fee | Total Appearances incl (subs) | Goals |
|---|---|---|---|---|---|
| KFC Verbroedering | 2008 | | | | |
| Lierse | 2006 | | Free | 11 | |
| Crystal Palace | 2004 | 2004 | Loan | 13 | |
| Bradford City | 2004 | 2004 | Loan | 6 | |
| Gillingham | 2003 | 2004 | Loan | 5 | |
| Birmingham City | 2001 | 2006 | | 63 | |
| Huddersfield Town | 1998 | 2001 | £80,000 | 154 | |
| KSC Eendracht Asist | 1995 | 1998 | | 34 | |
| Cercle Brugge | 1993 | 1995 | | 16 | |
| Tongeren | 1990 | 1993 | | | |

THE HEROES

**BARCLAYCARD PREMIERSHIP**

**birmingham city v arsenal**

barclaycard premiership
sunday 12th january 2003
kick off 4.05pm

match sponsor
**BARCLAYCARD**

associate match sponsor
Premier Holiday Caravans

match ball sponsor
System Chytel

programme sponsor
Primetime Recruitment

main club sponsor
phones 4u

bcfc's official airline
flybe. british european

# blues

the official matchday magazine of birmingham city football club   price £2.50

### Career in words
He spent his first professional season at Belgian sides Cercle Brugge and KSC Eendracht Asist and on 21 May 1998 moved to Huddersfield Town. He was sent off on his debut but went on to play 135 League games. On 18 June 2001 he signed for Blues, helping them to win promotion to the Premier League before a cruciate knee injury in March 2003 put him out of the game for nine months. On 24 December 2003 he went to Gillingham on loan for 45 days, during which he played five games. He had spells at Bradford City and Crystal Palace, with whom he took part in another Play-off victory in 2004. At the end of that season he re-signed for Blues for a further two years to compete with Maik Taylor, finally dislodging him in late 2005, but a 4–1 defeat at Manchester City in which he conceded a penalty and was later sent off proved to be his final first-team game prior to him being released at the end of 2005–06 season. He returned to Belgium with Lierse and retired. Since then he changed his mind and signed a contract with KFC Verbroedering Geel in 2008.

### About the man
#### Who would you say has been your most difficult opponents?
Thierry Henry, Dennis Bergkamp of Arsenal, Duncan Ferguson of Everton and Darren Moore of West Bromwich Albion.

#### Who is the best player you have played with during your career?
Christophe Dugarry for Blues and Dorinel Ionel Munteau of Romania, who I played with at Bruges.

#### Tell me about your League debut in England?
It was for Huddersfield against Bury at Gigg Lane, and I was sent off after just nine minutes! We had a corner which came to nothing, Bury broke quickly upfield and our defence was in a complete mess as most of them had gone up for the corner so I raced outside of the 18-yard box to clear the danger and their forward fired the ball at me and, although it hit me on the chest, the crowd went mad shouting 'hand-ball' and even though the referee was still down the other end of the field, he was intimidated by the crowd and gave me a red card – my first game in England!

#### How do you spend your leisure time?
I have children, so they take up a lot of my time ferrying them to and from school or ballet lessons, football training or tennis lessons or whatever they have got to do. On my day off I like to play golf or tennis with my fellow goalkeeper and good friend Maik Taylor.

# Patrick William Roger Van Den Hauwe

### Heroic claim to fame
Famously married Mandy Smith, the ex-wife of Rolling Stones bass player, Bill Wyman.

### Vital statistics
*Date of birth:* 16 December 1960
*Place of birth:* Dendermonde, Belgium
*Blues career:* 140 – 1 goal
*Blues debut:* 7 October 1978 (h) lost 1–2 v Manchester City. Crowd: 18,378
*Team:* Montgomery, Van Den Hauwe, Dennis, Dillon, Gallagher, Towers, Page, Ainscow, Givens, Emmanuel, Barrowclough
*First Blues goal:* 15 March 1983 (h) won 2–1 v Arsenal

# THE HEROES

*Club honours:* Blues – Division Two runners-up 1984–85; Everton – League Cup winners in 1985 and 1987, European Cup winners in 1985; Tottenham Hotspur – FA Cup winner 1991
*Representative honours:* Wales full 13 caps

## Playing Career

| Club | From | To | Fee | Total Appearances incl (subs) | Goals |
|---|---|---|---|---|---|
| Millwall | 1993 | 1995 | Free | 36 | |
| Tottenham Hotspur | 1989 | 1993 | £575,000 | 150 | |
| Everton | 1984 | 1989 | £100,000 | 184 | 1 |
| Birmingham City | 1978 | 1984 | Apprentice | 140 | 1 |

## Career in words

He was brought up in London and joined Blues as an apprentice in July 1977. He made his League debut at the age of 17. He was transferred to Everton in September 1984 for £100,000. Five years later he went to Tottenham Hotspur for £575,000 in August 1989 making his debut in a 2–0 defeat to Aston Villa on 9 September 1989. He made 110 League appearances for Spurs including six as a substitute between 1989 and 1993 but never scored. He finished his career at Millwall joining in 1993. At Goodison he won the League Cup in 1985 and 1987 and the European Cup in 1985. He won the FA Cup with Spurs in 1991. On 19 June 1993 he married Mandy Smith the former wife of Bill Wyman but they separated after two years before divorcing in 1997. He attracted the nickname 'Psycho' as he was fearless on the pitch and was as feared by opposition players.

## About the man
### Where are you living now?

In Capetown South Africa where I have been since 1995 following a sequence of events which saw me effectively flee the country: Ossie Ardiles taking over from Terry Venables at Spurs and not fancying me as a player, a year with Mick McCarthy at Millwall and my divorce from Mandy Smith.

### How did the move come about?

I was totally disillusioned and then I got a telephone call from a good friend of mine, a solicitor called Nick Traynor, who asked if I'd take an opportunity to play in South Africa. At first I was a bit funny with it. All you see on TV is the bad publicity and I thought 'I'm not going over there, I'll get killed knowing my luck and the stuff I was getting up to! But anyway I did go. I started playing and getting used to the people, and within a month I'd made friends. I decided to stay, and it's home now.

# Mark William Ward

### Heroic claim to fame
From Right Wing to B Wing.

### Vital statistics
*Date of birth:* 10 October 1962
*Place of birth:* Liverpool
*Blues career:* 84 – 8 goals
*Blues debut:* 26 March 1994 (h) won 1–0 v Middlesbrough. Crowd: 12,409
*Team:* Bennett, Scott, Frain, Cooper, Daish, Whyte, Ward, Claridge, Saville, Willis, Harding
*First Blues goal:* 2 April 1994 (h) won 3–1 v Stoke City
*Club honours:* Blues – Second Division champions 1995, Auto Windscreen Shield winners 1995
*Representative honours:* England Semi-Professional one cap

### Playing Career

| Club | From | To | Fee | Total Appearances incl (subs) | Goals |
| --- | --- | --- | --- | --- | --- |
| Northwich Victoria | 1997 | 1998 | | | |
| Wigan Athletic | 1996 | 1996 | Free | 5 | |
| Huddersfield Town | 1996 | 1996 | Free | 8 | |
| Birmingham City | 1994 | 1996 | £500,000 | 84 | 8 |
| Everton | 1991 | 1994 | £1,100,000 | 94 | 7 |
| Manchester City | 1990 | 1991 | £1,000,000 | 67 | 16 |
| West Ham United | 1985 | 1990 | £250,000 | 209 | 14 |
| Oldham Athletic | 1983 | 1985 | £10,000 | 92 | 12 |
| Northwich Victoria | 1981 | 1983 | | | |
| Everton | 1980 | 1981 | Apprentice | | |

### Career in words
His return to Goodison in August 1991 meant that The Toffees had paid £1 million for a player they released as an apprentice some 10 years earlier. He joined Blues on loan initially and although unable to save us from relegation that season he signed a permanent deal and settled in as the Blues' midfield playmaker and was inspirational in getting them promoted the following season.

Edwin Stein was an integral part of the Barry Fry regime that won the Division Two Championship in 1994–95 season, and he had this to say about Mark Ward's contribution to the triumph: 'Wardy was our playmaker and he did well considering his earlier season form was hampered by injury. He didn't have time to get a pre-season under his belt but played on. In the last few weeks he was inspirational. We never looked the same side without him. When he was on song we were in tune. His passing was superb and he scrapped away as well, which some players dropping from the Premiership to our division might not have done. The players definitely looked up to him which was not bad considering he's only four foot nothing'

### About the man
Although a fine midfield player, he will always be remembered for his imprisonment for the supply of cocaine. He was arrested after 4kg of cocaine with a street value of £645,000 were found during a raid at a house in Prescot, Liverpool, in May 2005. In October 2005 he was jailed for eight years, eventually being released from Kirkham Prison in May 2009 having served four years in Kirkham and in Walton

# THE HEROES

prison. Prisoner NM6982, aka Mark Ward, has never denied his involvement. Broke and with no permanent home at the time, he accepted £400 a week from an acquaintance to rent a house for an unspecified 'stash'. He knew it would be illegal but did not ask for details. He found out too late it was cocaine. He was sent down for eight years after declining to name names for a lighter sentence. He was married to Jane and they had a daughter Melissa who has made him a grandfather. In the early 1990s he had a big house, flash car, nice clothes, foreign holidays and a £2,000 a week contract, which was a lot of money in those days. But the playing days ended, and a desperate fight to stay in the game – at lower League clubs, then in Hong Kong and Iceland among other places – eventually had to be given up. A non-League management career at Altrincham lasted a year before finances helped lead to the sack. The decline led to crime, and prison. Walton jail is notoriously rough, full of drugs, and depressing by any standards. In summer 2005, just after Mark was sent there, there were three suicides within 17 days.

### What is your current job?
I am working for a company called GB Building Solutions based in Manchester. Paul Hill my Framework Director has given me an unbelievable opportunity to work alongside him. He has shown strength of character and understanding to help me get my life back on track.

### Who was your favourite player as a boy? And why?
I have been a life-long Evertonian, but when I was a kid it was Kevin Keegan who I admired, even though he played for Liverpool. He was all action dynamic player and he was small which gave me inspiration to realise my size was not going to be an excuse not to become a footballer.

### Which game in your career stands out in your memory?
My home debut for Everton. We entertained Arsenal the champions the second game of the 1991 season. It had taken me 10 long years to get back to the club who had let me go. Gordon Lee had told me I was not big enough strong enough or quick enough to become a footballer. I scored two that night past Seaman for a memorable win.

### Who was the best player you played with and why?
I played with some fantastic players over my career. Peter Beardsley, Niall Quinn, Billy Bonds, Liam Brady, etc, etc, but the best player I ever played with was Alan Devonshire.

**BIRMINGHAM CITY**  MODERN DAY HEROES

**If you could go back to your days at Blues what one thing would you do differently?**
My biggest regret at Brum was not staying a little longer and taking over from Barry Fry. I was the player-coach and organised the lads that season when we won the League and the Cup. I still believe I have the qualities to manage a group of men.

**What was your best moment while at St Andrew's?**
My best moment at Brum was winning the Man of the Match award at Wembley in the Auto Windscreens Trophy.

**What is your opinion of football today?**
The game today is not the same. I enjoyed my career. You could still make a tackle, you could still go out for a pint and have a conversation with your teammates. The only plus now is the wages. Players in my day played because they loved the game. I still could have played today because I was very athletic for my size. But I would have had to come to terms with the new rules…No tackling…

**If you could be one of today's Premier League stars who would you want to be and why?**
It has to be Ryan Giggs. His dedication and sheer brilliance…He has conducted himself so well…Exemplary…

# Christopher Anderson Whyte

**Heroic claim to fame**
Won the League with Leeds United.

**Vital statistics**
*Date of birth:* 2 September 1961
*Place of birth:* Islington, London
*Blues career:* 89 – 1 goal
*Blues debut:* 22 August 1993 (h) drew 2–2 v Wolverhampton Wanderers. Crowd: 15,117
*Team:* Miller, Hiley, Frain, Parris, Dryden, Whyte, Mardon, Smith (D), Peschisolido, Saville, McMinn
*First Blues goal:* 19 April 1995 (a) won 3–1 v Plymouth Argyle
*Club honours:* Leeds United – Division One champions 1991–92; Blues – Second Division champions 1994–95
*Representative honours:* England: Under-21 four caps

**Playing Career**

| Club | From | To | Fee | Total Appearances incl (subs) | Goals |
|---|---|---|---|---|---|
| HyPS (Finland) | 2000 | | | 10 | |
| Harlow | 1999 | | Free | | |
| Raleight Capital Express (USA) | 1999 | | | | |
| Rushden & Diamonds | 1997 | 1999 | Free | 2 | 1 |
| Oxford United | 1997 | 1997 | Free | 11 | |
| Leyton Orient | 1997 | 1997 | Free | 1 | |
| Charlton Athletic | 1996 | 1997 | Free | 13 | |
| Coventry City | 1995 | | Loan | 1 | |
| Birmingham City | 1993 | 1996 | £250,000 | 89 | 1 |
| Leeds United | 1990 | 1993 | £400,000 | 147 | 6 |
| West Bromwich Albion | 1988 | 1990 | Free | 93 | 9 |
| LA Lazers and New York Express (USA Indoor) | 1986 | | | | |
| Crystal Palace | 1984 | | Loan | 13 | |
| Arsenal | 1979 | 1986 | Apprentice | 113 | 8 |

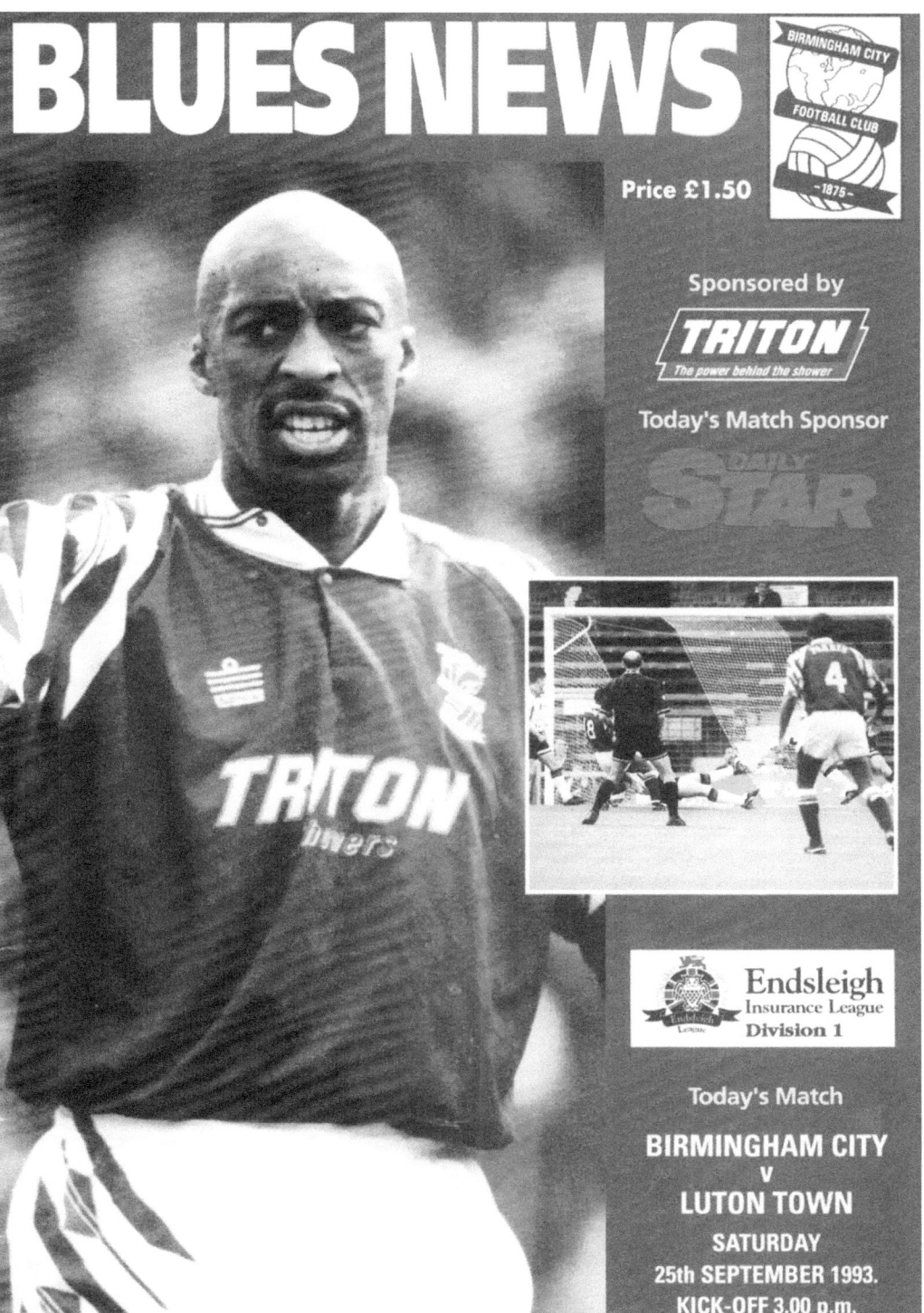

## Career in words

He began his career as a youth with Arsenal, turning professional in September 1978. He made his first-team debut v Manchester City on 17 October 1981, and during that season he played all but one of the League matches establishing a strong partnership with David O'Leary. He spent a loan period with Crystal Palace before being given a free transfer at the end of the 1985–86 playing 113 matches for the Gunners, scoring eight goals. As no domestic club offered him a contract he played for two years in the Major Indoor Soccer League for New York Express and Los Angeles Lazers. In the summer of 1988 he returned to England joining West Bromwich Albion in the Second Division. He made his Baggies debut in a League Cup tie v Peterborough United in September 1988 and was the club's player of the year for the 1988–89 season. He returned to the top flight when Leeds United paid £400,000 in 1990 becoming a near ever-present for the next three seasons putting in 147 apearances as Leeds United won the 1991–92 First Division title. In 1993 he joined Blues winning the 1994–95 Second Division title. After a brief spell at Coventry City on loan he left St Andrew's in 1996 going on to play for Charlton Athletic, Leyton Orient, Oxford United and Rushden & Diamonds. He then returned to the USA with Raleight Express in the A-League before coming back to England to play for Harlow Town in the Ryman's League Division One on 4 November 1999. In 2000 he was in Finland with HyPS.

## About the man

After Blues had secured the Division Two title in 1994–95 season the following article appeared in *The Blues Special* produced by the *Birmingham Evening Mail* on Monday 1 May 1995:
'Whyte man for job'
Chris Whyte added his title medal to the First Division Championship honour he won when at Leeds United. The 33-year-old Blues veteran did so playing in a role he never had filled before – at left-back. Whyte was drafted in at Brentford on October 22 as John Frain was injured, and Gary Cooper was at loggerheads with the club. He had lost his central-defensive place after being given compassionate leave after the death of his father in America. Whyte slotted in so well at left-back that he played 15 consecutive games there until injury struck. 'To be perfectly honest, it was no problem. I was just delighted to be involved and in the side. I adapted OK. At the end of the day my job was a defender and that's what I concentrated on doing. The full back position gave me less responsibility than I had when I was in the middle and I was able to distribute the ball better' Whyte returned to his accustomed role after Dave Barnett's achilles problems began and scored his first Blues goal in the win at Plymouth Argyle, one of the most important results of the season. 'When we went down last season it was the worst feeling I've had in football and I never want to experience it again. I felt it like the fans and everyone else did at the club. Coming back as we did, winning the double was the perfect way to respond. Everyone has played their part and I'm glad for David Sullivan and the Gold brothers because they have put their money where their mouths are and showed they want the club to go places. Whyte said the atmosphere among the Blues squad was at a similar high octane to that when he was a member of Howard Wilkinson's Champions. Without a doubt the spirit is as good. I cannot say Leeds was any better than it has been at Birmingham. Leeds are a big club but by no means and I'm not just saying this any bigger than us. The support shows it and the ambition does.

Edwin Stein had this to say about Chris Whyte's contribution to the Division Two Championship triumph: 'The Bear was a man for all seasons. A great professional from whom you could not have asked for more. He played at centre-half and left-back when John Frain got injured and adapted like he'd played there all his life. That says a lot about him. He was part of the defence that was rock solid on that 25-game unbeaten run.'

Chris is the only Blues player to be sent off during the Auto Windscreens Shield competition on 31 January 1995.

THE HEROES

# Peter Withe

### Heroic claim to fame
Two spells at Blues over a decade apart.

## Vital statistics
*Date of birth:* 30 August 1951
*Place of birth:* Liverpool
*Blues career:* 48 – 11 goals
*Blues debut:* 30 August 1975 (a) lost 2–4 v Ipswich Town. Crowd: 22,659
*Team:* Latchford (D), Martin, Bryant, Kendall, Gallagher, Hope, Francis (T), With, Hatton, Pendrey
*First Blues goal:* 20 September 1975 (h) won 4–0 v Burnley
*Club honours:* Portland Timbers – 1975 Division winners of NASL, 1975 Soccer Bowl finalist; Nottingham Forest – 1976–77 Anglo-Scottish Cup winners, 1977–78 Football League Cup winners 1977–78, First Division champions 1978, FA Charity Shield winners; Aston Villa – 1980–81 League Champions, 1981–82 European Cup winners, 1982–83 European Super Cup winners.
*Representative honours:* England – 11 full caps 1 goal

## Playing Career

| Club | From | To | Fee | Total Appearances incl (subs) | Goals |
| --- | --- | --- | --- | --- | --- |
| Huddersfield Town | 1989 | 1990 | | 38 | 1 |
| Birmingham City | 1987 | | Loan | 8 | 2 |
| Sheffield United | 1985 | 1989 | | 74 | 18 |
| Aston Villa | 1980 | 1985 | £500,000 | 182 | 74 |
| Newcastle United | 1978 | 1980 | £400,000 | 76 | 25 |
| Nottingham Forest | 1976 | 1978 | | 75 | 28 |
| Birmingham City | 1975 | 1976 | | 40 | 9 |
| Portland Timbers | 1975 | | | 22 | 17 |
| Wolverhampton Wanderers | 1973 | 1975 | | 17 | 3 |
| Arcadia Shepherds | 1973 | | | | |
| Port Elizabeth City | 1972 | 1973 | | 2(4) | |
| Barrow | 1971 | 1972 | | 1 | |
| Southport | 1971 | | | 3 | |

## Career in words
Peter is a veteran traveller. At 20, he left Liverpool with his wife Kathy, having never before lived outside the city, to play in South Africa. In 1974, after two seasons at Wolverhampton Wanderers, he played in the North American Soccer League. During the summer of 1975 he had one season in the USA with Portland Timbers of the NASL scoring 17 goals and seven assists in 22 games gaining them first place in their division, they played two home Play-off games attracting crowds of 30,000 which was unheard of in US soccer at the time. The Timbers advanced to Soccer Bowl 1975 losing to Tampa Bay Rowdies 2–0. Peter won the First Division title with Nottingham Forest but left prior to their European glory to join Newcastle United as Brian Clough wanted to raise funds for the purchase of Trevor Francis, Cloughie got £400,000 for Peter with the Magpies becoming his ninth club in less than eight years. Ron Saunders signed him for Aston Villa on the eve of the 1980–81 season spending £500,000 on the 29-year-old striker, the club's record signing at the time. He formed a formidable strike partnership with Gary Shaw, and he scored 20 goals in 36 games to finish joint top scorer in the Division One with Steve Archibald of Tottenham Hotspur as Aston Villa won the title. After five years he moved to Sheffield United. He was the first-ever English player playing for Aston Villa to feature in a World Cup Finals squad: Spain 1982. He went into football management with the Thailand National team and also managed Indonesia until 18 January 2007.

BIRMINGHAM CITY                                                    MODERN DAY HEROES

He was sacked due to his failure to get past the first round of ASEAN Football Championship, a tournament he had won with Thailand in 2000 and 2002 then finished the runner up with Indonesia in 2004. He was given a touchline ban for wearing shorts at an international match with the United Arab Emirates v Thailand – the Thai FA felt he should wear a suit!

He had a spell as manager of Wimbledon, being recruited from his role as reserve-team coach with Aston Villa in October 1991, but unfortunately he only won one game in 13 and was replaced after just

105 days with the players complaining about his style of man management. He finished his playing days at Huddersfield Town, where he began coaching in 1990. A year later he was back at Villa, working alongside Czech manager Josef Venglos. It was while back at Aston Villa, this time as chief scout, that he landed the job as Thailand coach in 1998.

### About the man
Currently he lives on the Joondalup Golf Resort in Joondalup, Perth, Western Australia, playing a lot of golf. His son Jason followed in his father's footsteps, and his brother Chris was also a professional footballer.

### Tell us about the day the Tsunami hit.
When the Tsunami struck north-west Indonesia on Boxing Day, I had not long left my apartment in Jakarta. It was 7.58am and I was about to take a training session. I never felt anything, Jakarta was too far south to be hit directly [it was 1,000 miles south-east of the earthquake's epicentre], but as news of the disaster came through things changed. People were in a state of shock and despair.

### But football carried on?
Less than 48 hours after more than 220,000 Indonesians died and thousands more saw their homes swept away, the national team were to play Malaysia in the first leg of the Tiger Cup semi-final – the South-East Asian football championship. A 2–1 home defeat was followed by a 4–1 away win, to set up a Final against Singapore. In a country fanatical about football (110,000 crammed into a Jakarta stadium to watch the first leg of the Final on 8 January), I was aware of the role football was playing. I arranged for two giant screens to be placed outside the ground so the thousands of fans who were locked out could still see the match.

It was only a game, but to the people it was more than that, it was a release for them. I don't know anyone that died, but almost every team member knew someone who had been affected. My assistant coach, Fachri Husaini, and one of my players, Ismet Sofyand, are both from Aceh [the devastated northern province] and were still waiting to hear from missing relatives. During one team-talk, my interpreter broke down in tears, unable to convey my thoughts. It was hard for them to think about football, but I told them it was a chance to unite the nation. It's not much, but what else could I do? The 3–1 defeat that followed was disappointing (they also lost the second leg, 2–1 on 16 January), yet I felt my team had, if nothing else, entertained a lot of people.

### What was the football like when you arrived?
There are a lot of technically good players out here, though it is taking longer to sort the team out than I had hoped. When I arrived, Indonesia was full of players who were professional in name only. Everything they did seemed to be in slow motion. There was no pride. Everyone walked with a slouch. Trying to communicate what playing for their country should mean has taken a while, but I think they realise now. The game in Thailand was in a mess when I took over. They had been suspended by FIFA, along with Indonesia, over a Tiger Cup match which neither side wanted to win. Victory would have meant going to play Vietnam in Hanoi, somewhere they didn't want to go. Indonesia ended up winning 1–0 after an own-goal.

### What were the problems you encountered?
My first task was to change the players' way of thinking, though I couldn't do it through my favoured technique of shouting and swearing. Unable to speak the language, I had to rely on other skills, such as body language and physical demonstrations, in order to get the best from my players. I succeeded, as Thailand won the Tiger Cup in 2000 and then again in 2002.

### What happened then?
Just as things looked to be going well, I came under pressure because of an unlikely fashion *faux pas*: I wore shorts during matches. Despite the improvement in results, the president of the Football Association of Thailand, Vijitr Getkaew, told me that I should be wearing a suit, not shorts. It was never about the shorts,

it was because we'd lost to the United Arab Emirates and failed to qualify for the Olympics. He made an issue where there wasn't one. I told him they were my work clothes and that I like to go on the pitch before a game to take the warm-up. The temperature is normally in the 90s; why should I wear a pair of trousers?

However trivial the row sounds, I was suspended, a decision that effectively ended my time in Thailand. We decided to take a break and move on again, This time, though, to a place of my wife's choosing. We ended up in Perth, Australia. Kathy has always been there for me when and wherever I've needed to go for 30 years. I thought it was time we lived somewhere she wanted to.

### But you were not without a job for long
Within a year, I had been offered the Indonesia job. I wasn't looking to go back to the Far East specifically, but when I was offered the job I couldn't refuse it. Jakarta is very different from anywhere I've been before, even Bangkok, where I lived for four years. The roads are completely chaotic. If you try to drive yourself around it's a total nightmare, there is so much traffic. The last domestic season should be in the Guinness Book of Records, it took so long. What with Ramadan and three elections, it took almost a year. The entire game needs modernising. I've introduced the players to heart-rate monitors and changed their eating habits. I've also brought in a sports psychologist. Indonesian players have got the physical attributes to play at the top level, but it's going to take time to get there.

### But surely you must miss home?
Not really – you can get a pint of Tetley's pretty much anywhere these days.

# The Final Word

I apologise to the players listed below who missed inclusion in this book but nevertheless played their part in Birmingham City's recent history by being involved in promotion campaigns and Cup successes:

Ken Armstrong
Des Bremner
Lee Carsley
Wayne Clarke
David Holdsworth
Raidi Jaidi
Fabrice Muamba
Tony Rees
Andy Saville
Steve Vickers
Mark Yates

# CARLING LEAGUE CUP FINAL

**27 February 2011**
This is the day Bluenoses have been waiting for; the last time we were at Wembley was in 1994 and the last time we won a major trophy was 1963.

But this is 2011, it is the new Wembley, the League Cup is a passage to European competition and the Blues are a Premier League side.

But would the result be any different? Could we beat the Arsenal who are competing in four competitions; the Premier League, the Champions League, the FA Cup and the League Cup? The bookies think not as the Gunners are odds on favourites and a 2–1 win for the Blues is 22 to 1.

My journey began on Thursday 24 February when I finally held in my hands my ticket for the Carling Cup Final at Wembley. Entrance K, Section 501, Row 4, Seat 8. On the halfway line, next to the Arsenal fans and a bargain at £86.

The morning of the match arrived, and I wore not only my home shirt (with long sleeves) but my scarf from the Millenium Stadium Worthington Cup Final in 2001. As I joined the queue for Platform One at Solihull station for the 11.22 train, I saw Malcolm Page and Alan Campbell in among the excited Bluenoses as the rain came down.

Upon arrival it was into the Ibis Hotel for shelter and a drink but it struck me that many of the Brummies outside in the rain were unlikely to see the end of the game in anything other than a drunken stupour. Well it is sponsored by a major lager brand! As I made my way towards the stadium from the hotel the burning of an Arsenal scarf had brought the unwelcome attention of the police.

After fish 'n chips Wembley style (how do they manage to take out the natural taste of the fish and the chips?) I settled down to watch the pre-match activities. A passionate video about Birmingham generated a huge response from the West end of the stadium that was well populated an hour before the kick-off in direct contrast to the East seats where there were very few occupants. Still, I guess they only had a six-mile walk from the Emirates stadium!

The team was announced and McLeish's game plan was revealed: a five-man midfield with Zigic upfront alone. Blues played like every Bluenose hoped they would – with energy, commitment and a dogged belief that today could be their day to be awarded the title of 'Modern Day Heroes'.

The game was 'kicked off' when Bowyer was fouled in the penalty area only to be ruled off side, which was later proved to be an erroneous decision.

Larsson's corner was met by Johnson, and Zigic out-jumped the Arsenal defenders to deflect the ball into the net – Blues were winning 1–0! It was inevitable that the Gunners would equalise, and sure enough Van Persie scored. The fact that Arsenal had also hit the woodwork in the first 45 minutes did not bode well for the second period.

Although Arsenal increased the pressure in the second half, Ben Foster proved his 'England Number One' claim with a succession of saves and stops, and it was Fahey who hit the woodwork. Then with a few minutes left the unbelievable happened, a mix up between Laurent Koscielny and Wojciech Szczensy resulted in the ball dropping at the feet of Martins, and Blues were 2–1 up.

When the final whistle went I felt stunned! There is no other way to describe it.

For all my time as a Bluenose I have been programmed for 'defeat and disappointment'; when we took the lead, the equaliser was expected – as full-time approached I was saying to myself 'Well at least we've not been humiliated' and 'It will be like 2001, a meaningless extra-time period and defeat in the penalty shoot-out' so when the winner went in, I was stunned!

After all those years of disappointment the Blues had won something – the League Cup – and no one could deny that they deserved it!